How to Survive and Thrive When Bad Things Happen

T0243493

How to Survive and Thrive When Bad Things Happen

9 Steps to Cultivating an Opportunity Mindset in a Crisis

Jim Taylor, PhD

ROWMAN & LITTLEFIELD
Lanham • *Boulder* • *New York* • *London*

Published by Rowman & Littlefield
An imprint of The Rowman & Littlefield Publishing Group, Inc.
4501 Forbes Boulevard, Suite 200, Lanham, Maryland 20706
www.rowman.com

86-90 Paul Street, London EC2A 4NE

British Library Cataloguing in Publication Information Available

Library of Congress Cataloging-in-Publication Data

Name: Taylor, Jim, 1958–, author.
Title: How to survive and thrive when bad things happen : 9 steps to cultivating an opportunity mindset in a crisis / Jim Taylor.
Description: Lanham : Rowman & Littlefield, [2019] | Includes bibliographical references and index.
Identifiers: LCCN 2018049540 (print) | LCCN 2018051495 (ebook) | ISBN 9781538108567 (electronic) | ISBN 9781538108550 (cloth : alk. paper) | ISBN 9781538185391 (paperback : alk. paper)
Subjects: LCSH: Adjustment (Psychology) | Crises—Psychological aspects. | Crisis management—Psychological aspects.
Classification: LCC BF335 (ebook) | LCC BF335 .T39 2019 (print) | DDC 155.2/4—dc23
LC record available at https://lccn.loc.gov/2018049540

♾️™ The paper used in this publication meets the minimum requirements of American National Standard for Information Sciences—Permanence of Paper for Printed Library Materials, ANSI/NISO Z39.48-1992.

Contents

Acknowledgments

I want to express my appreciation for my nine chapter assistants who generously gave their time, energy, and good cheer in support of the preparation of *How to Survive and Thrive*: Marina Salman; Samantha Sanderson Brown, PhD; Dylan Christian; Toby Larson; Nina Rois-Doria, PhD; Michael Clark; Hope Williams; Michael Walker; and Ashley Fryer. Thank you all for your unbounded generosity of spirit.

I would like to give special recognition to Samantha Sanderson Brown. Samantha started out as a chapter assistant (as noted above), but thanks to her remarkable editing contributions to her assigned chapter, I asked her to be my manuscript editor (a first for me). Her ability to see "the forest from the trees" and her keen knowledge of structure, flow, and grammar has taken *How to Survive and Thrive* to a new level of clarity. Even with seventeen authored books to my credit, I am now a better writer thanks to you, Samantha.

I also want to thank everyone at Rowman & Littlefield for their confidence in my ability to contribute to the marketplace of ideas. *How to Survive and Thrive* is my third book with R&L and my first self-help book. I look forward to more collaborations with you in the future.

Finally, I want to express my deepest gratitude to my wife, Sarah, and my daughters, Catie and Gracie. Their unwavering support throughout my career as a consultant, speaker, and author has made it a journey full of meaning, fulfillment, and joy. I love you all madly!

Introduction

"Between stimulus and response there is a space. In that space is our power to choose our response. In our response lies our growth and our freedom."—Victor Frankl, noted psychiatrist [1]

In his 1933 inaugural speech, President Franklin Delano Roosevelt addressed the nation as it was being consumed by what came to be known as the Great Depression. One of his most memorable statements from that now-famous speech is "The only thing we have to fear is fear itself." FDR wanted to instill a sense of confidence, calm, and hope into citizens who were truly terrified of what had happened and what lay ahead for the US economy. What you may not know, however, is the full context of that declaration: "So, first of all, let me assert my firm belief that the only thing we have to fear is fear itself—nameless, unreasoning, unjustified terror which paralyzes needed efforts to convert retreat into advance."

FDR was certainly right about that crisis. He realized that economic conditions and how we respond to them are powerfully influenced by the psychology of the times. FDR also knew that the panicked mentality overtaking our country would prevent it from taking the actions it needed to recover quickly.

THE GREAT RECESSION

The economic crisis of the late 2000s was dubbed the Great Recession. Much as the Great Depression was influenced by the psychology of its time, the more recent crisis was affected by an unrealistically optimistic psychology—what the former Federal Reserve chairman Alan Greenspan referred to as "irrational exuberance"—and quickly descended into what might be called "irrational despair." Once again, a mentality of fear took hold of our country and the world. That ineffective mentality made it even more difficult to weather the economic storm at every level of our financial system, from the global financial markets and national economies to industries and companies to individual investors and workers. Consumers began saving instead of spending, investors put their money in safe places, companies cut costs, banks started hoarding cash, and countries imposed austerity on their citizens.

So, yes, negative mentality played a big role in the emergence and long-term impact of the Great Depression and the Great Recession. At the same time, contrary to what FDR said, many of the crises we experience, whether global, societal, organizational, or individual, are justifiably frightening. The Great Depression and Great Recession were exacerbated by psychology, but they were grounded in economics and finance. To a large extent, we were at the mercy of uncontrolled market forces, both small and large. Some of the forces were close to us—for example, easy credit, reckless consumerism, and the housing bubble. Other forces rose from the financial miasma—such as subprime and predatory lending, the creation of risky investment products, and over-leveraged financial institutions. Still other forces imposed themselves from the halls of government in the form of economic policy—such as deregulation, the bailout of banks that were deemed "too big to fail," and changes in monetary policy.

What we know now is that in reaction to the lit tinderbox of global finance, a pessimistic mentality fanned the flames and spread like wildfire across our country and around the world. We witnessed a mass exodus from the stock market, investors withdrawing money reflexively, knee-jerk reactions from politicians, rioting in the streets, and hasty and poorly thought-out "solutions" by governmental policy makers. As the crisis played out, we saw progress in response to the crisis in fits and starts, often driven by political ideology rather than sound economic theory and evidence, as our country and the world struggled to move beyond its visceral reactions to a calmer and more deliberate answer.

Yet almost a decade after its supposed conclusion, the aftereffects of the Great Recession are still present, with individuals, companies, industries, and nations continuing to struggle between the calm voice of reason and the shrill voice of fear, frustration, and anger.

Both the Great Depression and the Great Recession offer us powerful lessons about the right and wrong ways to respond to the crises we inevitably experience in our lives—as individuals, communities, nations, and the world. It's easy to get so absorbed in the powerful and visceral reactions we feel when faced with a crisis that we underestimate or completely miss the valuable lessons we can learn about how to deal with crises of all sorts. More importantly, we have the power to regain control of our own psychology when a crisis strikes. We can allow this unproductive mentality to overwhelm us. Or we can embrace a positive, composed, and constructive psychology to both help us when a crisis arises and also better prepare us for future crises.

WHAT IS A CRISIS?

Before I go further into an exploration of crises, I want to step back and ask a simple yet important question: What is a crisis? The answer to this question might seem obvious, as we all intuitively know what a crisis is—it is when something bad happens suddenly. At the same time, I believe in the power of words. I also believe that we must all not only fully understand the depth and implications of words but also—given the many meanings words can have—be assured of having shared meanings. Here are definitions of *crisis* that can be found in several dictionaries:

- A time of intense difficulty, trouble, or danger
- A time when a difficult or important decision must be made
- A crucial or decisive point or situation; a turning point
- An unstable condition, as in political, social, or economic affairs, involving an impending abrupt or decisive change
- An emotionally stressful event or traumatic change in a person's life

All of these definitions add texture to our understanding of what a crisis is, but, in my view, none fully capture what a crisis really means. In an attempt to capture the full depth and breadth of what a crisis is and its impact on us, let me offer this definition: an event or situation that arises suddenly or reaches a tipping point in its severity that has the effect of significantly disrupting lives and threatening the status quo, and that may also have long-term, harmful consequences on individuals or groups.

Qualities of a Crisis

These definitions vary in certain ways, yet they all have common themes. First, crises are unexpected. They occur without warning or reach a new threshold suddenly. As such, they produce shock and, as I will discuss throughout *How to Survive and Thrive*, trigger an immediate, powerful, and primitive reaction that doesn't serve us well in most modern crises.

Second, crises, by their very nature, create instability—what was once solid is no longer. For example, think of the crisis caused by the 2010 earthquake in Haiti. Certainly, the physical and economic damage was staggering, but also consider the psychological damage. Do we trust anything more than the ground under our feet? All of a sudden, Haitians lost that "rock-solid" stability.

Third, what was once familiar, predictable, and controllable ceases to be so. In its place is a sense of uncertainty, a sense that we can longer count on the past and present to predict the future.

Fourth, the instability and uncertainty that emerge from a crisis are experienced as trauma in many forms, including physical, psychological, social, political, emotional, and economic. This profound distress takes a toll on us and exacts substantial short-term suffering. Just as importantly, crises produce a delayed and extended reaction that often isn't realized for years.

Fifth, as I will discuss shortly, a crisis triggers a sense of urgency, a perceived need to act immediately and with force. The impetus behind this exigency is the need to control in the hope of minimizing the damage caused by the crisis and reestablishing a sense of normalcy after a period of disruption and destabilization. These five attributes are what make a crisis so challenging to experience and so difficult to overcome.

The Nuances of a Crisis

If we explore the linguistic roots of the word *crisis*, what emerges is a different, and more nuanced, understanding that has meaningful implications in how we perceive, feel about, experience, and respond to a crisis. For example, in Hebrew the original meaning of *crisis* refers both to something broken and to a solution, suggesting a crisis is something that is damaged and needs to be repaired or replaced. Interestingly, in Hebrew *crisis* also denotes a birth, indicating something positive emerging from an episode of pain.

The Greek derivation of crisis, *klinein*, has neither positive nor negative connotations associated with it. Rather, a crisis simply involves the need to form a judgment or make a decision. This meaning removes the threatening undercurrent of a crisis and with it, presumably, the oftentimes negative reactions that crises provoke and that can add fuel to the fire of the five qualities mentioned previously.

Interestingly, as John F. Kennedy noted, "When written in Chinese, the word 'crisis' is composed of two characters—one represents danger, and the other represents opportunity."

At best, the modern-day use of the term *crisis* doesn't do justice to its rich and potentially beneficial aspects. At worst, our contemporary use is so laden with baggage that it creates a perception about and an emotional reaction to the situation that we deem a crisis; as a result, we begin our response to the situation from a decidedly negative, defensive, and counterproductive posture.

How to Survive and Thrive aims to take into account both the origins and the current use of the term *crisis* as a means of broadening our understanding of the experiences we label *crises* and better positioning our perceptions and emotional reactions to those situations. Ultimately, my goal is to liberate us from our limiting and often harmful beliefs about crises and our internal responses when faced with a crisis. I also hope to increase the range of (constructive) reactions we have available in the face of a crisis.

> "When is a crisis reached? When questions arise that can't be answered."—Ryszard Kapuscinski, journalist[2]

Examples of a Crisis

Crises can be experienced in every area of life, from the personal to the societal to the natural. They vary in their specifics but share the common qualities I just discussed. Crises can be placed into a number of general categories:

- Personal (e.g., gender, emotions, substance abuse)

- Health (e.g., illness, injury, aging, dying)
- Safety (e.g., harassment, violence, property crime)
- Relationship (c.g., divorce, family estrangement, death)
- Transition (e.g., child to adult, single to married, new parent, empty nest)
- Career (e.g., job loss, job dissatisfaction, return to work)
- Financial (e.g., stock market crash, bad investment)
- Technological (e.g., hacking, identity theft, cyberbullying)
- Corporate (e.g., deception, fraud, negligence)
- Governmental (e.g., politics, corruption, scandals)
- Societal (e.g., poverty, education, health care)
- Environmental (e.g., pollution, unsafe drinking water, food shortage)
- Natural disaster (e.g., hurricane, flood, earthquake)

A CRISIS IS A CRISIS

How to Survive and Thrive is an exploration of all crises—large and small; physical and psychological; short-lived and ongoing; personal and professional; individual, family, corporate, community, governmental, and societal. The reality is that we face various crises every day in the form of unexpected challenges, obstacles, setbacks, and failures. Moreover, crises are a test of our psychological, emotional, and leadership mettle. In a way, crises tell us a lot about who we are because our best and worst qualities reveal themselves most prominently during the stresses of a crisis. Given the fact that crises are a normal, though certainly unpleasant, part of our lives, if we can become masters of crises then we become masters of ourselves and, in fact, life itself.

> "Life isn't meant to be easy. . . . Life is one crisis after another."—
> Richard M. Nixon, thirty-seventh US president[3]

OUR PRIMITIVE CRISIS WIRING

A crisis triggers our most primitive reaction: ensuring our survival. This ancient response evolved in our ancestors when they began walking upright. Threats to their survival mobilized emotional, physical, and psychological resources in reaction to the perceived crisis. Back then, threats generally had simple solutions; for example, threat of starvation could be solved by killing some game, and threat from a rival tribesman could be removed by doing battle or running away. Reducing the threat, by either vanquishing it or distancing it, resulted in survival being ensured.

Emotionally, our ancestors experienced immediate and intense feelings. If they had a chance to survive by fighting, they felt extreme anger that motivated them to attack the crisis with ferocity. If they had a better chance to survive by fleeing, they experienced fear that drove them to run away from the crisis with the utmost haste. These strong emotions catalyzed rapid physiological and psychological changes, which, in turn, produced immediate action. Without these responses, our ancestors would have died and their gene pools wouldn't have been propagated.

Physically, our ancestors' survival instinct prepared them by sharpening their senses, increasing their strength and stamina, and reducing their perception of pain. In response to a threat, our ancestors felt a rush of adrenaline. Their hearts pumped hard and fast, directing blood flow to parts of the body needed to respond to the crisis, for example, to their legs when confronted by a wild animal or a rival tribesman. Their breathing became forced and shallow. These essential physical changes produced the maximum amount of strength and agility to fight or the speed and endurance to flee; without these changes, our primitive forbearers were dead.

Psychologically, our ancestors' focus honed in on the cause of the crisis and their decision making shifted into hyperdrive. These instantaneous changes in psychology ensured their minds locked onto the crisis, raced through the various options, and worked feverishly to determine the best course of action in response to the crisis. Without a laser-like focus, quick thinking, and rapid decision making, our earlier predecessors wouldn't have survived.

In primitive times, those who didn't emotionally, physically, and psychologically react to the crisis the fastest didn't, as they say, live to tell the tale. They either were killed before they had time to respond or lacked the capabilities to fight with sufficient rage or flee with adequate urgency.

WHAT WORKED THEN DOESN'T WORK NOW

Unfortunately, what worked for us as cave people doesn't usually work in the twenty-first century. You may ask, why wouldn't a reaction that has served us so well—first, as animals when we crawled out of the primordial muck some 300 million of years ago and then for the past 250,000 years as *Homo sapiens*—work now? The answer lies in the increased complexity of life that has evolved as humankind has become more civilized and as technological advancements have changed our individual, social, and work lives.

The notion of survival and how best to ensure it has changed dramatically since the earliest days of humankind. For most people in the developed world, it's no longer about staying alive in the face of an immediate crisis. It's not even about putting a roof over our heads, clothes on our backs, or food on the table. These essentials haven't changed much since we lived in caves (though our "caves" have gotten larger, our clothes fancier, and our food better tasting).

Today's crises have complex dimensions that were unheard of for our ancestors and that our ancient survival instinct is now ill unprepared for. Today's crises have a different makeup than those faced by our ancestors. Present crises are often not foreseeable or even understandable. For example, the Great Recession and its continuing aftermath, with its incomprehensible credit default swaps, collateralized debt obligations, and subprime mortgages, have demonstrated how complex our lives are: even the CEOs of the companies that sold those arcane financial products didn't understand how they worked or their implications on the financial markets.

Many of today's crises are distant and their impact is indirect. For example, the wars in the Middle East that America has been fighting for almost twenty years are occurring thousands of miles from US shores, yet they profoundly affect us as individuals and as a country. Current crises are also often amorphous—their effects diffuse, their causes unclear, and as a consequence, their solutions elusive.

Today's crises are frequently delayed and then lingering. The housing crisis of the late 2000s, for example, was years in the making and, more than a decade later, is still being felt.

Lastly, many crises these days are beyond individual or even institutional control. During the Great Recession, as many of us watched our jobs disappear, our homes foreclosed on, and our investment portfolios decimated, we were helpless to intervene. Even more scary, as our entire economy slumped so dramatically, we saw that industry and government had only limited ability to exert control and turn our economy around.

The survival instinct that was triggered in response to crises and worked so well for our forbearers is now far too simplistic and binary to effectively overcome the varied nature of modern-day crises. In fact, not only is it not effective, but it is usually counterproductive to our survival and to the survival of companies, industries, societies, and even our Earth.

Moreover, in the last two decades the crisis landscape has changed significantly compared to just fifty years ago, much less fifty thousand years ago. As I will describe in *How to Survive and Thrive*, the economic, political, technological, and cultural shifts of the last two decades have been truly tectonic in their impact on our lives. Many of the paradigms, practices, and solutions that were applicable in the twentieth century are no longer relevant or useful. Thanks to the technological revolution we have seen since the start of the new millennium, we can no longer respond to twenty-first-century crises using the tried-and-true answers from the past, distant or recent. These changes require us to look at crises in new and different ways and to seek innovative and untested solutions to the crises we are confronted with if we have any hope of overcoming them.

THE NEXT STEP IN OUR EVOLUTION?

This exploration clearly demonstrates that the *crisis mentality* of primitive times has outlived its usefulness. In an ideal world, this outdated instinctive response would go the way of the dinosaurs (being extinct) and the appendix (having no impact)—except, perhaps, in reaction to mugging and other personal threats to our lives. Yet, the crisis mentality is not going away any time soon. This ancient reaction to crisis, which is coded into our very genes, cannot be immediately exorcised from our psyches; it will take many millions of years for it to evolve out of us. So instead of removing it from us, our only hope is to remove its power over us, neutering it, you might say, so that its influence becomes negligible.

To do this, we must understand the crisis mentality and learn to gain mastery over it, so that while others react to a crisis as our ancestors did (with, for example, fear, pessimism, and panic), we remain calm, optimistic, and purposeful in response to it. This transition from the crisis instincts of our distant past to a more effective psychology of our present and future is essential if we are to respond positively to the crises that we will inevitably face in our lives in the twenty-first century and beyond.

> "There cannot be a crisis today; my schedule is already full."—Henry Kissinger, American statesman[4]

Opportunity Mindset

If this crisis mentality, which is so deeply woven into our DNA, no longer fulfills our most basic survival instinct, what can we do to survive in the concrete, metal, and wired world in which we now live? As with earlier forms of evolution, we need to adapt to our surroundings and produce a shift in the crisis instinct that will be more effective than the survival instinct that served us so well for these hundreds of thousands of years. We need to develop what I call an *opportunity mindset*. As Rahm Emanuel, President Obama's former chief of staff, stated, "A crisis is a terrible thing to waste." In other words, it is an opportunity to take positive action. Notably, this new approach is also more in line with the linguistic origins of crisis.

Just as I defined crisis in a deep way so that we may have a shared and understood vocabulary, I also want us to have a collective understanding of what I mean by an *opportunity*. An opportunity is defined as "an occasion or situation that makes it possible to do something that you want to do or have to do; a favorable juncture of circumstances; a good position, chance or prospect, as for advancement or success." As these definitions suggest, we normally see opportunities as positive situations from which we can gain considerably, which would seem a far cry from what crises present to us.

However, although crises are, by their very nature, negative, they have two positive aspects: First, navigating crises successfully requires a positive orientation, an opportunity mindset or can-do attitude rather than a defeatist attitude. Second, as many people who have weathered crises will tell you, the challenges that arise from a crisis can lead to new and healthy realizations, perspectives, growth, and, yes, opportunities that have a very positive impact on our lives. In other words, crises can, ultimately, be life affirming and life changing in the most positive ways.

Additionally, I found a definition of opportunity in a business dictionary that really hits the nail on the head: "exploitable set of circumstances with uncertain outcome, requiring commitment of resources and involving exposure to risk." This definition, like the more nuanced understanding of crisis discussed earlier, sees opportunity as both positive and potentially negative. Interestingly, then, crisis and opportunity have much more in common than we might initially think. Given this richer exploration, we may conclude that crisis and opportunity really differ less in the substance of the situation than in how they are perceived. And it is those divergent perceptions that set people on very different roads as they confront a crisis.

> "Close scrutiny will show that most 'crisis situations' are opportunities to either advance, or stay where you are."—Maxwell Maltz, author of *Psycho-Cybernetics*[5]

Forks in the Road

The primitive crisis mentality is so instinctive and powerful that you may feel as if you have no choice but to respond to it; like being on a highway with no exits, you're going to stay on that road because you have no way to get off. Developing an opportunity mindset involves recognizing that your response to a crisis is not an immutable path governed by evolution and your genes, but rather a modifiable route in which you can choose how to react based on thought and reason. Instead of seeing one road of crisis mentality, you will see *forks in the road* from which you can select an opportunity mindset. This book explores nine essential aspects of your psychology; your ability to recognize and choose a different road in each of these nine aspects will determine whether you are able to resist the ineffective crisis mentality and embrace the more constructive opportunity mindset.

Forks in the road arise when your crisis mentality compels you to take the road that worked for our ancestors but probably won't work in today's world. In other words, that road you are propelled down by your crisis mentality will lead to some form of "death"—a psychological, social, professional, financial, physical, or other form of demise that may result from a crisis. Although you may not have been aware of it in the past, there are other roads—good roads!—you can take that are much more effective in a crisis. In fact, opportunity mindset begins when you recognize these forks when you experience immediate and overwhelming negative emotions (e.g., fear, anger, or despair) or intensely negative thinking (e.g., "I'm sure I'm going to lose my job."), or when you begin to engage in destructive behavior (e.g., attacking your boss).

But recognition is not enough to take the good road. Rather, it only gives you the opportunity to make a better choice. Your crisis mentality is still deeply ingrained and strong, so you will likely go through a period in which you recognize the good road when you arrive at it but still take the bad road. You shouldn't be discouraged by this internal battle; your crisis mentality has been around a long time and is not easily overcome. At this point you must muster the calm, confidence, and determination to reject your crisis mentality and take the good road of opportunity mindset. *How to Survive and Thrive* is devoted to showing you how to recognize and take these good roads.

> "Character is not made in a crisis, it is only exhibited."—Robert Freeman, photographer[6]

BEING HUMAN IN A CRISIS

I'm not suggesting that you become cold, detached, and distant from a crisis; that is, quite frankly, impossible given that we are human beings. In other words, I'm not encouraging you to shed your humanity to protect yourself from the crisis or to become an unfeeling automaton who responds to crises in a preprogrammed or disengaged way.

To the contrary, I want you to fully embrace your humanity and leverage every aspect of being human, not just your primitive side, to respond positively and constructively to the crises life throws at you. Being human means accepting that a crisis mentality will envelop you at first; you can't resist millions of years of evolution so easily. In fact, if you try to resist the powerful emotions and physiology you experience in a crisis, you will actually do yourself more harm than good. Being human in a crisis involves acknowledging and accepting the crisis reaction as part of the deal; it's natural and normal. And, paradoxically, not immediately pushing the crisis reaction away is a sign of strength that you should embrace rather than a sign of weakness to ignore. You can use that initial wave of crisis mentality to fuel and focus yourself.

At the same time, because most crises we face in the modern world tend to unfold at a slower pace than those of our forbearers, being human also means that you don't allow the crisis mentality to consume and overwhelm you and dictate your long-term reactions. Thanks to our evolved brain—what separates us from animals—we don't have to fall victim to our primitive urges. Instead, we have the ability to corral and harness them, release ourselves from their control, and make full use of the more evolved aspects of our humanity, with the end goal of responding more purposely and productively to the crises we face.

WHAT LIES AHEAD

The purpose of *How to Survive and Thrive* is to give you the power to escape from the hardwired grip of the outdated and ineffective crisis mentality and replace it with a modern-day and beneficial opportunity mindset that will enable you to emerge from a crisis not only surviving but also thriving.

How to Survive and Thrive is comprised of nine chapters that explore the essential psychological areas that most impact your reactions to crises. In each chapter, you will be presented with three forks in the road that determine whether the crisis mentality of fear, negativity, and panic controls you or whether you impose the opportunity mindset of calm, confidence, and determination on the crisis.

How to Survive and Thrive explores the meaning and power of crisis and how it impacts us. Compelling examples are drawn from notable crises, both recent and historical, well-known and unfamiliar, to bring these issues alive. Illustrations from government, large and small business, and ordinary people highlight who responded well and who did not. With these lessons explained, I then provide you with deep insights, useful information, and practical tools to ensure that you break free of the crisis mentality and embrace an opportunity mindset in all aspects of your life.

"There was always an opportunity in crisis, however desperate things seemed."—Gemma Malley, English journalist[7]

Part I

Your Amygdala

We humans like to think of ourselves as highly evolved beings at the top of evolutionary hierarchy and clearly different from the animals from which we came. Gosh, we have opposable digits (that is, thumbs), which are rare in the animal kingdom, and unlike our animal ancestors, we have a cerebral cortex, which enables us to think, evaluate, organize, and plan our actions. We certainly are special, aren't we? Well, yes, there are many things about us that separate us from animals, which I will discuss in detail in part II. For now, let's look at how we are far more similar to those creatures lower down the evolutionary ladder, much to the chagrin to those who hold an "exceptionalistic" view of human beings. These similarities become most evident when we are faced with a crisis. We humans most resemble other animals in how we respond to crises.

> "In the animal kingdom, the rule is, eat or be eaten. In the human kingdom, define or be defined."—Thomas Szasz, former professor and critic of psychiatry [1]

The part of the brain that often reduces us to animals when confronted by a crisis is the amygdala, two small, almond-shaped chunks of gray matter located at the base of our brain (the area commonly referred to as the primitive brain), with one chunk on the left side and one on the right. An in-depth exploration of the amygdala's neuroanatomy is beyond the scope of this book, but a basic understanding will illuminate how we typically respond to crises and hopefully show us how to control this primitive reaction.

Let's begin by traveling back in time, about three hundred thousand years, to the Serengeti in Africa when bipedal beings finally earned the designation of *Homo sapiens* (i.e., human being). Back then, when an individual faced a crisis, such as a saber-toothed tiger or a rival tribesperson with a really big club, the amygdala processed this life-threatening information, bypassed our higher-order thinking ability (no time for that!), and immediately triggered emotional, psychological, and physical changes that mobilized action in the name of survival.

Now this reaction sounds all well and good, doesn't it? And it was for our ancestors and may still be useful in the twenty-first century when confronted by, say, a mugger on a dark street or a mountain lion while on a hike. But the activation of the amygdala produces changes in our brain and body that are less effective for managing many of today's crises. For example, the amygdala told our ancestors' cerebral cortex to shut up because they didn't have time to think when faced with an immediate threat like a tiger. When our amygdala is activated, we lose our ability to think, analyze, evaluate, and plan before we act because back in primitive days, our ancestors didn't have the luxury of time before reacting. Plus, our cerebral cortex didn't have the firepower it has now because we didn't need those evolved functions when encountering someone or something that wanted to kill us. Our options were simple, clear, and instinctive.

Part I focuses on the specific ways in which our amygdala impacts our thoughts, emotions, and reactions to a crisis. It also introduces you to the forks in the road you can take to gain control over your amygdala (gosh, if we couldn't do that, then we'd really still be like other animals!). We will use what makes us a more evolved species to respond in ways that work when faced with crises of today instead of what worked many millennia ago.

Chapter One

Instincts

Primitive or Evolved?

Instincts lie at the heart of a crisis mentality. They are the starting point for all of the reactions we have toward a crisis. So, what is an instinct? Basically, it is a complex, genetically hardwired action (meaning it doesn't have to be learned through experience) that serves a specific purpose in our lives related to survival. As I have previously suggested, most human instincts are not much different from those of our primitive ancestors or, in fact, most other animals. Examples include fear, suckling, and sex.

Instincts are also the first obstacle to establishing an opportunity mindset. For us to gain control of and, if necessary, override our instincts when confronted with a crisis, we must understand the role that instincts play in how we respond to crises.

When we experience a crisis, we regress back to acting like our primitive ancestors did; we literally go caveman or cavewoman. We fall back on the deeply ingrained instincts and habits that have enabled us to survive for eons. Most notably, as I mentioned in the part I introduction, the amygdala is triggered the same way that the amygdalae of other animals are, and our body prepares to take action. These instincts evolved in us for a very good reason: they helped ensure our survival. Yet, as I noted in the introduction, what worked then doesn't necessarily work now. Those instincts that have served us so well for so long are no longer helpful in most modern-day crises.

In a crisis, more than any other situation, you need to have all of your most highly evolved capabilities firing on all cylinders. Many of today's crises—for example, financial, health, or interpersonal—are either highly complex, more cerebral than physical, or occur at a distance. As a result, modern-day crises are not typically solvable by way of immediate physical action, which is why your primitive instincts can prevent you from responding positively to and overcoming the many crises that occur today.

> "The wise are instructed by reason; ordinary minds by experience; the stupid, by necessity; and brutes by instinct."—Marcus T. Cicero, Roman philosopher and statesman [1]

There are three instinct forks in the road. These will appear when you are confronted with a crisis. Many of us fall victim to a crisis mentality because it's our natural instinct. By working to instill opportunity mindset "instincts," you will increase your awareness of the three forks and the probability that you will take the good road when faced with a crisis.

SURVIVAL VERSUS THRIVAL

The specific purpose that instincts serve is grounded in humans' most powerful instinct, survival. Since animals climbed out of the primordial muck and our early ancestors rose from all fours to walk upright, evolution has been guided by its ability to ensure our individual survival and, by extension, the survival of our species. Yet, as I will describe shortly, humans possess an instinctive drive that other animals do not. This instinct extends beyond just surviving and is based in a drive to thrive by growing, improving, and, well, continuing to evolve.

> "Nearly all men can stand adversity, but if you want to test a man's character, give him power."—Abraham Lincoln, sixteenth US president [2]

Survival

Just about everything that humans have become—how we think, what emotions we experience, and the ways we behave and interact with others—serves the essential purpose of ensuring our survival. In fact, Daniel Kahneman, a psychologist who won the 2002 Nobel Prize for economics, has demonstrated that how we think has clear evolutionary value. The way we process and remember information, solve problems, and make decisions is driven by what he calls "cognitive biases." Although this approach doesn't always result in the most accurate or best outcomes, it is the most efficient in terms of time and energy expenditure. These biases are guided by the basic principle: what is "good enough" for our survival.

Our emotions have also evolved to be of great benefit to our survival. "Hot" emotions, such as surprise and disgust, are experienced instantaneously and powerfully. These emotions signal an imminent threat to our survival (e.g., an attacker or rotten food), which initiates urgent action that increases our chances of survival. In contrast, "cool" emotions, like joy and love, typically take longer to be felt and are usually less intense initially. Simply put, there isn't a pressing need to experience cool emotions strongly or right away because they don't signal a threat to our lives.

The way we think and the emotions we feel that are immediate and intense have survival value, meaning they produce reactions that increase our chances of survival. Possibly the best-known expression of our survival instinct is our fight-or-flight reaction to a perceived threat to our survival (to be discussed in detail later in this chapter). Without this instinct to survive, our primitive forbearers would have died, their genes wouldn't have been passed on, and we wouldn't be living in the twenty-first century.

Unfortunately, in an odd sort of way, our primitive survival instinct has become outdated for many aspects of our modern lives. Back in the Serengeti three hundred thousand years ago, this instinct ensured our physical survival in the face of daily threats in the form of predatory animals, hostile tribes, starvation, and pestilence. Yes, sadly, many people in the world still face some of these same challenges. At the same time, for those who live in developed countries (and, admittedly, who are most likely to read this book!), times have changed, such that primitive physical challenges are no longer a daily existential threat.

Instead, survival in the twenty-first century has taken on new meanings that require a different understanding of survival and an evolved survival instinct that focuses on modern-day crises related to finances, marriage, child rearing, education, career, politics, and global events. In all of these threats, the danger isn't often physical death but rather other forms of "death," such as psychological (e.g., self-identity, self-esteem), cmotional (e.g., shame, sadness), social (e.g., rejection), and professional (e.g., failure). This new conceptualization of the survival instinct demands a very different set of responses than those triggered by the old-school fight-or-flight response.

Thrival

Our understanding of and means for ensuring this new form of survival in the twenty-first century have changed significantly compared to primitive times. A more appropriate definition of survival for modern times may be "the state of continuing to live one's normal life, typically in spite of an accident, ordeal, or difficult circumstances." In other words, survival is the ability to get by or maintain the status quo despite challenging conditions.

At the same time, as the immediate threats to our physical survival have receded, another instinct more aligned with our times has risen to the forefront—what I call our "thrival" instinct (yes, it is actually a word). Derived from the word *thrive*, thrival can be defined as "to prosper; to be fortunate or successful; to grow or develop vigorously; flourish." In other words, to want to feel better, do better, and live better. The thrival instinct drives us to seek out our limits and to expand the world in which we live.

Now, keep in mind that the instinct to thrive isn't new in any way, shape, or form. The thrival instinct—that is, the drive to know more, do more, experience more, create more, and explore more—is what has produced all of the great advancements in human history. From the discovery of fire to the invention of the wheel to manifest destiny to the innovation of the Internet and every step of progress in between, the thrival instinct has driven humans to evolve.

Following the Industrial Revolution—when mass production and distribution of food made starvation for most a distant memory, mechanization and automation provided us with more leisure time, people began to live longer and healthier lives, and overall basic survival resources (e.g., food, water, shelter) became more abundant and readily available—the thrival instinct overtook the survival instinct. This trajectory has accelerated with each additional technological development, giving increasing numbers of Earth's population more security, resources, and leisure time, and along with these, more opportunity to not simply to survive, but rather to thrive.

Conflict between Instincts

The problem with these two instincts—survival and thrival—is that they are fundamentally in conflict with each other. Our survival instinct demands that we seek out safety, security, certainty, familiarity, predictability, routine, comfort, and control. In contrast, our thrival instinct drives us to seek out risk, novelty, uncertainty, insecurity, discomfort, and stress.

This conflict is inherently connected to the difference between a crisis mentality and an opportunity mindset, with the former being grounded in our survival instinct and the latter woven into our thrival instinct. As I show throughout *How to Survive and Thrive*, rejecting our survival instinct and embracing our thrival instinct is essential to shifting from a crisis psychology to a psychology of opportunity. With most of today's crises, thrival instinct qualities will better serve your efforts in responding to crisis challenges and enable you to adopt an opportunity mindset.

Given that most modern-day crises don't require immediate and urgent action, your goal is to not allow the deeply ingrained survival instinct to dictate your reactions and to replace it with the thrival instinct and the processes that spring from it. This entire book is devoted to encouraging the transition from crisis mentality to opportunity mindset, and this objective can be catalyzed in several initial steps.

First, when a crisis strikes and you experience the first wave of a crisis mentality, don't attempt to resist it. The fact is that you can't, because it has millions of years of evolution driving the instinct through you. Instead, acknowledge and accept that your survival instinct is responding naturally to the perceived threat. This acceptance will dull the intensity of your survival instinct's actions by not adding unhelpful emotions (e.g., frustration, anger) or physiological reactions (e.g., more adrenaline) to the situation. Acceptance will also allow you to let the psychological, emotional, and physical wave to pass more readily and quickly.

Second, the initial shock of your survival instinct and crisis mentality will either ebb to a more manageable level or mostly run its course. Then, you can invoke your thrival instinct by recognizing its attributes are better suited for twenty-first-century crises (I'll explain why and what part of the brain is activated to help this process in part II, Your Cerebral Cortex).

Third, expect and acknowledge that this shift from survival to thrival and crisis mentality to opportunity mindset will be uncomfortable. Millions of years of evolution will be screaming at you to not go there. But you must go there because the thrival instinct and an opportunity mindset give you the best chance of coming out of your crisis as intact as possible.

Finally, make a commitment to your thrival instinct and your opportunity mindset. Stay conscious of and vigilant to your survival instinct and crisis mentality creeping into your mind and body and attempting to kidnap you back to your primitive self. Then, use that commitment as the foundation for everything I offer you in *How to Survive and Thrive*, which you can then apply to crises that you confront in your life moving forward.

THREAT VERSUS CHALLENGE

How you respond to a crisis starts with how you look at it. I have found that a simple distinction lies at the heart of whether you adopt a crisis mentality or an opportunity mindset: do you perceive the crisis as a threat or as a challenge? (Think glass half empty or half full, lemons or lemonade.) Whether you view crises as threats or challenges sets into motion a diametrically opposed cascade of thoughts, emotions, and actions that results in either constructive or harmful responses.

> "We're programmed to believe that time is the enemy, that it takes away from us or that it diminishes us. I have found that it's done the opposite to me. Life is in perfect balance. It's just that our perception of it isn't."—Queen Rania of Jordan[3]

Threat

The problem is that whether you respond to a crisis as a threat or a challenge is initially driven by your deeply ingrained instincts. The threat instinct arises instantaneously to protect you from the perceived danger: you experience visceral and dramatic emotions, including fear and anger; your body is mobilized through powerful physiological changes that were designed to help you survive; and your focus narrows to guarantee that you pay attention solely to the presenting threat.

As I emphasized earlier, this reaction served humans well in primitive times when the crises were obvious and immediate. Back then, people had to respond immediately and urgently if they wanted a chance of survival. However, due to the amorphous nature of most crises today, this defensive posture more than likely decreases your chances of survival or successful navigation of the crisis at hand (e.g., holding onto a job, protecting your retirement portfolio, or keeping your marriage intact). The painful irony of the threat instinct is that it once ensured the future of humanity, but today it can actually exacerbate, rather than mitigate, a crisis.

Challenge

The ability to respond to a crisis as a challenge separates us from our primitive forbearers because we must resist our most basic instincts. The fundamental goal behind the challenge response is to pause rather than act instinctively, engage our cerebral cortex, and figure out a way to overcome the crisis. More importantly, we now strive not only to survive but to thrive in the difficult environment the crisis has created.

This challenge mindset goes beyond simply creating a physical and psychological state that enables you to direct all of your resources to removing—or at least minimizing—the threat that the crisis presents to you. Although crises are not relished or sought out, using the challenge approach allows you to view them as opportunities to be embraced rather than misfortunes to recoil from. With this challenge perception, you are focused on responding to the crisis with commitment, confidence, and courage while minimizing counterproductive emotions like doubt, worry, or fear. Challenge is associated with embracing what needs to be done to overcome the crisis rather than obsessing about potential harm that might result. This can-do state acts as the foundation for the opportunity mindset by creating a positive lens through which you view and experience the crisis.

The challenge reaction prompts a vastly different emotional response to the crisis than the threat instinct. Whereas the threat reaction involves negative, unpleasant, and unhelpful emotions (e.g., fear, frustration, anger, and despair), challenge emotions include hope, pride, inspiration, and equanimity. These much more pleasant and productive emotions propel you toward confronting the crisis rather than avoiding it or sabotaging your efforts to alleviate it.

In turn, these emotions activate a physiological state that better prepares you for responding positively to the complex nature of crises today. You experience just the right amount of adrenaline to make you feel ready to perform your best, your muscles are loose, and your breathing is deep and controlled. Unlike the intense and uncomfortable physical changes associated with the threat instinct, the challenge approach leads you to feel physically comfortable and in control of your physiology. You may feel relaxed yet energized or, perhaps, even fired up to take on the crisis.

This calmer condition allows your mind to be clear and intentional. You will be confident that you have the capabilities to surmount the crisis. Maintaining relative calm in the storm of a crisis enables you to focus on the depth and breadth of the situation: analyze possible options, set reasonable goals, make sound decisions, plot appropriate courses of action, and pursue them with vigor that wouldn't be possible in the frenzied state of the threat instinct.

> "The most authentic thing about us is our capacity to create, to overcome, to endure, to transform, to love and to be greater than our suffering."—Ben Okri, African poet [4]

From Threat to Challenge

It is unrealistic to expect that you will never again experience the threat instinct in response to a crisis. We would all love to be cool, calm, and collected when faced with a crisis, but that's rarely the case, at least initially. Because the threat response has been wired into our brains through millions of years of evolution, some feelings of threat are an inevitable part of crises. As such, the presence of the threat instinct is less important than whether you continue to react to the crisis like our primitive ancestors did or let go of the threat instinct and shift to a challenge orientation.

Recognize the Threat

The first step in making the shift from a threat reaction to a challenge response is to recognize that your threat instinct is being triggered. Often, our threat responses are so strong and ingrained that we have no conscious awareness of our reactions to the threat; fight-or-flight kicks in and we're swept away by its immediacy and intensity. Without recognizing the response's presence, you can't engage your evolved brain and stop your outdated threat instinct from continuing to control your response to the crisis.

Gaining awareness of your threat instinct when it happens isn't magic; it's just a matter of having your "radar" on when crises arise. Just by learning the differences between your threat instinct and a challenge response, you are better attuning yourself to occasions when your threat instinct is activated. At first, you may not be conscious of your threat instinct going off until it has already passed (for a short-lived crisis) or until you are well into the crisis (for a lasting crisis). Over time, however, as your sensitivity to your threat instinct increases, you will find that your recognition moves closer and closer to the fork in the road of threat versus challenge, until one day when you are confronted with a crisis, you will have an epiphany: "My threat instinct is kicking in, and I can now do something about it."

> "Awareness is like the sun. When it shines on things, they are transformed."—Thich Nhat Hanh, Vietnamese Buddhist monk and peace activist[5]

Accept the Threat

The next step in overcoming your threat instinct is to accept it as normal. How normal, you ask? So normal that billions upon billions of human beings before you, over hundreds of thousands of years, have experienced the same response. Unfortunately, the threat itself isn't the only problem when you experience a threat instinct in reaction to a crisis. Three things can exacerbate the impact a crisis has on you.

First, allowing the threat instinct to consume you and drive your thinking, emotions, and reactions. Relying on this primitive and outdated instinct to help you through a modern-day crisis will certainly not end well.

Second, attempting to ignore or distract yourself from the crisis in the hope that it will just go away. The fact is that crises don't usually just run their course. Instead, they tend to persist and grow if not actively staunched. Plus, crises tend to be big and powerful like an eight hundred–pound gorilla in the room. That means you won't be able to ignore it for long, and by then, it might be too late to resolve the crisis in a positive way.

Third, not realizing that your perception of the crisis in the near term is through the lens of the threat instinct. Not only do you experience the trauma of the crisis and the unpleasantness of the threat instinct, but you also feel terrible for feeling both in the first place. It's bad enough to have to deal with a crisis and the threat instinct on their own, it's even worse to then beat yourself up about feeling as if you are weak for succumbing to them. These feelings can create a psychological and emotional vicious cycle that compounds the impact of a threat instinct many times over. You feel bad about feeling bad, which makes you feel even worse and that increases the perception of the threat and the harm that will be incurred by the crisis.

When your threat instinct is triggered, cut yourself some slack by accepting it as a natural—although not ideal—response to a crisis. This acceptance takes the pressure off of this threat feeling, lessens your internal turmoil and conflict, and makes the threat less menacing and more realistic. Not adding the insult of a cacophony of negative thoughts and emotions to the injury of the threat instinct itself will not only feel better but also take away much of the power that the threat has over you and free up energy to put you in a better position to shift to a challenge orientation.

> "Acceptance doesn't mean resignation; it means understanding that something is what it is and that there's got to be a way through it."—Michael J. Fox, Canadian-American actor and activist[6]

Understand the Threat

With your threat instinct in its proper perspective and its psychological and emotional volume turned down, you are now in a position to begin the transition from threat reaction to challenge response. This shift starts by understanding the precise nature of the crisis and what makes it so threatening. Crises commonly threaten important areas of our lives, including our careers, finances, relationships, and health. When you have a clear understanding of what is threatening about the crisis, it becomes something more tangible, more clearly defined, and more manageable, rather than an amorphous feeling of threat to your survival.

Crises often create a double whammy when it comes to the threat instinct. There are the obvious threats such as a serious health issue or financial ruin. But these overt crises often trigger internal "crises of self" that threaten our perceptions of ourselves. For example, losing your job can jeopardize your view of yourself as a competent person. An illness can prompt existential worry about your mortality. To move from threat to challenge, you must understand and address both levels of the threat present in crises.

"Any fool can know. The point is to understand."—Albert Einstein, German theoretical physicist[7]

Respond to the Threat

A strong indication of your transition from threat to challenge is your ability to resist this deeply ingrained instinct that has governed our responses to crises for as long as humans have walked the Earth. If you can recognize that fork in the road and take the "good road" rather than the "bad road," you will score a big victory in your shift to a challenge response and your ability to confront the crisis in a positive and constructive way. Developing the ability to recognize this fork in the road is so important that it's taught in the military. They label the fork in the road Courses of Action Development in which they assess risk, identify possible outcomes, and then choose a course of action that best diminishes the threat.

Most often, taking the good road when confronted by a crisis begins by not doing anything. This pause from the immediacy, intensity, and urgency of the just-presented crisis enables you to stop the threat instinct before it can fully take hold of you and before it does any harm (more on this shortly).

"Two roads diverged in a wood, and I— / I took the one less traveled by, / And that has made all the difference."—Robert Frost, "The Road Not Taken"[8]

You can then decide what is the best "big picture" road to take in addressing the crisis. This is perhaps the greatest challenge when faced with a crisis. A threat instinct causes us to focus on the most present and obvious signs of the crisis. In other words, we become so absorbed by the "trees" that we can't see the "forest." As noted, this reaction worked for our ancestors, but it won't work when faced with today's complex crises. The goal of responding positively to a crisis is to see and respond to both the trees (the immediate threat) and the forest (the larger crisis). A response that is calm, deliberate, reasoned, and solutions based will accomplish that goal.

Embrace Challenge

Your ability to make the complete transition from viewing crises as threats to viewing them as challenges relies on embracing and ingraining certain beliefs about yourself. These beliefs act to override the threat instinct when confronted by a crisis. By their very nature, these perspectives remove the deafening alarm of threat (think Chicken Little, "the sky is falling") and replace it with a battle cry of a challenge (think Paul Revere, "the British [crises] are coming, the British [crises] are coming"). I have identified five such beliefs that lay this foundation. One thing to note about these beliefs is that they build on one another, from the first to the last.

> "The last three or four reps is what makes the muscle grow. This area of pain divides the champion from someone else who is not a champion. That's what most people lack, having the guts to go on and just say they'll go through the pain no matter what happens."—Arnold Schwarzenegger, former professional bodybuilder, actor, former governor of California[9]

"I Am Competent."

One of the most threatening aspects of a crisis is the feelings of being over your head and out of control. In other words, feeling like you're not capable of overcoming the crisis. When you have a fundamental faith in your capabilities, you believe that you have what it takes to surmount anything that comes your way. This sense of competence can be both specific and general. In an ideal world, you would possess the specific capabilities to deal directly with a crisis. For example, it would be great if you were a lawyer with a legal crisis, a physician with a health crisis, or a family therapist with a child crisis.

Unfortunately, specific competencies rarely align with the crises we experience. When this misalignment exists, having a general sense of competence provides a feeling of relative comfort that mitigates the impact of the threat instinct and increases the confidence to seek out support, guidance, and information that will help you constructively navigate the crisis. With belief in your competence, you remove the potentially intense threat associated with the possibility of surrendering to the crisis and its consequences ("I don't have a chance!"). Then you can focus on mustering all of your resources to conquer the crisis.

> "Some people say that I have an attitude—maybe I do. But I think that you have to. You have to believe in yourself when no one else does—that makes you a winner right there."—Venus Williams, American professional tennis player[10]

"I Am Responsible for Myself."

This belief in ownership of yourself results in your ability to see that you control how you respond to a crisis and that your response (what you think, feel, and do) frequently determines how the crisis affects you. It prevents you from falling into a victim mentality where you feel ineffective and helpless. As a result, you believe that your response to the crisis is within your control even though the cause of the crisis is often outside of your control. As a result, you take responsibility for your reaction, look inward for strength and direction, and decide for yourself how to move forward in the face of the crisis.

"I Am Determined."

One of the most common reactions when confronted by a significant crisis is to surrender to what might seem inevitable. Yet, a steely resolve and an unwavering determination is what will drive you to persist in the face of the potentially formidable obstacles that a crisis presents. That persistence is what often separates those who survive and even thrive in a crisis from those who don't. This determination draws its energy from the two previous beliefs because, if you see yourself as competent and take ownership of your response, then you will believe you can overcome the crisis if you persist. With these beliefs, you will harness and focus your energy with your fullest efforts toward a positive resolution of the crisis, regardless of potential obstacles and the uncertainty of the outcome.

"I Can Handle Adversity."

By their very nature, crises are rife with adversity, whether it is the cause of the crisis, its breadth, or the resulting problems that might ensue. Your belief that you can overcome whatever adversity crises throw at you is essential to seeing them as challenges rather than falling victim to your threat instinct.

You can develop an "I can handle adversity" belief in several ways. First, you can cultivate this belief by reflecting on past experiences in which you've marshalled your resources and succeeded in overcoming the adversity of previous crises. These experiences demonstrate to you that you had what it took to overcome prior crises, and you'll have what it takes this time. Second, because it's unrealistic to think that you will have previous experience specific to every crisis you face, you'll need to tap into your general knowledge, abilities, and tools to handle adversity and confront the challenges of the current crisis.

"You, me, or nobody is gonna hit as hard as life. But it ain't about how hard ya hit. It's about how hard you can get hit and keep moving forward. How much you can take and keep moving forward. That's how winning is done!"—Rocky Balboa, *Rocky* [11]

"I Can Effect Change."

The preceding four beliefs act as the wellspring for the basic yet powerful belief that you can catalyze positive change even in response to a crisis whose sheer size or force may seem to preclude such change. Realistically, due to the intangible, complex, and oftentimes incomprehensible nature of today's crises, the change you seek to resolve a crisis is often outside of your control. So, depending on the type of crisis, when I speak of change, I am referring to changing your beliefs about your ability to change the way you think, feel, and act in response to the crisis. The belief that you can effect change arises from your experience, knowledge, capabilities, tools, and support that you bring to bear as you face the crisis in front of you.

In sum, when you embrace these five fundamental beliefs (or perhaps just remind yourself that these beliefs are true and powerful), you create in yourself a foundation that enables you to confront a crisis with confidence and determination. This foundation allows you to let go of your primitive instincts, disconnect from your amygdala, fully engage your evolved cerebral cortex, and access your entire arsenal of abilities. In turn, you will be prepared to respond positively to whatever life throws at you, even in the direst of crises. Finally, in adopting these five beliefs, you complete the transition from threat reaction to challenge response and are one step closer to adopting an opportunity mindset in the face of a crisis.

Reaction versus Self-Possession

A defining feature of how our amygdala responds to threats to our survival is its immediate, reflexive reaction regardless of the degree to which that reaction is unfocused, undirected, or ineffective. Our amygdala and its accompanying instincts "believe" that any reaction is better than inaction, which, back in primitive times, was very likely true. However, such mindless reactions are not so effective in dealing with twenty-first-century crises. As such, the evolved "instinct" of self-possession will set the stage for your adoption of an opportunity mindset that is better suited for the crises you face today.

Reaction

This instinct produces reflexive actions that preclude thought, deliberation, or deliberate decision making. This reaction instinct produces instantaneous and urgent changes in us because the threats we faced in primitive times were immediate and life threatening. Our autonomic nervous system activates rapid emotional, psychological, and physical changes. Emotionally, we feel either fear or anger intensely. Psychologically, our senses are heightened and we're able to make instantaneous decisions with minimal thought because, in the past, if we took too long to figure out what to do, we would be beaten or eaten. Physically, we get a shot of adrenaline, our heart rate rises, blood flow is diverted to essential parts of the body, we experience greater strength and stamina, and our pain tolerance increases. Without these essential changes, our forebears would have died, their genes wouldn't have been passed on, and we wouldn't be living in the twenty-first century.

All of the changes we experience when our instincts tell us our life is in danger coalesce around what is famously known as the fight-or-fight reaction. Through evolution, we have learned that to increase our chances of survival, we must either fight or flee the threat. When we feel anger rising inside of us and the adrenaline coursing through our veins, we attack the threat. In contrast, when we feel fear overwhelming us and our heart jumping out of our throat, we run away from the threat as fast as we can.

Yet, these instincts are seldom effective in today's world where crises are rarely immediate, simple, tangible, direct, or readily resolvable. Let's consider how the fight-or-flight instinct often exacerbates rather than resolves many of today's crises. For example, you learn that you didn't get the promotion you had expected. Your primitive instincts are triggered, you feel threatened because the event jeopardizes your career aspirations and financial future. Being passed over for the promotion also threatens your deeply held perceptions of yourself as being highly competent and productive. It also challenges your belief that you are a likable person with whom others enjoy working. Your spontaneous reaction kicks in and you either fight (storm into your boss's office in a rage and threaten her life) or flee (leave the office in tears and never return). Clearly, neither of these actions will help your long-term professional or financial survival.

> "When we meet real tragedy in life, we can react in two ways either by losing hope and falling into self-destructive habits, or by using the challenge to find our inner strength. Thanks to the teachings of Buddha, I have been able to take this second way."—Dalai Lama, Tibetan monk [12]

Self-Possession

Given the very different nature of crises we experience today, involuntary reactions to them will not likely serve you well. Instead, your best bet in mitigating the impact of your most base and outmoded instincts and establishing an opportunity mindset is to create in yourself the quality of self-possession.

Self-possession is a word people use periodically, always in a complimentary way in describing someone. Yet, an informal survey among some of my colleagues indicated that few could adequately define it. So, to ensure clarity of meaning, I define self-possession as having full command of one's faculties, feelings, and behavior and control of one's emotions and reactions when under stress. I can't think of a better description of how you want to be when you experience a crisis. Moreover, self-possession is the antithesis of everything associated with the activation of the amygdala and the three instincts it unleashes. Only the complete authority over our thoughts, emotions, and actions that self-possession affords us will be sufficient to resist those instincts and replace them with measured thought, feelings of calm, a sense of mastery, and deliberate action. Ultimately, this state of self-possession results in an opportunity mindset.

To further illuminate the value of self-possession in dealing constructively with a crisis, it is useful to understand the origins of the word. The Latin derivatives of self-possession are to "hold in one's control, be master of, having power" and, interestingly, "to sit." These roots of self-possession have particular relevance for this discussion. These attributes of self-possession allow us to do several things that are essential for adopting an opportunity mindset and constructively responding to crises. Though much of *How to Survive and Thrive* is devoted to the steps I'm about to describe, I will summarize the key features of this process related to self-possession next.

"I am the master of my fate: / I am the captain of my soul."—William Ernest Henley, author and poet [13]

Control

Let's begin with the first derivation of self-possession because it lies at the heart of embracing a new set of evolved instincts that lead to an opportunity mindset. Whereas we often feel victims of our base instincts, self-possession gives us the ability to gain control over our minds and bodies. This mastery allows us to think, feel, and act in ways that constructively meet the demands of today's crises.

Taking control when a crisis strikes is no small feat because you have millions of years of evolution urging you to act now and with urgency. There is no easy answer to how to gain control of your primal urges when your mind and body are telling you that you must take action *now*! Yet, through awareness and self-control (and many of the strategies I will discuss), you can exert dominance over your amygdala and squelch its automatic reactions to a crisis.

Pause

The second origin of self-possession, "to sit," is precisely what our primitive instincts prevent us from doing ("I need to act now or I'll get eaten!"). Yet, there may be no more important thing you can do when faced with a crisis than to pause. Your ability to stop before you act on those primordial instincts prevents a torrent of psychological, emotional, and physical changes that impel you to act in ways that will only hurt you in responding to most modern crises.

This break should involve some sort of distancing from the crisis, either physically (e.g., get away from the source of the crisis), psychologically (e.g., do something that distracts you from the crisis), or emotionally (e.g., do something that produces emotions in opposition to those produced by the crisis). Rarely has damage ever been done when you briefly walk away from a modern-day crisis and then return with a calm heart and a cool head.

Reflect

Once you've hit the "Pause" button, you are now in a position to take the next step in using an opportunity mindset: reflect on the crisis before you act. In sum, reflection involves

- Considering the crisis's impact on you
- Identifying the key aspects of the crisis
- Gathering pertinent information
- Seeking relevant counsel
- Evaluating the various options available to you

> "People of the world don't look at themselves, and so they blame one another."—Jalāl Muhammad Rūmī, thirteenth-century Islamic scholar [14]

Decide

After weighing the options you've identified and determining the different forks in the road that lie ahead, you can then make an informed decision about the road that will result in the best possible outcome. As I will discuss in greater depth in chapter 9, self-possession plays an important role here because decision making is difficult in any complex situation, particularly in a crisis that is fraught with uncertainty and emotions. The confidence and calm that come from self-possession enable you to be as emotionally detached as possible and to ensure that information, experience, and reason override your primitive instincts, emotions, and reactions.

> "Each player must accept the cards life deals him or her; but once they are in hand, he or she alone must decide how to play the cards in order to win the game."—Voltaire, French philosopher [15]

Chapter Two

Emotions

I'm Feelin' It!

When confronted with a crisis, the fight-or-flight instinct that I described in chapter 1 is our initial emotional response, hardwired into us long before we began to walk upright. Historically, these feelings have served as our first line of defense against people and/or situations we perceived as a threat to our survival. These reactions were experienced by our ancestors as a wake-up call that danger lurked close by.

Our emotions have also evolved to become our greatest survival benefit. "Hot" emotions, such as surprise and disgust, are experienced instantaneously and powerfully. These emotions signal an imminent threat to our survival, which then initiates urgent action in response to the cause (e.g., an attacker or rotten food) that increases our chances of survival. Crisis emotions evolved to be really unpleasant for two essential purposes. First, they get our attention. When something doesn't feel good, we take immediate note. Second, they strongly encourage us to take action to remove the aversive feelings and to prevent them from happening again. In contrast, "cool" emotions, such as joy and love, typically take longer to be felt and are usually less intense initially because there isn't a pressing need to experience them strongly or right away. Plus, as you well know, they are very pleasant!

We experience crisis emotions in ways that guarantee we pay attention to them and heed their warning. Crisis emotions are immediate. In earlier times, any delays in recognizing or acting on these feelings could have meant certain death. Crisis emotions are visceral, meaning we feel them in every cell of our physical being. Cortisol is released in our brain, and adrenaline is released into our blood stream. These hormones activate the sympathetic nervous system, which heightens energy production and prepares our bodies for action. In addition, heart rate and respiration increase to maximize the oxygen distributed throughout our bodies. Our immune systems become suppressed to boost available energy, and our senses heighten to broaden our awareness of our surroundings. This physical shift is overwhelming and impossible to ignore because our bodies want to ensure that our minds receive a clear message that danger is near. If our ancestors missed or confused this message, they wouldn't have survived and we wouldn't be here today.

Which emotions you experience and the intensity with which you feel them depends on a variety of factors. Your emotional hardwiring influences the impact that crisis emotions have on you. There is clear evidence that temperament, which is the characteristic way in which we react emotionally, is innate. Some people are born highly sensitive and, as a result, are more likely to react emotionally to situations quickly and intensely. Conversely, other people are temperamentally impassive, meaning they aren't particularly emotional about anything, whether pleasant or unpleasant. Those stolid people don't get overly excited with good news or particularly upset with bad news. These "stoics," as a consequence, are less reactive emotionally and less likely to respond strongly or negatively to a crisis. Though I just described the two ends of the temperamental spectrum, there are many degrees of emotional reactivity in between. If you reflect on ways you've responded emotionally to crises in the past, you will be able to judge where you lie along the temperament continuum.

Your past experiences with emotions in general, and during crises in particular, also influence your immediate reactions. For example, those who have years of experience and a history of success in confronting crises are more likely to have developed constructive attitudes and effective strategies to react positively to crises; think of a senior executive in the financial services industry with years of experience seeing the stock market go up and down, a seasoned team of emergency room professionals, a squad of navy SEALs on a combat mission, or an veteran football team in the Super Bowl. In contrast, those with little experience in a field or who have struggled in crises in the past will probably have less confidence in their ability to successfully confront crises as they haven't had the opportunity to develop effective strategies for managing these stressful situations.

Your emotions will also be dictated by the degree to which the crisis threatens you directly and immediately. The closer you are to the crisis, in terms of distance, connection, or personal investment, the more strongly your emotions will likely be. For example, people who lived in New York City or knew someone who died in the 9/11 attacks probably reacted more intensely than those in other parts of the country or those who didn't know anyone there. Additionally, people who held more aggressive investment portfolios likely responded more strongly to the stock market crash of 2008 than those with a more conservative portfolio because the losses would have been greater and the financial pain inflicted more significant than those who had less at risk.

The resources you have available will also contribute to the intensity of your emotions during a crisis. Whether in the form of experience, information, support, money, time, or materials, the more resources you have, the less threatened you will feel in reaction to a crisis. These resources increase people's confidence in their capabilities to manage and overcome the crisis. For example, US Airways captain Chesley Sullenberger, "Sully," who piloted the 2009 "miracle on the Hudson" landing of a passenger jet on the Hudson River, used his years of experience and extensive flying skills to remain calm and save the lives of 150 passengers and crew. In contrast, a less experienced pilot lacking those resources would likely have had greater difficulty in successfully handling this intense and potentially catastrophic situation.

Finally, the amount of control you have or think you have in response to a crisis will influence how much the crisis affects you emotionally. Generally speaking, the more control you feel over a crisis, the less intense your emotions will be and the less they will interfere with your ability to assert control and respond positively. Returning to the example of Captain Sullenberger, his well-trained and demonstrable capabilities—pilots regularly train in simulators that enable them to practice positive responses to precisely these sorts of potential disasters—instilled in him the belief that the crisis was within his control. This belief enabled him to stay calm and focused and make rapid—and correct—decisions that averted a tragedy. In contrast, the passengers on the plane likely felt helpless, and presumably terrified, when they realized their plane was going to crash into the water.

"You have to be able to center yourself, to let all of your emotions go. . . . Don't ever forget that you play with your soul as well as your body."—Kareem Abdul-Jabbar, six-time NBA champion, Los Angeles Lakers[1]

Interestingly, research has shown that simply the perception of control can reduce emotional reactions in response to a crisis. In other words, even in the absence of real control over a situation, if you believe you have control, you will react less emotionally. This phenomenon is exemplified by the desire some people have to gather information about and increase their knowledge of a crisis. Particularly for a crisis that is actually out of your control, gaining a better understanding of its causes and consequences doesn't change the degree to which you can control it but does increase your perceptions of control.

There are three emotion forks in the road. Emotions play an immediate and elemental role in how humans experience a crisis. Key aspects of this emotional influence include how strongly and negatively you react when a crisis strikes and your response to that emotional reaction. Your ability to recognize, understand, and overcome your initial emotions to a crisis may very well determine its long-term impact on you.

DEVASTATION VERSUS DISAPPOINTMENT

It never feels good to have a crisis in your life; crises produce a range of very unpleasant emotions. If you experience something that threatens some aspect of your life, you're going to feel bad. However, what specific negative emotions you feel, particularly in the initial stages of a crisis that might last a long time, can have a significant influence on how the crisis impacts you in the near term and in the future. Typically, people have one of two immediate emotional reactions to a crisis that can set the stage for either a traumatic outcome or a successful resolution: devastation or disappointment.

Devastation

Unfortunately, when a crisis strikes, particularly one that has significant implications on your life, it can be immediately and viscerally felt as devastation. When people believe what may be lost in the crisis is too much to effectively manage, they experience devastation. Imagine losing most of your retirement savings in the Great Recession, having your house go into foreclosure during the last housing bubble, learning that your spouse wants a divorce, losing your job, developing a drug problem, or being diagnosed with cancer.

This overwhelming emotion comes from two sources. First, devastation is associated with the perception that an event can cause significant harm to an important aspect of your life, known as an existential threat. The crises described in the previous paragraph are examples of existential threats. Second, a crisis is experienced as a *failure of the self*, meaning you perceive the crisis to be a direct attack on you as a person and on the life you lead and care so deeply about.

Devastation is a truly harmful emotion that not only interferes with your ability to respond positively to a crisis but is also unbelievably painful. It is an emotional state that encompasses a plethora of the worst possible emotions you can experience, including embarrassment, humiliation, shame, fear, grief, sadness, dejection, despair, jealousy, pity, bitterness, loneliness, and self-hate. Now that is one very depressing list of emotions! If this response is not addressed, the negative internal state can last for days, weeks, months, or even years after the crisis has run its course.

What makes devastation such a destructive emotion in response to a crisis is the natural reaction you have after feeling devastated; this reaction actually increases the likelihood that the crisis will overwhelm you in the future. This tsunami of hurtful emotions subsumed within devastation doesn't just make you feel really, really bad; it also causes your motivation and confidence to plummet, leaving you feeling uninspired, incompetent, and inadequate to respond in a constructive way to the crisis. In sum, devastation causes you to want to surrender to the crisis, rather than confront it. You are hit so hard by the crisis that you just want to flee from the painful experience. When feeling devastated, you will likely withdraw from people, mope around, look deflated, and feel sorry for yourself at a time when such responses will actually create more difficulty. The inevitable outcome of experiencing devastation as a crisis unfolds is a failure to overcome the crisis.

> "Each one of us has lived through some devastation, some loneliness, some weather storm, or spiritual super storm. When we look at each other, we must say 'I understand.'"—Maya Angelou, American poet, singer, and civil rights activist[2]

Disappointment

No one likes to be disappointed. You feel sad and defeated. Your heart aches for the consequences paid, the opportunity lost, and the goal not achieved. Certainly, disappointment is not a pleasant emotion; it feels really bad, in fact. But that doesn't mean it is a bad emotion to be avoided at all costs. To the contrary, disappointment is actually a very healthy and helpful emotion that plays an essential role in how you respond to a crisis. Disappointment is an emotional reaction to an unexpected situation that may have negative consequences. Disappointment occurs when you are unable to fulfill some hope, goal, or expectation; it involves feelings of thwarted desire and loss. A key element of disappointment that distinguishes it from devastation is that it is perceived as a *failure of a situation* rather than a failure of self. As a result, even though the situation may feel threatening, the crisis isn't experienced as painful or overwhelming because the problem is not perceived as an attack on you personally.

In fact, disappointment is hardwired into us to help when we are confronted with a crisis. It actually girds our resolve and mobilizes our resources to overcome a crisis. What is your natural reaction to disappointment? Most people initially go through a brief period of discouragement and withdrawal. Over time, however, disappointment morphs into determination to overcome the situation and to prevent it from happening again.

When you experience disappointment in the aftermath of a crisis, you should let yourself feel the emotion fully, even though it doesn't feel good. Allowing yourself to feel the disappointment in all of its power enables you to turn that energy toward the future and transform it into motivation to resolve the crisis that originally caused your disappointment. Your newfound understanding of disappointment will also take some of the sting out of it and actually make it easier to use as a positive force in your efforts to overcome the crisis.

After "falling off the horse" from the shock of a crisis, you will naturally feel a brief period of letdown, but then you must pick yourself up and get back on the horse; that is, get back to confronting the crisis with renewed vigor and resolve. Putting the disappointment behind you and directing your focus and energy to the present and the future allows you to experience more constructive emotions in response to a crisis, find new ways to overcome your setbacks, and return to your path toward your goals.

Rather than allowing the disappointment to be disheartening and cause you to feel bad about yourself, you can use the experience to affirm your capabilities by showing yourself that you can overcome your disappointment and confront the crisis productively. As difficult as it may seem, an opportunity mindset enables you to view the disappointment from a crisis as the chance to grow and become more resilient. You want to accept the crisis and the accompanying disappointment as an inevitable and unavoidable part of life and focus on what matters and how you react to the crisis.

Separate Yourself from the Crisis

Crises often have practical consequences in our lives: we get sick, lose our jobs, or get divorced. However, it isn't just the tangible effects of a crisis that can lead you down the rabbit hole of devastation. In addition to the tangible effects, the level of your personal investment can cause an extreme emotional reaction. When I talk about personal investment, I mean the degree to which your self-identity, self-esteem, and life goals are attached to the crisis. In other words, when the crisis represents a threat to your perceptions of who you are, your worth as a person, and what you want to achieve in your life, your negative emotional reaction will be stronger and your vulnerability to devastation will increase (more on investment in chapter 5).

Although a crisis is threatening at many levels, whether you experience it as devastation or disappointment largely depends on whether you perceive it as an existential threat to your "psychic integrity." Think of yourself as a puzzle sitting on a table during an earthquake. The tremors will undoubtedly dislodge some pieces. A few displaced puzzle pieces are easy to return to their rightful place, but if many pieces are dislodged and some are lost, regaining the completeness of the puzzle will be very difficult. The difference between disappointment and devastation is how many pieces are displaced. If few are displaced, you will experience disappointment at the damage done to the puzzle and at having to reassemble it. If many are dislodged or lost, you will likely feel devastation because even the idea of restoring the puzzle to completion seems daunting.

In addition, the cause of the crisis determines the level of ego threat you may experience and whether you feel disappointment or devastation. A crisis caused by forces outside of your control—for example, a wildfire that destroys your home—is relatively less threatening because it can't be seen as an indictment on yourself. Yes, you have to accept the painful consequences, but the crisis is in no way a reflection of who you are. On the other hand, a crisis that is caused by your own hand, like losing your job because you berated a colleague, is directly attributable to yourself. This type of crisis is likely to be a threat to your perceptions of yourself and, in this case, your future professional prospects. Therefore, when confronted with a crisis, do your best to separate yourself from it as much as possible to minimize the ego threat that is likely to occur.

In crises in which there is a high ego threat, your best bet for separating yourself from it is to see the crisis as an isolated incident rather than as a reflection of who you are, even if you actually caused it. Being able to accept that you are human and that you make mistakes allows you to soften an otherwise harsh self-assessment that can lead to devastation. This acceptance also enables you to more easily take ownership of your role in the crisis and to use that accountability to take action to resolve the crisis.

Additionally, in making the shift from a crisis mentality to an opportunity mindset, especially when a crisis exposes your vulnerabilities, it can be helpful to shift your focus away from the threat of the crisis. Instead, focus on the opportunities the crisis presents and identify the personal capabilities you bring to the situation, which alters the perceived level of threat. In this move, what once appeared so devastating can now seem only disappointing.

> "We cannot change the cards we are dealt, just how we play the hand."—Randy Pausch, professor and author of *The Last Lecture*[3]

Gain Perspective

One way to ensure that your response to a crisis is one of disappointment rather than devastation is to put the crisis in perspective. Placing an experience in the context of your whole life changes your attitude toward or the way you look at the crisis. Do you see the crisis as catastrophic to your life or merely a substantial setback that you must surmount? Do you focus on the terrible consequences of the crisis or how you can best respond to it? Do you see the crisis as beyond your control, or do you see yourself as capable of resolving it?

Clearly, your perspective toward a crisis will dictate how you think about, feel about, and respond to it. Unfortunately, as noted previously, when confronted with a crisis, our focus and actions zero in on its immediacy and urgency; in other words, our perspective shrinks in breadth, depth, and length to what is right in front of us. As your focus and your perspective contracts, the crisis appears to grow before your eyes and assume gargantuan proportions.

This narrowing of perspective evolved from primitive times when the only perspective that mattered was short term and reactive to ensure survival. These days, however, such a perspective likely does more harm than good. This primitive reaction can result in a loss of big-picture perspective, that is, how the crisis fits into the gestalt of your life. When you focus on a crisis, it may seem immense, but when the lens is pulled back, you may come to see the crisis as just one unfortunate part of an otherwise fortunate life. For example, a serious health issue is truly existential in its threat to your life, yet your reaction to it may be tempered by putting it in the context of your overall life, which might include wonderful family and friends, a satisfying career, and enjoyable avocations. This perspective won't resolve the crisis, but it will shift your emotional reaction from overwhelming devastation to manageable disappointment and enable you to better respond to the challenges it presents.

> "As someone who has faced as much disappointment as most people, I've come to trust not that events will always unfold exactly as I want, but that I will be fine either way."—Marianne Williamson, spiritual teacher and author[4]

Follow the Three Ps

Patience is another key quality that can turn the volume down from devastation to disappointment. When a crisis strikes, you want it to conclude quickly, even if the outcome isn't ideal. Often the uncertainty—the not knowing—can be even more stressful than the final outcome itself. One of the nice things about primitive crises is that cave people knew the outcome right away: they were either killed or they survived. Not so with today's crises. With a health or financial crisis, for example, the full extent of its impact may not be known for a long time, sometimes years.

When you begin to experience devastation in realizing the enormity of the task that lies ahead, you can remind yourself that resolution takes time and that you need to hang in there no matter what happens. Taking the long view puts the immediate consequences in a broader context that makes the crisis seem smaller and more manageable.

Along with patience, embracing *persistence* and *perseverance* can help temper your response. *Persistence* means you commit to doing what is necessary for as long as it takes, and *perseverance* is your acceptance of, and your willingness to continue to tackle, the inevitable ups and downs that you will experience as you face the crisis at hand. This long-term perspective and commitment to what will certainly be a tough road ahead will not completely relieve you of feeling bad, but it will encourage the shift from devastation to disappointment. This shift will allow you to more easily respond to the crisis in constructive ways.

An essential part of making the shift from crisis mentality to opportunity mindset is for you to look at disappointment that comes out of a crisis as a chance to grow and become more resilient. The reality is that crises are disappointing because they are often intense, uncontrollable, and difficult to sort out with their many setbacks and failures. Experiencing disappointment gives you the opportunity to embrace that emotion and learn how to deal with it in a positive and fruitful way. You can think about disappointment as emotional adversity. When you welcome it and then learn how to respond productively to it, you become a better person more capable of dealing with disappointment and other difficult emotions in the future.

> "Patience is not passive waiting. Patience is active acceptance of the process required to attain your goals and dreams"—Ray A. Davis, author[5]

FEAR VERSUS COURAGE

There is no more fundamental emotion than fear. When a crisis arises, it hits us like a sucker punch to the gut; it's unexpected and painful, and can send us reeling. It can numb our mind and paralyze our body. As I discussed previously, the strength of our fear response depends on whether we initially view the crisis as a disappointment (low to moderate situational threat) or devastation (high existential threat). At the same time, we possess courage, which can help us move beyond the fear. Courage can enable you to face or let go of your fear and direct your efforts at overcoming the thing you fear most in a crisis.

> "The brave man is not he who does not feel afraid, but he who conquers that fear."—Nelson Mandela, South African activist and political leader[6]

Fear

Despite how truly unpleasant fear feels, it is actually a good emotion. Why? Because it sends us a necessary and urgent message: we are faced with an immediate threat to our survival. Fear is instantaneous by its very nature; if fear didn't arise immediately, we probably wouldn't react quickly enough to avert the threat and survive. As Gavin de Becker, author of *The Gift of Fear*, has noted, "True fear is a gift, unwarranted fear is a curse." It is up to us to reject the curse, accept this gift, and use the gift wisely.

Unfortunately, as I noted in chapter 1, this fear reaction that was so effective in ensuring our survival in primitive times can work against us in the face of many modern-day crises. Our primal experience of fear as an instigator of immediate action is, most often, more destructive than constructive when we confront today's complex crises. Where swift and instinctive reactions once served us well, they now may cause us to act in ways that are rash and ill-advised. The negativity and panic that have been fear's constant companions for eons now prevent us from reasoned thought, sound problem solving, and cogent decision making, which are all essential to effectively overcoming today's crises.

Also, fear is an all-encompassing emotion that impacts how we think, what emotions we experience, how our bodies feel, and the actions we take in response. And one thing is certain about fear: the reaction can't be prevented; three hundred million years of instinct can't be readily undone. Rather, the best you can hope for during the early stages of a crisis is to move from the amygdala, where fear originates, and shift to the cerebral cortex. This change allows you to gain control of your emotions when a calm heart and a cool head are necessary for your survival. Though fear can't be avoided, it can and must be mitigated. Your goal is to limit the intensity and duration of the fear that you experience when faced with a crisis, so that your more highly evolved capabilities can assert themselves and guide you toward a solution.

Courage

Courage is among the most admired attributes in people and one that we all aspire to possess and demonstrate. We revere acts of courage from our military, political activists, first responders, and ordinary people placed in extraordinary circumstances. Courage is defined as "the state or quality of mind or spirit that enables one to face danger, fear, or vicissitudes with self-possession, confidence, and resolution." Few people know whether they have courage because the only way to know is to be faced with a situation that requires you to act courageously. In modern society, there are relatively few opportunities to demonstrate courage in noticeable ways such as the passengers on United Flight 93 who overcame hijackers to prevent the plane from crashing into the White House. Yet, people act bravely in many ways, big and small, every day of their lives—a parent advocating for her children at school, a student confronting bullies, or someone proposing marriage to his significant other.

Myths about Courage

Despite what seems obvious and intuitive about our understanding of courage, people hold some mistaken beliefs about it. First, many believe that courage is the absence of fear. To the contrary, if you ask most people who act bravely, they will likely tell you that they were "scared s&%#less!" What distinguishes people who show courage is not their fearlessness, but rather their ability to overcome their fear. Think of a soldier fighting in a war, a downhill ski racer hurtling down a mountain at eighty miles per hour, or even J. K. Rowling, whose first Harry Potter book was rejected twelve times before she found a publisher. The fact is that just like our primitive forbearers, you may not be around very long if you don't experience fear in a crisis. If for nothing else, fear tells you to wake up and pay attention because there's something very important you need to know. It's what you do after you take notice that determines whether you are courageous.

Second, many people believe they are born either gutsy or timid in the face of challenges; that's just the way they are, and there's nothing they can do about it. There is little doubt that some innate influence on courage exists. We all know people who have been risk takers since they were babies; these sorts are often drawn to paths in which courage is a necessity, like mountain climbing or entrepreneurship. At the same time, as I often say, "genetics is not destiny"; in other words, even if you aren't bold in the obvious sorts of ways you can still develop courage in your daily life or when confronted by a crisis.

Third, many people believe being courageous is about who you are, instead of what you do. You may already have some preconceived notions about how courageous you are. You may think yourself to be a very brave person, or you may believe you are as fearful as the Cowardly Lion of *The Wizard of Oz*. Yet, to label yourself in a binary way—you're either courageous or you're not—doesn't do justice to the complexity and malleability of humans.

In fact, courage is not necessarily a trait that applies to all aspects of life. Instead, courage can be situation specific. For example, you may have courage when it comes to physical activities like mountain biking. Or you may be brave enough to quit your job and seek out a new career path. Yet, you may lack courage when confronted with a spider or certain social situations, like asking someone out on a date or speaking up at a work meeting. Importantly, for you to embrace courage, you must believe that you are capable of it in the face of fear. Think of it this way. How do you know when you're courageous? Courage isn't based on what you think, what you say, or even who you are; it is based on actions. Did you act courageously? If so, then you are brave.

Fourth, people think of courage in a fairly narrow way that focuses on extreme behavior. For example, Alex Honnold is a free solo rock climber who puts his life on the line every time he climbs, alone and without ropes. What courage that takes; one slip means certain death. But, some years ago, a group of extreme athletes were asked what kinds of people they believed were really brave, and their answers were surprising. Many didn't see themselves as particularly courageous because they learned the consequences of their extreme behavior immediately (and often painfully). Instead, they believed the people who had the most courage were entrepreneurs who commit their lives and their livelihoods to businesses that can take years to determine their success or failure.

> "Ideas are easy. Implementation is hard."—Guy Kawasaki, founder of AllTop[7]

Developing Courage

Courage is required for any situation that you perceive as threatening in some way, whether it be a physical danger, a financial risk, a serious injury, or a new relationship. It is also necessary when you don't feel confident or capable of overcoming the crisis.

As I just stated, courage is determined, not by your thoughts, emotions, or intentions, but rather by your actions. Acts of courage lie at the end of a sequence of internal events that begins when a crisis strikes and culminates in actions that either resolve the crisis or better enable you to manage it.

The first step in developing courage is to identify the cause of the fear, that is, what is the underlying issue that is threatening you? It might be financial ruin, death due to illness, loss of a job, or the end of a marriage. Having a deep understanding of what the crisis represents to you can make the amorphous nature of modern-day crises seem more tangible and manageable, thus reducing your fear.

As part of this exercise, I have found that making a list of things you fear most in the crisis has multiple benefits. First, writing them down acts as a cathartic that releases those emotions from your psyche and body. I encourage you to record them with a pen and paper rather than typing them into your computer, tablet, or phone because the simple act of writing appears to have a more beneficial effect than typing. Second, listing the fear-provoking items makes the crisis more concrete and manageable, which can also lead to insights, realizations, and potential new courses of action in response to the crisis. As you write, you engage your evolved brain and disengage your amygdala, thus replacing emotion with reason. In doing so, you separate irrational fear from rational concerns.

Third, you can assess the resources you have available to respond to the crisis. These resources can be either specific to the crisis or related to the general capabilities you can bring to bear on the crisis, including experience, knowledge, skill sets, strategies, and support. As part of this appraisal, you can recall past crises in which you demonstrated courage and overcame the situation; doing so reminds yourself that you are capable of prevailing over the current crisis. In addition, you can acknowledge the range of competencies you bring to the table. You can also reach out to others who can help you through the crisis. This evaluation shows you that you possess certain abilities to resolve the crisis.

Fourth, acting with courage is risky because, by definition, it involves facing something that poses a threat and can't be easily resolved. The most powerful force that fuels courage and the willingness to accept those risks is confidence. If you believe you can overcome the crisis, you will more readily put yourself out there and take the risk of showing courage. Your confidence will grow and, by extension, so will your willingness to act courageously by bringing the crisis to a more understandable and controllable level and recognizing all of the resources you have at your disposal to confront the crisis.

Fifth, you should get organized in responding to the crisis. This planning includes gathering all relevant information, exploring options, and making decisions. After planning, create a plan A for how you will take action to resolve the crisis. Part of this plan should include an analysis of various scenarios, including what could realistically go wrong. Next, based on that analysis, develop a plan B and, if needed, a plan C for when Murphy's Law strikes. By breaking down into more manageable chunks the enormity of the task presented to you by the crisis, these plans make what had been scary and overwhelming more familiar, predictable, and controllable. In this process, you actively engage your evolved brain and create separation from your initial primitive emotional reactions to the crisis. All of which will further bolster your confidence and make acting courageously easier.

Finally, to act with courage, you must accept that you may not be able to resolve the crisis to your satisfaction. Despite your best efforts, the sad reality is that crises don't always turn around. In some cases, marriages end, family members die, and careers don't rebound. These are not feel-good endings to be sure, but they're not foregone conclusions either. Regardless of the outcome, without courage, crises rarely end well. In other words, without courage, the odds go from bad to worse that the crisis will resolve in your favor. In contrast, while there are no guarantees of a happy ending, acting courageously dramatically increases the chance of a good resolution.

"Courage is resistance to fear, mastery of fear, not absence of fear."—
Mark Twain, American author[8]

FRUSTRATION VERSUS EQUANIMITY

Although fear is the most immediate and powerful emotion triggered by a crisis, it is not the only emotion that can be unproductive. If you become overwhelmed with a crisis mentality and are unable to break free of its grip, the visceral fear you feel is only the beginning of a cascade of destructive emotions that will increasingly interfere with your ability to respond constructively to the crisis. These feelings may ultimately render you helpless as the crisis engulfs you, which is why creating distance from fear is so important. The second emotion you are likely to experience if you are unable to readily resolve the crisis is frustration. As you will soon learn, frustration has some benefits, but it also has some significant liabilities, particularly in response to modern-day crises. Thankfully, we have evolved a counterbalancing emotion that you can tap into when frustration rears its ugly head: equanimity.

Frustration

We've all experienced the feeling of frustration in our daily lives when we feel our efforts are not producing the results we want: we feel stuck, we get stressed, and we feel helpless. The best way I can describe the feeling is *aarrgghh*! It is a truly infuriating feeling. And when felt in the context of a crisis, where the impact and consequences are amplified exponentially, the experience is much more uncomfortable, destructive, and, well, frustrating.

Despite our shared intuitive familiarity with frustration, being able to clearly articulate what it is and what causes it is another question all together. Think of a crisis as a massive obstacle in the path of your survival and thrival and you're not able to easily clear that path in a timely manner. Frustration is born out of a loss of control and a feeling of helplessness: "I'm in this situation and I can't get out of it!" Simply put, frustration arises when the path toward your goals is blocked.

Most people think of frustration as a bad emotion, but it is actually more complex than that. Frustration, like fear, is hardwired into us and helps us survive. Frustration starts out as a good emotion because it motivates us to remove the obstacle that is blocking our path toward our goals. We try harder, and that extra effort often results in clearing that path, enabling us to continue our journey to our goals.

Let's go back again to early humans. A caveman needed to hunt and kill game for his family to survive. If he was one of the unlucky cavemen within whom frustration didn't evolve, this caveman would throw his spear at his prey a few times and if he missed, would give up and go home. His family would starve, die, and wouldn't pass on their genes to future generations. In contrast, if another caveman was fortunate enough to have frustration in his DNA, he might miss his target a few times, get frustrated, and redouble his efforts until he killed some game. The happy ending? He would feed his family, and they would survive and strengthen the human gene pool.

If only life were as simple today. Yes, in the face of a crisis, frustration can start out as a helpful emotion, causing you to intensify your efforts to overcome the crisis. At the same time, crises these days have attributes that make frustration largely ineffective. Because of the magnitude, complexity, and oftentimes amorphous nature of many of today's crises, our instinctive efforts to remove the obstacles in our path or minimize their damage will have little effect on resolving the crisis, which will only cause more frustration. Despite your best efforts, if you can't overcome the roadblocks that the crisis presents, frustration can become a destructive emotion as it impels you to continue to do the same thing, only more frequently and with more intensity. In doing so, you violate Albert Einstein's law of insanity: doing the same thing and expecting different results.

If you are unable to clear the blocked path, frustration becomes just the first link in what I call the "negative emotional chain" in which the frustration you experience morphs into other emotions that further impede your ability to overcome the crisis you are faced with. The farther along the negative emotional chain you go, the more your amygdala and its associated emotions overwhelm and take control of you, and prevent you from mustering a constructive response to the crisis.

Anger

If your frustration isn't dealt with quickly and effectively, it can shift to the next emotion in what I call the negative emotional chain: anger. Most people believe that anger is also a bad emotion because it doesn't feel good and seems to do more harm than good in most situations. But, like frustration, it has both positive and negative aspects.

Anger starts out as being helpful because it is motivating. Let's return to our primitive roots. Responding with anger when faced with a threat was hardwired into us, the purpose of which was to cause us to fight ferociously and overcome the source of the threat, usually a rival tribesman or a vicious animal. Even today, anger causes us to want to go after the thing that is causing our anger, whether it be a punitive boss, a former love interest, or a new and seemingly unfair tax law. Unfortunately, in most crises these days, anger swiftly becomes a harmful emotion. For example, it can result in verbally berating or physically attacking the source of our anger—but it doesn't do much good to yell at Congress or cancer, and you can't beat up the stock market. Given that the source of the anger has changed drastically since prehistoric times, our instinctive response doesn't prove to be much help in resolving modern-day crises.

Because most crises today require deliberate thought rather than instinctive action, anger has a particularly detrimental impact on our crisis psychology. Yes, anger can motivate you to address the crisis, but how that motivation is expressed is no longer useful. Like frustration, anger tends to cause us to do whatever we were doing with more intensity. Back in caveman days that meant people would fight more forcefully or run faster and farther, but most modern-day crises are far too complicated for an anger-driven reaction to work effectively. Additionally, a more-of-the-same approach just won't work for crises that typically demand we do something differently than we do during normal conditions.

Further, focus narrows and we become inflexible in our thinking when we become angry. This reaction was adaptive to our ancestors because crises tended to be singular and immediate in nature, and this response ensured that we directed all of our attention to the threat. Crises today, however, are often multifaceted and require a broad focus and agile thinking that involves paying attention to and processing many cues simultaneously. For example, missing one or two important pieces of information in relation to a diagnosis, the prognosis, and possible treatment plan because of an overly narrow focus or rigid thinking could mean the difference between crisis worsened and crisis averted.

Additionally, as we all know, our thinking tends to become clouded when we are angry. This means our ability to analyze, interpret, problem solve, and make good decisions diminishes, which are all essential processes to effectively confront contemporary crises. These changes, which once benefited the fight-or-flight reaction, are decidedly unsuited for the crises we experience today. More importantly, these changes are actually counterproductive to a beneficial response to current crises.

"When anger arises, think of the consequences."—Confucius, Chinese teacher and philosopher[9]

Despair

By this point, if you're not able to overcome a crisis, your emotions may shift to the final crisis emotion in the negative emotion chain: despair. You have tried and tried and tried and still can't resolve the crisis to your satisfaction. At this point, the natural desire is to want to quit; what's the point of continuing to try if nothing you do works? For our primitive ancestors and their modern-day counterparts alike, despair is not a good emotion when faced with a crisis. For our forbearers, despair led to surrender, which was usually followed closely by death. Despair these days leads to giving up and the loss of any opportunity to overcome the challenges of the crisis. In some cases, this can mean death as well. For example, research found that more than ten thousand suicides can be attributed to the Great Recession of the late 2000s (suicide is the ultimate outcome of despair).

At the heart of despair is a sense of futility or defeat and a loss of hope. These experiences sharply contrast to the first three crisis emotions of fear, frustration, and anger, which involve a marked increase in physical activation and mental acuity aimed at complete mobilization of all available resources in response to the crisis. Despair, on the other hand, is associated with physical changes related to surrender, including a depressed mood, significantly lower physiological activity, and feelings of lethargy.

The psychological and cognitive shifts of despair include a dramatic decline in motivation, confidence, and focus, as well as a diminished desire or capacity for assessment, analysis, judgment, and decision making. In other words, everything that mobilizes you to action in a crisis disappears, which pretty much guarantees that you will fall prey to whatever crisis you are facing. My experience has shown that if you proceed down the negative emotional chain from frustration to anger to despair, the crisis will likely consume you or, at the very least, significantly slow your constructive response to the crisis.

Equanimity

Equanimity is one of those personal qualities that, like self-possession, we all admire in others and wish we had, particularly in a crisis. It is defined as "mental calmness, composure, and evenness of temper, especially in a difficult situation." Boy, doesn't that sound like the right medicine when confronted with a crisis? As with most personality attributes, there is likely an innate temperamental component to equanimity; some people are just born to be more equanimous than others when faced with challenges. At the same time, as I emphasize throughout *How to Survive and Thrive*, beneficial traits such as equanimity can also be developed. Plus, equanimity isn't just a quality you possess or a feeling you have; it's a course of action you take in response to a crisis. I can't magically bestow upon you the quality of equanimity, but I can describe how you can act to develop equanimity. And, in acting with equanimity, you become equanimous.

Despite the powerful impact that the negative emotional chain can have in our daily lives, much less a crisis, most of us were never taught how to deal with our frustration, anger, and despair in constructive ways. You may have figured it out on your own, but most people don't handle frustration well at all. Responding to crises with equanimity involves learning to stop the negative emotional chain at frustration by responding positively to frustration when it first arises. Here are several clear steps you can take.

Take a Break

When frustration first arises, your initial innate response is to take action to clear the path to your goals. But, as I described earlier, that rarely works in contemporary crises because either the crisis is too complex to immediately know what to do, it is at a distance, or it is outside of your control, so prompt action is pointless. Instead, you should take a break from the situation that is causing the frustration. By separating yourself from the source of the frustration, you can create physical and emotional distance, and that feeling naturally diminishes.

As a part of taking a break, you can take two more useful steps. First, frustration causes stress and concomitant physical changes such as increased heart rate, a shot of adrenaline, muscle tension, and choppy breathing. To relieve these unpleasant symptoms of frustration, change your physiology by taking deep breaths, relaxing your muscles, and calming yourself down. Second, you can do something during the break that creates emotions that are the opposite of frustration, for example, listen to music, be goofy, watch a funny movie or TV show, or talk to friends. This step lessens the uncomfortable physical symptoms that accompany frustration and generates positive emotions, such as happiness or joy, that can counteract the feelings of frustration, thus reducing its influence on you.

Another great way to counter the feelings of frustration is to do something at which you are competent and can experience success. In your initial response to an unexpected crisis, your confidence, sense of control, and motivation take a hit, which will make you feel less capable of and willing to engage with the crisis. By doing something you are highly competent at, you replace those feelings of loss of control and helplessness with feelings of confidence, control, and determination, thus generating positive emotions such as pride, hope, and inspiration.

Finally, when you get frustrated, your body experiences considerable strain at a time when you need all of your physical resources to respond positively to the crisis. As a result, though it might seem trivial at first glance, ensuring that you're properly rested, fueled, and hydrated can help. Unfortunately, your body's response to the stress of a crisis is to keep you awake and suppress your appetite and need for hydration when you most need sleep, food, and liquids. Hunger and thirst can contribute to vulnerability to frustration because your body is in a weakened and needy state; think "hangry," that recently popular portmanteau (a word combining the meanings of two others) referring to irritability due to hunger. Refueling can give you the energy you need to resist the pull of frustration, help you respond better to the crisis, and make it less likely that frustration will arise in you again.

Identify the Cause

At this point, you have relieved yourself of most of the physical, psychological, and emotional expressions of frustration. But you still aren't ready to return to the crisis because whatever aspect of the crisis that caused your frustration is still there; if you reengaged with the situation now, you would simply become frustrated again.

The next step, then, is to identify the cause of your frustration. Within a modern-day crisis, this is no small task because the source of your frustration may be amorphous, distant, or not readily reducible to a single cause. Yet, when you isolate the proximal cause (it may not resolve the crisis writ large), you empower yourself to take one action step against the crisis, which will have instantaneous emotional and practical benefits.

Find a Solution

Now that you know what the immediate problem causing the frustration is, you are now in a position to find a solution. Even if it's not a complete resolution of the crisis, at least you have shifted from a reactive and defensive crisis mentality to a proactive and constructive opportunity mindset.

Sometimes, the solution to the cause of your frustration may be obvious and easy to put into action. Other times, it may be too big to act on en masse. In this case, it can be useful to break down the bigger problem presented by the crisis into smaller, more manageable ones and seek incremental solutions to those. For example, you can start by gathering as much information as you can about the crisis. Then, you can identify the many resources you may have available to respond to the crisis. In doing so, you will maintain a greater sense of control over the crisis, you are less likely to slide back into the negative emotional chain, and you'll be able to maintain your emotional equilibrium. All of which will serve you well as you peel away the onion of the crisis until you reach its essential core and, hopefully, a solution to it.

If All Else Fails . . .

The reality is that you can't always identify the cause and find a solution to the crisis immediately. So, continued efforts in addressing the crisis at that time may be both futile and discouraging. The barriers may be just too great to surmount on that day. If you feel as if you have exhausted every resource you have to remove the barriers, you have two options.

First, you can change your goals to ones that you feel capable of striving for and achieving that day in response to the crisis. For example, rather than trying to address the crisis directly, you could decide to learn about similar previous crises. This increases your understanding of the current situation, distracts you from its emotional impact, and provides information that you can use when you choose to reengage fully with the crisis.

Second, there are going to be days when you just aren't going to make any progress in responding to the crisis. In this situation, continuing to try without success will just further frustrate and dishearten you and actually hurt your efforts in the long run. In this case, it may be wise to put your efforts on pause and decide to fight another day. If you choose this path—and this should be your path of last resort—then go do something else that is enjoyable in another part of your life. By taking your mind off of the crisis and producing positive emotions, you will counter the negative emotions that stem from the crisis and you'll put yourself in a better position to reengage with the crisis later.

> "Almost everything will work again if you unplug it for a few minutes, including you."—Anne Lamont, political activist and author [10]

Chapter Three

Reactions

Knee-Jerk!

To help you gain a clear understanding of how the amygdala drives your reactions to a crisis, let's think about your response to a crisis as being a car. Your instincts function as the engine that initially propels you down a certain road when a crisis first strikes. Your emotions act as the fuel for that engine, powering you forward. And your reactions determine the initial road you take in your journey through the crisis. If your amygdala is in the driver's seat and you're in the passenger seat along for the ride, then your reactions will be driven by your instincts and emotions.

Just as the instincts and emotions described in chapters 1 and 2 evolved to ensure our survival, so did our reactions. In the world of our ancestors, knee-jerk reactions were absolutely essential to survival because the threats to their lives were direct and urgent. Anything less than an immediate and vigorous reaction usually ended in death.

Yet, as noted previously, what worked then won't work in the crises we often face today. In today's world, crises are often indirect, emerge slowly, last for extended periods, and require brain functioning more sophisticated than our amygdala, and the resolution is often outside of our control. Not only are those knee-jerk reactions no longer useful; they are often detrimental.

Since our instincts and emotions can't readily be avoided, the challenge is to experience them without acting upon them. That's right, you can acknowledge the presence of your instincts and withstand the discomfort without allowing them to dictate your reactions. Doing this allows you to choose the response that will serve you best in the crises we most commonly face in the modern world.

> "It's not what happens to you, but how you react to it that matters."—
> Epictetus, Greek Stoic philosopher [1]

There are three reaction forks in the road. Your reaction to a crisis is where the rubber meets the road. Your instincts and emotions certainly trigger many powerful internal states, but no harm can be done until you actually take action. Understanding the surge of instincts and emotions and their impact in reaction to a crisis, is important because the first action you take often determines the direction of your ongoing reactions. In turn, this initial reaction may govern how the crisis affects you in the long term.

> "Life is ten percent what happens to you and ninety percent how you respond to it."—Lou Holtz, former Notre Dame football coach [2]

STRESS VERSUS CALM

Crisis psychology activates an instantaneous and intense physical reaction to a crisis that includes a rush of adrenaline, a racing heart, tight muscles, and restricted breathing. This survival response produces increased strength and endurance, greater tolerance for pain, and a sharpened focus. It helped primitive humans to either resist or flee the perceived threat.

Some of today's crises can benefit from the extreme physical transformation of this caveman physiology. Escaping from a fire in your home or saving a drowning child both require swift and immediate action. At the same time, many of today's crises are more cerebral than physical, such as financial, interpersonal, or health-related situations that are not solvable by way of physical action that benefits from a stress reaction. As a result, this primitive reaction can prevent you from responding positively to many modern-day crises.

What is tricky is that we experience a stress reaction viscerally through our amygdala before we process any emotions or thoughts related to the crisis with our cerebral cortex. This is why it's so important to address the physical aspects of a stress reaction immediately.

Only a physiology of calm will give you a chance to be composed, have clarity of mind, and relax your body to confront a crisis with an opportunity mindset rather than a crisis mentality.

"There is nothing either good or bad, but thinking makes it so."
—William Shakespeare, English playwright[3]

Stress

What I refer to as "going caveman" (or cavewoman) is what is called stress in modern times. For anyone living or working in a high-pressure environment, just mentioning stress likely causes them to cringe because they know what stress feels like (not good!). Stress is an inevitable, and often unavoidable, part of our lives, but the suddenness, severity, and consequences of crises take the stress of daily life and turn the volume way up.

In addition to affecting us physically, stress also takes a toll psychologically and emotionally. Stress causes you to worry because the source of the stress is so threatening. You will likely have doubts and become pessimistic because of the undesirable consequences that can arise from a crisis. This shift to the "dark side" can produce a cascade of negative emotions, including fear, frustration, anger, and despair, none of which are helpful as you confront the crisis.

You may have already made the connection, but stress is the physiological and psychological reaction to the survival instinct discussed earlier in *How to Survive and Thrive*. What we experience as stress can be more accurately described as our body's reaction to a perceived threat; it is logical that a crisis would generate a massive stress reaction because it is so threatening. Unfortunately, unlike for our ancestors, stress is not your friend when it comes to overcoming many of today's crises.

"Make sure your worst enemy doesn't live between your own two ears."—Laird Hamilton, big-wave surfer[4]

Calm

Stress is an inevitable part of experiencing a crisis. Since the physiological manifestations of stress are immediate and intense, your ability to constructively confront a crisis depends on your ability to lower the volume or turn off your stress or prevent that switch from being flipped in the first place. Your ability to stay calm makes it easier to disengage your amygdala before it climbs into the driver's seat and takes you for a rough ride. When faced with a crisis, your goal is to alleviate, or at least dampen, the stress as much as possible as soon as possible.

Your ability to rise above the stress of a crisis and remain calm greatly depends on your ability to withstand the toll that it takes on your body and your mind. One way to think about preventing stress is by comparing it to preventing an injury. To reduce your chances of sustaining an injury, you exercise to strengthen your body. Similarly, by working out and strengthening your stress "muscles," you increase their ability to flex rather than tear when you're faced with a crisis where they are strained. In other words, by taking steps to bolster your ability to let go of the physical experience of stress, you will be in a better position to remain calm and encourage a positive response in the face of a crisis.

Coping is a common term you'll see when reading about stress, and experts often talk about coping with stress as the goal to reducing it. But I don't like the word *coping* because it carries the connotation of struggling, getting by, or just dealing with stress. The reality is that just getting by is not going to be enough to overcome the challenges that come with a crisis. Additionally, just barely staying ahead of the stress will probably only create more stress. Instead, I use *mastery* to describe the best way to respond to the stress of a crisis. You want to have command over your stress, to control and dominate it, to conquer and overcome it. When you have mastery over your stress, you aren't caught off guard when it arises; you know how to reduce it and actively prevent it when necessary.

You can use a variety of stress-busting techniques to help your body and mind resist the stress that you experience and seek a state of calm during a crisis. These strategies act to lessen the immediate physical and psychological symptoms and help you feel more calm, comfortable, and in control.

Don't Overdo It

You may be laughing at this suggestion because you believe that the only way to overcome a crisis is to devote as much time and energy as possible toward the resolution. While you have to do what you have to do in response to the crisis, keeping your nose to the grindstone for extended periods of time will catch up with you and cost you in the long run. Fatigue, discouragement, and loss of motivation often result from committing too many resources and can make it virtually impossible for you to maintain a positive response to the challenges of a crisis. The result will actually be a decline in the quality of your efforts to respond to the crisis at a time when you need to be at your best. Yes, there is work that needs to be done, but place reasonable limits on the time and energy you devote to a crisis. Setting aside time to rest, recharge, and refocus are essential for maintaining a constructive response, as well as continuing to put your best efforts into overcoming the crisis.

> "Stand up to your obstacles and do something about them. You will find that they haven't half the strength you think they have."—Dr. Norman Vincent Peale, American minister and author [5]

Have Healthy Outlets

One of the best ways to relieve stress is to engage in activities that provide the opposite emotions of what you experience during a crisis. For example, feelings of fear, frustration, anger, and despair are common in response to a crisis, not to mention anxiety, worry, and doubt. When your resources become depleted from the stress of a crisis, it's important to refuel by doing things that produce enjoyment, excitement, meaning, satisfaction, inspiration, and pride. Common outlets include sports, cultural and spiritual pursuits, cooking, reading, watching movies, and other hobbies. All of these act as healthy distractions and respites from the intensity required to resolve a crisis.

Increase Your Resources

One of the primary causes of stress during a crisis is believing its demands exceed your available resources. In other words, you feel that you lack the capabilities to overcome the challenges of a crisis. A direct way to reduce this stress, while simultaneously enhancing your ability to surmount a crisis, is to increase the resources at your disposal. These can include giving yourself more time to address the crisis, getting help from others, and gaining relevant information and skills. As you gain resources, you are able to tip the scales in the other direction until your resources exceed the demands of the crisis. That is when you will have the ability to respond to the crisis calmly and constructively.

Exercise

While stress attacks the body and the mind, attempting to break down and defeat them, research shows that exercise resists those assaults. Physical activity releases stress-reducing neurochemicals and bolsters your body's immune system. In addition, it increases your strength and stamina, which lessens the wear and tear that stress places on your body. Finally, exercise also increases your energy, gives you confidence, sharpens your mental acuity, and improves your ability to sustain your intense efforts to surmount the crisis.

Rest

As human beings, we have physical, cognitive (thinking), and emotional limitations that prevent us from going at 100 percent for extended periods. Unfortunately, the severe stress that accompanies a crisis causes our bodies and minds to go into overdrive. The result of this persistent strain is the tearing down and weakening of our bodies and minds in the form of exhaustion, illness, or injury.

That is why you must ensure you have sufficient rest to repair the damage to your body and mind. Although you may not think you have time to rest during a crisis, the physical and cognitive consequences of fatigue will do far more harm than taking time for a needed respite from the stress. Essential tools that allow your body to rejuvenate and prepare for the crisis-related stress include a good night's sleep (eight hours according to the latest research), naps, meditation, and yoga.

> "Take rest; a field that has rested gives bountiful crop."—Publius Ovid Naso, Roman poet[6]

Eat Well

The simple reality is that your body can't survive, much less perform at a high level, without adequate fuel. Think about driving your car. If you're racing to a destination at high speed, you're going to run out of gas at some point. Ultimately, you need to stop and refuel if you want to get to where you want to go. During a crisis, time is in limited supply and urgency seems to be a priority, which often results in a change in eating habits. Often food quality declines, and the quantity you eat can increase or decrease depending on a number of factors (e.g., emotional eating, decreased hunger, limited time to eat). What you eat and drink is the fuel that powers your body and enables it to resist the debilitating forces of stress during a crisis, yet eating habits are one of the first things to change in reaction to stress and are often outside of your awareness. If you put quality gas into your car so it runs its best, why wouldn't you do the same for your body?

Unfortunately, the lifestyle that a crisis creates saps you of energy and makes you more vulnerable to stress. For example, there's little time to prepare healthful meals, so you may use caffeine and sugar to keep yourself awake and alert, and fast food that is readily available. In contrast, a healthy and balanced diet every day bolsters your immune system, helps your stamina for the long days, and gives you the energy to keep ticking even when your body is taking a licking.

Breathe

I'm sure you're familiar with the expression "choking under pressure." What you may not know is that the muscles in your respiratory system actually contract, so you're literally not getting sufficient oxygen when you're under stress. In a very real sense, you are choking. As a result, something as simple as slow and deep breathing has a direct physiological impact on your body under stress. These deep breaths provide the oxygen your body needs to slow your heart rate, reduce stress-inducing neurochemicals and hormones, relax your muscles, calm your body, and most importantly, increase your sense of comfort and well-being.

Breathing also calms your mind. During a crisis where so much can feel out of control, deep breathing helps you feel in control of your body. As a result, this renewed sense of control helps buttress your confidence in your ability to respond positively to the crisis. In addition, breathing helps you to redirect your focus away from the chaos of the crisis. Not only does this reduce the stress reaction, but it allows you to focus on how you can constructively respond to the crisis.

Relax

In response to what your body believes is a threat to its survival, your muscles tense up. Unfortunately, this hardwired reaction has the opposite effect of its original purpose and actually makes us more vulnerable to the stress from a crisis. Engaging in relaxation exercises, such as through the use of targeted muscle relaxation practices, stress-related muscle tension is relieved. The outcome is that your body feels more comfortable, functions better, and is prepared to withstand the ongoing stress of a crisis.

Take a Moment

Sometimes you don't have the time to engage in elaborate calming strategies, but you need to do something to settle yourself down during a crisis. In these situations, it can be enough just to take a brief break. During this respite you can create some physical and emotional distance from the stress of the crisis, take a few deep breaths, and slow yourself down, and then refocus on the task at hand. Once you "return to the fray," you will be calmer and better able to respond positively to the crisis.

> "Every now and then go away, have a little relaxation, for when you come back to your work your judgement will be surer. Go some distance away because then the work appears smaller and more of it can be taken in at a glance."—Leonardo da Vinci, Italian Renaissance artist and scientist[7]

Use Positive Self-Talk

A stress reaction sends a signal to your mind that you may not be capable of overcoming the crisis. It can cause you to fall into a vicious cycle of negativity (e.g., doubt, worry, pessimism), which further turns up the volume on your stress, producing even more negativity. Thoughts such as, "This is too overwhelming for me to handle," "I'm not up for this," and "I'm doomed" may pop into your head. Unknowingly, these can come to dominate your thinking about the crisis.

Being aware of your negative thoughts is especially important during a crisis, because it is a time when you need to be your best ally. That's why you want to make a concerted effort to replace your negative self-talk with positive self-talk. I don't mean start saying things to yourself that you don't or can't possibly believe. For example, crises are defined by the threatening impact they have on our lives, so saying to yourself, "This is no big deal" or "This will be easy" is unrealistic and you will reject such statements immediately.

Instead, you want your self-talk to be realistic and within your control. For instance, you could say to yourself, "I'm going to confront this crisis one step at a time" or "I know this crisis will be difficult for me, but I'll get through it." Even if the pessimistic part of you continues to pull you to the dark side, do your best to stay optimistic about the crisis you are facing by replacing your negative thoughts with positive and constructive self-talk.

"We cannot solve our problems with the same thinking we used when we created them."—Albert Einstein, German theoretical physicist [8]

Laugh

One of the best medicines for stress is simply to laugh. Laughter has been shown to have physical, psychological, and emotional benefits, including enhanced immune system activity, pain relief, increased life satisfaction, and improved mood. What makes laughter so powerful, especially in a crisis, is that the physiological and psychological states it produces are in direct opposition to those generated by stress. Through laughter, your body relaxes, your mind clears, and your spirits rise, even when it seems there isn't much of a reason to laugh.

A good follow-up question may be, how do you get yourself to laugh? Some common ways are to watch a funny movie or TV show, go see a comedian perform, read a humorous book, or just hang out with funny people. In doing so, you're no longer consumed by the crisis you're facing; you have time to calm down and create space to enjoy yourself. Laughter is another way to take a brief respite from the stress of a crisis.

Journal

There's no doubt that a crisis can get into your head and not want to leave. Its demands can cause you to obsess over it and clutter your mind, even when there's no immediate action to take. It's a real challenge to let go of these ruminations, distract yourself, or even just turn your mind off for a while. When this happens, I've found that the best way to break free from this crisis preoccupation is to journal, that is, write down your thoughts and feelings. It's as if the thoughts and feelings are trying to escape, and writing them down allows you to clear your mind of the junk related to the crisis.

So, when you find yourself fixating on and becoming enveloped in a crisis, clear out that clutter in your mind by writing down your thoughts and feelings, doubts and drama, worries and fears. Your writing may start out as quite negative (because that's how you're thinking and feeling), and journaling can act as a helpful cathartic. You can then shift your mind in a more constructive direction by writing down your strengths and resources, hopes and dreams, plans and goals, and everything in your life for which you're grateful. In doing so, you let go of a lot of the crap (apologies for the language) associated with the crisis, at least temporarily. You also pull your mind out of the negative tailspin a crisis can cause and orient yourself in a positive direction. This change also creates an entirely different set of emotions that can counter the stress of the crisis, including gratitude, inspiration, and pride.

A final point about journaling is the importance of writing by hand. In this age of technology, your natural tendency when someone says to write something down may be to type it into your computer, tablet, or smartphone and save it as a document file. But I encourage you to actually put pen to paper. Research has shown that the simple act of writing invokes a level of cognitive processing and memory consolidation that can't be replicated by typing on a keyboard. The physical act of writing allows you to channel your crisis-related angst from your brain, through your hand, into the pen, and onto the paper in a way that keyboarding your thoughts and feelings simply cannot do.

Realize That Stress Can Be Productive

Of course, none of these mastery steps will alleviate all of your stress during a crisis, but you don't actually want that. The kind of stress you experience with a challenge reaction actually helps you during a crisis. A manageable amount of this stress enables you to work hard toward surmounting the crisis by staying motivated, energized, positive, and focused.

PANIC VERSUS PURPOSE

Chances are that you've felt panic at some point in your life. As it coursed through your veins in reaction to some unexpected threat, you likely felt fear, your body went into overdrive, your mind raced in all directions arriving nowhere, and your actions were chaotic. You would have done anything to extricate yourself from the situation. In all likelihood, your panic actually caused more harm than good.

Unfortunately, panic rarely ever produces a good outcome in response to a modern-day crisis. In contrast, you set yourself up best to deal with a crisis in a positive and constructive manner when you respond in a purposeful way.

Panic

The course of crisis psychology culminates in panic, which is defined as "a sudden overwhelming fear, with or without cause, that produces hysterical or irrational behavior." Panic is experienced as a veritable torrent of negative emotions (e.g., fear, worry), unpleasant physiological changes (e.g., sweating, rapid heart rate), and unsettling thinking (e.g., "I can't handle this") that produces intense and directionless reactions.

Moreover, panic isn't just an individual reaction as it can spread from one person to another. The panic reactions of one individual can go viral and trigger mass hysteria. Panic becomes a "contagion" that can infect everyone affected by the situation. When I think about panic, I envision a stampede when someone yells "Fire!" in a theater, the reaction to the stock sell-off that occurs during a financial crisis, or the widespread panic reaction to the now-famous 1938 radio broadcast of H. G. Wells's *The War of the Worlds*.

Panic was quite functional back in prehistoric days because it triggered our ancestors to either engage in a frenzied attack or frantically retreat from the threat. Yet, panic these days doesn't usually work out well. Whether it's a decision that results in the end of a life, loss of hard-earned money, or, in the case of *The War of the Worlds*, looking a bit foolish, panic often produces actions that are ill-advised and more destructive than helpful. Where there should be patience, there is haste. Where there should be reasoned deliberation, there is thoughtlessness. Where there should be calm, there is fluster.

The importance of being aware of panic and not reacting to it is taught to us indirectly from childhood. A simple example of this is "stop, drop, and roll." When someone's clothing, skin, or hair catches fire, they may instinctively start to run around. Their thought may be that the wind will blow out the fire, but it's more likely that the person had no intentional thought process. Running around increases the rate oxygen fuels the flames, which makes it worse, not better. Instead, the majority of us were taught stop, drop, and roll, which smothers the flames. This engrained response removes the necessity for us to think clearly in the event that what we are wearing catches fire.

Purpose

By their very nature, crises are surprises—true shocks to your system psychologically, emotionally, and physically. They can leave you feeling discombobulated, out of control, and thoroughly unprepared to handle the aftermath. These feelings can be overwhelming, and panic is a natural, albeit unproductive, reaction because you just aren't ready for the crisis in front of you. Therein lies the power to turn a crisis mentality into an opportunity mindset—preparation. You can gain control over a panic reaction by preventing it from occurring or mitigating the impact of a crisis when one does arise.

Preparation is the foundation of a constructive response to crises. There are some basic things you can do to ensure that the most likely crises you may experience don't hit you like a ton of bricks. In fact, we prepare for worst-case scenarios all the time in our lives. Imagine if you have a health scare and what it would be like without health insurance. How would you react? Now, imagine how you would respond if you do have health insurance. Another example is losing your job. How would you react if you didn't have a rainy-day fund to cover your expenses while you're in between jobs? What would your response be if you did? In either case, the crisis will be stressful, but far less so if you're prepared for it.

So, one way to mitigate or prevent panic is to prepare yourself for potential crises. A simple, yet compelling example of this sort of preparation is the lifeboat drill the navy uses with its sailors. They practice man-overboard and abandon-ship drills over and over and over again until they are second nature to every sailor. Every crew member knows the rapid actions they must take immediately. For instance, they know what station they should go to and how to put on a life preserver. They prepare to the point that, rather than panicking, going to the appropriate station and putting on the life preserver becomes their instinctive response when the alarm sounds.

How does this translate into life outside of the navy? Start by identifying areas in your life in which crises could potentially occur. Common areas to think about include health (e.g., illness, injury), finances (e.g., job loss, poor investments), natural disasters (e.g., earthquakes, forest fires), crime (e.g., theft, violence), technology (e.g., hacking, identify theft), and divorce (e.g., fifty-fifty split of assets). Prioritize these potential crises differently depending on your circumstances. Then, determine and implement strategies to prevent or lessen a crisis should one occur. For example, buy health insurance, save money, create a fire-defense zone around your home, install a security system, protect your identity online, and consider a prenuptial agreement if you're not already married.

Of course, you can't prepare for every crisis you may face. In these situations, you can't take specific steps to alleviate the shock of a crisis and the ensuing panic reaction; however, you can create a general plan for responding with purpose. This preparation enables you to establish some semblance of control over a crisis shortly after its onset. If you anticipate that a crisis might occur and develop a plan to respond positively to it, you create the means to shift from the primitive crisis mentality to an evolved opportunity mindset.

To help you get started, here is a basic plan that will help create purpose, ensure preparation, and lessen panic immediately after a crisis strikes:

1. Articulate your strengths (builds hope, optimism, and confidence).
2. Analyze the crisis (provides a realistic perspective).
3. Evaluate possible consequences (establishes realistic expectations).
4. Gather relevant information (increases understanding).
5. Identify resources (fosters feelings of support).
6. Set goals (provides a constructive direction).
7. Create an action plan (enhances feelings of control).
8. Take action (creates momentum toward resolution).

There are two valuable aspects of establishing purpose early in a crisis. First, it engages your evolved brain, which allows deliberate thinking to override your amygdala's emotional reactions. Second, establishing purpose is a catalyst for creating a virtuous cycle in which the increased sense of purpose reduces feelings of stress and panic, which enables you to devote more energy to confronting the crisis in a constructive way.

> "Give me six hours to chop down a tree and I will spend the first four sharpening the axe."—Abraham Lincoln, sixteenth US president[9]

ISOLATION VERSUS SUPPORT

As humans, we rarely experience crises alone as they usually have an interpersonal component to them. A crisis might impact a large number of people, such as a natural disaster or financial meltdown. Also, while a crisis may appear to only affect you (e.g., a serious injury), the reality is that others are either affected by it, including your family, or play a vital role in how you respond to it, such as your medical team.

Isolation

As the sermon by the English author John Donne goes, "No man [or woman] is an island entire in itself." Yet, our natural tendency is to get on that island and isolate ourselves from others when a crisis hits. Back when we were cave people, this distancing acted to protect us from the perceived threat. These days, this separation is driven by our attempts to avoid the crisis in the hope that it will just go away, usually to our detriment. We often feel a strong desire to curl up in a ball in our bedroom and lock the door to our house; we just want to be left alone! Unfortunately, this isolation feeds our crisis mentality and prevents us from confronting the crisis head-on.

Think about what you are likely to do when you separate yourself from others during a crisis. With no outward distractions, your focus turns entirely inward toward your own internal machinations around the crisis. Without any outside perspective, you view the crisis through only one lens, your own mind's eye. Your thinking can become stubbornly rigid, fatalistic, and catastrophizing. Your emotions can become negative, intense, and overwhelming. And your stress levels can escalate as your negative thinking and unpleasant emotions feed on themselves. In your isolation, you build a silo around yourself that leaves you psychologically, emotionally, physically, socially, and practically unprepared to confront the crisis that lies before you.

Support

One of the most daunting aspects of a crisis is feeling that you have to face it on your own. This perception can make you feel unprepared, incapable, overwhelmed, and just plain alone. To continue John Donne's verse, "Every man is a part of the continent, a part of the main." When you recognize that you are part of a larger group of people who can help you surmount a crisis, you give yourself a much better chance of a successful resolution.

One of the most robust findings in the research is that social support is one of the best buffers against the stresses of a crisis. Studies have found that it lessens the impact of stressful events, reduces the intensity of the negative reactions caused by a crisis, and inspires new and healthier ways of responding to the stress. Interestingly, social support doesn't just have a psychological influence; it also has physical benefits such as improving cardiovascular health, bolstering immune system activity, and reducing the impact of stress-related hormones.

When you actively seek out positive connections with others, you foster an opportunity mindset in several ways. First, considerable research has demonstrated that keeping difficult emotions to yourself during periods of stress leads to more harmful reactions to stress. Conversely, sharing negative emotions during stress can effectively mitigate their impact. Also, as the saying goes, "Two (or more) heads are better than one," which applies here because more people means more ideas aimed at overcoming the crisis. Finally, both support and solutions are more likely to encourage a psychology of opportunity.

As you can see, social support is a vital aspect of overcoming a crisis. Let's explore this further. Social support can be divided into four categories: emotional, technical, practical, and shared experience.

First, emotional support comes primarily from family and friends and is shown through love, care, and encouragement. This support will help you generate more beneficial emotions to counteract the inevitable unpleasant emotions that come from a crisis. In addition, it acts as an outlet for negative emotions associated with a crisis, such as sadness and frustration, that you would otherwise keep to yourself. Emotional support includes others giving you a healthy perspective and more positive ways of looking at the crisis. Simply put, emotional support can lift you up psychologically and emotionally when you're feeling down.

Second, technical support comes from people with specific expertise related to a crisis, such as health-care professionals, therapists, and financial experts. Technical support provides you with information you can use to better understand and respond to a crisis. In a crisis situation, the saying "Knowledge is power" means that the knowledge gathered through technical support can increase your familiarity and control over the crisis. Ultimately, information enhances your confidence, strengthens your resolve, and provides you with solutions to the crisis you face.

Third, practical support comes from a variety of sources and involves providing you with useful strategies for coping with a crisis. When faced with a crisis, you must usually do many things to overcome it. For example, to respond constructively you may need financial management tools, dietary regimens, or a place you feel safe. Unfortunately, unless you happen to be an expert in the particular area where the crisis strikes or you have experienced the crisis before, you often don't know what you can do to respond to it constructively. Practical support has many benefits, including a greater sense of control, improved confidence, increased determination, less stress, and more positive emotions.

Fourth, you can seek out people who are confronted with the same crisis and receive shared-experience support from them. One of the best-known examples of this type of support is Alcoholics Anonymous. There are support groups for just about every kind of crisis from health to finances to relationships. Shared-experience support can provide emotional, technical, and practical support in a setting of "We totally know what you're going through."

My bottom-line message here is that despite the part of you that wants to close yourself off from everyone, your best bet when facing a crisis is to proactively reach out to and connect with others. In doing so, you give yourself a far greater chance of successfully overcoming the hurdles you face. As I've just described, the various types of support have many psychological, emotional, and physical benefits that will serve you well as you progress through the crisis and continue developing an opportunity mindset.

"Alone we can do so little, together we can do so much."—Helen Keller, American author, political activist, and lecturer [10]

Part II

Your Cerebral Cortex

In part I, Your Amygdala, I described the ways in which our primitive brain first reacts to a crisis. As I have noted throughout part I, the instincts, emotions, and reactions elicited by your amygdala evolved to help other animals and then humans to survive in a very different world than the one in which we currently reside. In fact, those primordial urges frequently fail us when confronted by most modern-day crises, which are vastly different than those encountered by our forebears. Thankfully, we twenty-first-century humans have something that animals didn't have and that our ancestors didn't take full advantage of— our cerebral cortex. This "evolved brain" has the ability to neutralize our amygdalae and bypass our ancient instincts before they do more harm than good.

When you pause in the face of a crisis, you interrupt the processing taking place in your amygdala and give yourself time to engage your cerebral cortex. An important part of your cerebral cortex is the prefrontal lobe, which is the part of the brain located behind your forehead associated with "executive functioning," which involves

- Memory
- Regulating emotions
- Impulse control

- Weighing risks and rewards
- Assessing short- and long-term consequences
- Judgment
- Decision making
- Planning
- Complex problem solving

Additional relevant functions of the cerebral cortex as a whole consist of perception, recognition, sensory processing, reasoning, and language.

It just so happens that all of these purposes are central to overcoming the amygdala's primitive reactions that we no longer find useful. This part of *How to Survive and Thrive* introduces you to five areas in which the cerebral cortex can help you to use its many beneficial functions to meet the challenges presented by today's crises.

Chapter Four

Values

Foundation, North Star, and Road Map

Values are defined as "the principles that help you to decide . . . how to act in various situations." Further, "values have a major influence on a person's attitudes and behavior and serve as broad guidelines in all situations." Values are so important to our daily lives because they act as the lens through which we look at our life experiences. They give clarity to the options we have in our lives, prepare us to confront challenges when they arise, and guide us in making the best decisions when required. We face a wide variety of situations in our lives, and values give us standards of behavior we can strive to meet consistently. Even more powerfully in the context of crises, research has shown that the simple act of reflecting on values reduces the hormonal responses to stress.

> "When your values are clear to you, making decisions becomes easier."—Roy E. Disney, former senior executive of the Walt Disney Company [1]

Values dictate the choices you make and determine the direction your life takes. They influence your relationships, education, career path, and other activities. Despite this importance, few people consciously choose, give much thought to, or are even aware of their values. Instead, they simply adopt the values of their parents and those dominant in society. In all likelihood, the values you internalized as a child remain with you through adulthood (yes, in some cases, people reject the values of their upbringings, but it is rare). Unfortunately, these values may not be well suited to help you respond positively to a crisis that arises in your life.

TYPES OF VALUES

As just noted, values have a broad range of influences on your life. Consequently, they impact how you respond to a crisis in many different ways. To help you gain a deeper understanding of the values you hold, particularly in the context of a crisis, I have placed them into categories:

Personal values guide the kind of life you create for yourself. These values emphasize how you wish to live your life (e.g., integrity, independence, health, education, quality of life, intellect, and creative avocations).

Social values determine what is important to you in your relationships with others and are expressed in the connections you have with family, friends, community, society, and the world as a whole.

Emotional values involve the role that different emotions play in your life and the ways in which you express them (e.g., love, happiness, inspiration, anger, fear). They provide a starting point for how you react emotionally to the many intense experiences that accompany a crisis.

Spiritual values focus on the role that faith plays in your life (e.g., belief in a higher power). They can be related to a formal religious system or may simply be a personal set of beliefs about spirituality, including atheism or agnosticism.

Aspirational values relate to the importance you place on striving for and attaining goals in different parts of your life, including education, career, physical, creative, and other endeavors in your life.

> "I have learned that as long as I hold fast to my beliefs and values, and follow my own moral compass, then the only expectations I need to live up to are my own."—Michelle Obama, former first lady[2]

As you explore your values, these categories can help you to increase your insight into them, organize them, get a better understanding of how they fit together, and use them most effectively as you respond to a crisis. Additionally, it is important to be aware that values can also have a negative impact on you when confronted by a crisis. First, here are some values that may inhibit your response to a crisis:

- Certainty
- Comfort
- Consistency
- Contentment
- Continuity
- Control
- Ease
- Harmony
- Order
- Security
- Stability
- Structure

Second, values can assist you in responding positively to a crisis. Here are some values that will likely help you respond constructively:

- Accountability
- Boldness
- Challenge
- Change
- Decisiveness
- Determination
- Discipline
- Energy
- Flexibility
- Humor
- Inventiveness
- Learning
- Openness
- Optimism
- Patience
- Persistence
- Poise
- Pragmatism
- Proactivity
- Resourcefulness

- Self-control

> "Life's up and downs provide windows of opportunity to determine your values and goals. Think of using all obstacles as stepping stones to build the life you want."—Marsha Sinetar, author[3]

As you explore your values as they relate to crises, you can refer back to the preceding categories to guide you; however, there are literally hundreds of values, and my lists are abridged. Therefore, I encourage you to do an Internet search of "list of values" to find a more comprehensive list that you can draw from as you deconstruct and then reconstruct your values.

SHAKY VERSUS SOLID

Think of your life as a house. Over time, you have come to trust that it's solid and stable. You have learned that the floor under your feet and the roof over your head will protect you from the elements. Then an earthquake strikes, and what you had trusted implicitly for so long has been shaken or even damaged. If your house was built on landfill, the disruption would be significant, traumatic, and long lasting. Conversely, if your house was built on bedrock and a concrete foundation, some damage may have been incurred, but your home would maintain its structural integrity and the disturbance would be measured and short-lived.

Metaphorically speaking, values act as the foundation for your life. They provide the solidness under your feet and enable you to weather periodic upheavals, such as crises, that are an inevitable part of life. The more you know and live by your values, the more you can use them to remain standing and balanced when faced with a crisis that unsettles the ground beneath your feet. Values have also been found to help increase persistence when facing situations of trial and tribulation, as well as alleviate the effects of stress.

Values are also like plants: to grow and flourish, they must be nourished and regularly tended to. A watchful eye must be kept for any disease or parasite, such as unhealthy messages from our culture, that might harm them. Values must be brought into the light daily so they can grow stronger and be appreciated for their meaning in our lives. It's easier to water and feed values when they are brought down from that hard-to-reach top shelf and placed within easy reach. Making them more accessible in your daily life allows them to be expressed and used more readily, giving you the opportunity to exercise them in preparation for trying times that arise with a crisis. Values should be connected to every thought you have, emotion you feel, and action you take. This nurturing of your values prepares you to use them to their best advantage when a crisis strikes.

> "We all get so caught up in the moment of what we're doing every day, it's hard to hit that reset button and get pulled away from all that and see life from a different perspective."—Tony Stewart, race car driver [4]

Shaky

Unfortunately, many of us have lost touch with the importance of values in our lives. Values have been commandeered by political, social, and religious groups to satisfy their own agendas instead of our own. Many of us think that values are ethereal entities that are floating somewhere outside of the "real world." They've become ideals chiseled into stone on the sides of buildings or inscribed in the emblems of universities. The frenetic pace of twenty-first-century life has interfered with our ability to stay connected to our values. We've become overworked, overscheduled, stressed out, and exhausted to the point that we no longer have the time or the energy to give values the consideration they deserve. The rigors of daily life have taken precedence over the values on which our lives should be based. As a result, many of us have become disconnected from the meaning of values and have lost sight of what values really are, the very real role they play in our lives, and how they impact every aspect of our lives.

This perceived distance from and lack of awareness of our values in everyday life are two contributing factors to values losing their essential influence over us. We no longer recognize, think about, see, feel, experience, or leverage values in our daily lives. Nonetheless, values continue to be very real, very powerful, and ever present in our everyday lives. Further, they express themselves throughout each day regardless of our level of awareness. More importantly, they become even more significant when confronted by a crisis that disrupts our lives.

Without knowing what your values are and the impact they have on your life, the ground under your feet and the foundation on which you built your life will remain shaky. The problem is that under normal circumstances, you may not notice that your life is unsteady in the first place. It may only be when a crisis strikes and the foundation of your life is shaken severely that you will see that you don't have a solid foundation of values to rely on as you face the crisis.

Solid

When a crisis presents itself, everything that had been familiar, predictable, and controllable is upended. Without a clearly defined and accessible set of values to stand on, it can be very difficult to maintain your psychological and emotional equilibrium, resulting in a significant destabilization of your life. In the moment of a crisis, you don't have the time, focus, or energy to examine and formulate your values. In these moments, you need values at your fingertips, available for immediate access to stabilize your life. Therefore, a deep exploration of your values when life is solid and stable will prepare you for when you experience a metaphorical earthquake in your life.

> "Before you tell your life what truths and values you have decided to live up to, let your life tell you what truths you embody, what values you represent."—Parker Palmer, founder, the Center for Courage and Renewal[5]

Deconstruct Your Values

To truly understand what values you possess and live by, you must deconstruct them until you are able to clearly see the precise values you hold most dear and understand why you hold those values. The first step of deconstructing your values is to look openly and honestly at the way you were raised and the values that were instilled in you while growing up. Think back to your childhood and ask yourself several questions:

- What values were emphasized and expressed in the way your parents lived their lives?
- What values were stressed in your family?
- What values were reflected in the way your family spent their time and money?

The next step in the deconstruction process involves looking at your present life and the values your life reflects:

- Where do you live—in a high-rise apartment in a city, in the suburbs, or in the country—and what led you there?
- How do you spend your free time and what cultural, physical, religious, political, and social values are reflected in those activities?
- What do you talk about most often: politics, religion, the economy, popular culture, sports, the arts? What does that tell you about your values?
- What do you spend your money on: a home, cars, travel, clothing, education, art, charity, technology?
- What values are you presently living in accordance with?

You can then determine how you came to your current values by reflecting on these questions:

- Have you adopted the values of your upbringing?
- Have you gone through a period of examination and reconsideration?
- Have you consciously chosen the values you currently live by?
- Have you experienced life-changing events that inform your current values?

Finally, consider the relationship between your values and your reaction to a crisis by asking these questions:

- How would the values you have identified influence your response to a crisis?
- What values would be of benefit to you during a crisis and why?
- What values would be a detriment to you during a crisis and why?

After completing these steps to deconstruct your values, you should have a clearer idea of what you value, the values that create the foundation for your life, and those that will impact your response to a crisis positively and negatively. Now you're ready for reconstruction of your values.

Reconstruct Your Values

It is one thing to identify what values you live by and to acknowledge that some of them may or may not serve you well when confronted by a crisis. It is an entirely different thing to have a deep understanding of how your values will actually help you respond positively to a crisis.

This process requires reconstructing your values, which is the next step toward creating a foundation for constructively responding to a future crisis. In addition, this process may help you live a better life that could reduce the likelihood of a crisis occurring.

The transition from a crisis mentality to a psychology of opportunity continues with identifying the values that will facilitate this change. Your goal is to align your values with an opportunity mindset, thus providing a solid foundation from which you can vigorously pursue the resolution of the crisis.

LOST VERSUS NORTH STAR

"It's about finding your values, and committing to them. It's about finding your North Star. It's about making choices. Some are easy. Some are hard. And some will make you question everything."—Tim Cook, CEO, Apple[6]

You may be thinking, "This whole deconstruction thing seems pretty easy." Yes, recognizing the values you were raised with, identifying the values that currently guide your life, and coming to understand the values that will help you through a crisis is the relatively easy part. The real challenge is the reconstruction as you may have to jettison unhealthy values and learn to embrace the beneficial values you've identified and must apply to your life, particularly when a crisis strikes.

Your life prior to a crisis may be familiar, predictable, and quite comfortable. It's likely that you have lived this way for many years, and the values and life habits that have arisen are deeply ingrained in you. Yet, when your life gets upended by a crisis, that life that you knew so well changes and may come to no longer exist. With that, your previously held values may no longer be helpful. In addition to the seemingly cataclysmic upheaval a crisis causes, one of its most difficult aspects is feeling absolutely lost about what to do, in what direction you should head, or what should come next.

In addition to your values acting as the foundation for your response to a crisis, they also serve to help you identify your "North Star"—the ultimate goal you want to achieve in resolving the crisis. Your North Star provides you with direction when you begin to wander and inspiration when your future looks grim. For example, your North Star in a health crisis may be to return to a healthy life. In a marriage crisis, your

North Star may be the reestablishment of a healthy relationship with your spouse.

Lost

One of the most unsettling aspects of a crisis is that much of your life is turned upside down and what had once been is no longer. Where there had been familiarity, predictability, and control there is now strangeness, uncertainty, and chaos. What had been a world you knew well is now one in which you feel lost and scared. What had once worked no longer does. Whatever future you had envisioned may no longer be possible.

As the crisis unfolds, this new world can cause your amygdala to take charge. In doing so, your primitive instincts, emotions, and reactions come to the forefront and guide you. Your mind is seeking anything that will provide purpose and direction in reaction to a modern-day crisis, regardless of how misguided the response may be. In turn, those primordial forces cause a cascade of negative thinking, emotions, and actions (or inaction), which can be overwhelming. At the very least, this negative torrent thrusts you down a road that will lead you astray in your attempt to resolve the crisis to your satisfaction.

When experiencing a crisis, feeling lost because you don't know what direction to take can also lead to feeling defeated. As you can imagine, feeling beaten even before you've begun to battle the crisis can psychologically and emotionally hurt you in so many ways. Feeling as if you've already failed can make you lose your motivation and confidence; becoming overcome with doubt, worry, and fear; and focusing more on all that has gone wrong rather than on what you can do to make things right.

North Star

To prevent or mitigate these feelings of being adrift, vulnerable, and helpless, you can fall back on your values to identify your North Star shortly after the advent of the crisis. Your North Star will provide you with clarity, purpose, and direction as you recover from the initial shock of the crisis. It will also help you pinpoint the values that will help you overcome the crisis. To identify your North Star, start by answering the baseline question for your life moving forward:

Where were you in your life before the crisis struck (e.g., psychologically, emotionally, physically, socially, financially, other areas that might bc impacted by the crisis)?

Once this question is answered, continue with the following questions:

1. Where is your life (in the areas listed in the preceding parentheses) now that the crisis has occurred?
2. Where do you want your life to be once the crisis has been resolved or has passed?
3. What strengths do you bring to the crisis that will help you overcome it?
4. What limitations do you bring to the crisis that will interfere with your success?
5. What resources do you need to leverage in support of your efforts to resolve the crisis?
6. What values will you need to enlist to provide the foundation to achieve your North Star?

Research has shown that simply identifying your values isn't enough to help you in a crisis. Rather, you must identify how your values apply specifically to the current crisis and which ones you can leverage to guide your efforts toward a resolution. Your North Star, and the relevant values you've identified, provide you with a clear direction in which you can head toward the resolution of the crisis.

One real challenge that arises when confronted by a crisis is that the way you lived your life before may no longer be possible. You may have well-entrenched ways of thinking, feeling, and acting that no longer work. For example, you may not have been a very assertive person, may have been laissez-faire in your approach to life, or may have avoided relying on others for help. Until the crisis is resolved, you may need to set aside these values, attitudes, beliefs, and habits that have been a part of you for your entire life. Because the uncertainty and instability that accompanies a crisis and the need to change can be intimidating, if not downright terrifying, you may cling to the comfort of your old ways, regardless of their ineffectiveness.

As the crisis evolves, there will be a point when you must accept that you can't keep doing what is familiar and comfortable because, quite simply, it doesn't work anymore. You need to recognize and decide that making a change is absolutely necessary. This is where having determined your values prior to this crisis allows you to identify your North Star and embrace a specific set of values required to move toward it. Once you make that commitment to pursuing your North Star, learning to live your new values will be easier. One thing you will learn when you see and pursue your North Star is that it gets easier the longer you do it because it is inherently self-rewarding. When you have clarity of purpose and are moving in that direction, you see that good things happen. In turn, that realization inspires and motivates you to continue to pursue your North Star and strengthens your desire to resolve the crisis even more.

AIMLESS VERSUS GPS

While knowing your North Star when a crisis hits is essential to overcoming the crisis, simply knowing where you want to go isn't enough. Of course, you could drive around aimlessly in the hopes of miraculously arriving at your desired destination. At best, it would take you a long time to get where you want to go. At worst, you would never get there at all.

Back in the day, if you wanted to drive somewhere, you would get a road map; figure out north, south, east, and west; make a list of directions; and attempt to decipher the ensuing lefts, rights, and straights required to arrive safely at your destination. These days, with technology such as GPS, Google Maps, and Waze, you just type in (or speak) the address where you want to travel, and these navigation tools guide you turn by turn to your journey's end. Although there are no precise directions for plotting a course through a crisis, you can create a road map that points you in the general direction of your North Star, allowing you to begin your trip. Then, as you get closer and your destination becomes clearer, you can gradually develop more detailed directions that will provide you with the most direct route to the successful resolution of the crisis.

> "Your vision will become clear only when you can look into your own heart. Without, everything seems discordant; only within does it coalesce into unity."—Carl Jung, founder of analytical psychology[7]

Aimless

When a crisis strikes, not only do you feel lost, but you can also feel confused and paralyzed about what to do next. Unfortunately, as previously mentioned, this state of shock can cause your amygdala to take charge and trigger your base instincts, emotions, and reactions. Due to the complexity of today's crises, this reaction would be similar to running around like a chicken with its head cut off. You would be moving but without clear purpose or direction. Even worse, the more you wander without a clear direction to overcome the crisis, the more disoriented and lost you will become and the less confident you will be that the crisis can be resolved.

GPS

When I talk about having a road map for arriving at the destination of a conclusion to a crisis, I don't mean a step-by-step plan detailing specific actions that you will take to resolve the crisis. That aspect of the response will be discussed later. Instead, I'm talking about having clarity on what values you will need to set you on the initial psychological and emotional road to surmounting the crisis.

So, this discussion leads us to a final question: What values do you need to turn a crisis mentality into an opportunity mindset so you can respond positively to a crisis? Earlier in this chapter I provided lengthy lists of values that can either hurt or support your efforts. I encourage you to review the two lists, identify the values you possess that may interfere or help in a crisis, and make note of those that you want to develop for a constructive response.

As an alternative, you may not have time to do such an exhaustive analysis or you may need help with how to start. I have landed on several values that appear central to helping most people navigate most crises. They are described next.

Resilience ("an ability to recover from a misfortune") lays the foundation for a value-driven approach to resolving crises. If you start from the position of "I'm capable of dealing with whatever this crisis throws at me," you establish a hopeful and optimistic tone for the crisis. Rather than focusing on the many negatives of the crisis, this approach enables you to view the crisis with a positive can-do attitude.

Resolve ("firmness of purpose or intent") is an absolutely essential value to have when a crisis knocks you down. In response to each setback, you must have the resolve to keep getting up and going forward, even when the going gets tough.

"Fall seven times, stand up eight."—Japanese proverb[8]

Crises are scary experiences that threaten many aspects of your life. If you succumb to the resulting fear, the crisis will certainly overwhelm you. As a consequence, *courage* ("the quality of mind or spirit that enables a person to face difficulty, danger, pain, etc.") is another indispensable value. Courage enables you to confront the crisis head-on and stand up to threats, risks, and challenges that you will inevitably face.

As I mentioned in a previous chapter, when confronted by a crisis, our tendency is to fall back on old and deeply ingrained ways of thinking, feeling, and acting. Unfortunately, because crises often present new and different problems, those old ways simply won't work. As a result, *adaptability* ("able to adjust oneself readily to different conditions") enables you to be agile in your approach to the crisis and to adjust to the ever-changing landscape that a crisis presents.

Also, as mentioned earlier, crises can cause you to want to isolate yourself from the world in the mistaken belief that the crisis will just go away. Regrettably, this distancing does more to hurt than help in a crisis. In contrast, *connection* ("having supportive relationships with others"), not isolation, actually provides vital benefits to help you navigate the crisis, such as emotional support, information, and additional resources.

Adopting and applying these values to your life before a crisis would certainly help you leverage them fully when a crisis strikes. Ideally, they would be deeply entrenched in your life and, as a result, readily accessible. At the same time, when life is rolling along smoothly, there is little incentive or sense of urgency to adopt values for future, unknown crises. Yet, it is still possible to embrace these useful values when a crisis arises and still gain their benefits.

First, presuming you completed the earlier values exercise, you want to remember these values and bring them to the fore shortly after a crisis hits. This engagement involves consciously identifying the values, understanding what they mean, and recognizing the benefits they offer to your response to the crisis. It also means looking for immediate ways to incorporate these values into your initial reaction to the crisis. When you use your values as your GPS early in your journey through a crisis, you set yourself on the road to a positive response. At a neurological level, you make it easier to bypass your amygdala and engage your cerebral cortex because the values, and the accompanying evolved-brain activity, are readily available to you. At a psychological level, you feel empowered to embrace an opportunity mindset in which these values become your default guides for your thoughts, emotions, and actions. The result is that you quickly begin your journey on a road of your choosing toward your North Star.

> "You have brains in your head. You have feet in your shoes. You can steer yourself in any direction you choose."—Dr. Seuss, American children's author[9]

Chapter Five

Investment

Bet It All on Red!

There is no doubt that a crisis is an unpleasant experience that we wish to avoid at all costs. As I have discussed previously, crises threaten some important aspect of our lives, whether it be our health, finances, relationships, or safety. At the same time, there is another side to that threat that goes beyond the objective harm (e.g., death, financial ruin, divorce, loss of a home). Though it's natural to have an initial negative response in many of the ways described in part I, Your Amygdala, the severity of your reaction, your ability to recover, and the speed at which you can reorient yourself in a positive direction depend primarily on your investment in the outcome of the crisis, not on the objective impact it has on your life.

When I talk about investment, I don't mean something tangible, like the amount of money you stand to lose from a financial crisis or the degree that a health crisis may impact your physical functioning. While those have very real and practical implications on your life, what I'm talking about here is the psychological and emotional investment you have in the long-term effect of the crisis. Given that a crisis is, by definition, significant, you will invariably have substantial investment in its outcome. At the same time, there is a fine line between being reasonably invested and overly invested in a crisis. Similarly, it's challenging to respond appropriately to a crisis and not excessively or in a way that interferes with your ability to overcome it.

There are three investment forks in the road. To help you better
understand the role that your investment in the outcome of the crisis
may play in how you react to it, I've identified three investment forks
in the road. Each of the forks will explore your degree of investment,
how that investment impacts you, and how you can establish a level of
investment that will improve your response to the crisis with which you
are faced.

OVERINVESTMENT VERSUS INVESTMENT

The degree to which your self-identity, self-esteem, and goals are de-
pendent on how the crisis turns out determines your level of investment. What defines a crisis as a crisis in the first place is that it threatens some sort of harm, so it's natural and healthy to be invested in a
crisis. It means you care about the end result and are willing to put in
sufficient time and effort to ensure a positive outcome. However, when
you are overly invested in the crisis, you perceive it to have a potentially catastrophic effect on you and make yourself vulnerable to the primitive instincts, emotions, and reactions described in part I, Your Amygdala. As you may recall, the result of being driven by your amygdala is
definitely not the one that will produce a desirable outcome for you.

> "Change the way you look at things and the things you look at
> change."—Wayne Dyer, self-help author and speaker [1]

Overinvestment

An imbalanced self-identity, fragile self-esteem, and highly and deeply
held goals can make you vulnerable to overinvestment in a crisis. Becoming overly invested can lead you to getting caught up in, and ultimately driven by, your most basic instincts, emotions, and reactions.

Self-Identity

Self-identity is basically the catalog of who we perceive ourselves to
be, both as an individual and within the context of others. It includes
our personal qualities (e.g., determination, compassion, generosity),
abilities (e.g., intelligence, discipline, detail-oriented), and interpersonal roles (e.g., spouse, family member, friend, colleague). Self-identity
can be summed up in a simple question: who am I?

Even though self-identity can be targeted with a straightforward question, the answer is far more complicated. While innate influences help shape our self-identity, it's ultimately something we develop over time that is based on the accumulation of our life experiences and interactions with others. One key aspect of self-identity is that we come to associate positive (e.g., "I'm a hard worker.") or negative (e.g., "I'm a terrible student.") attributes to ourselves. Regardless of their direction, these statements influence our thoughts, emotions, and behaviors. Another thing about self-identity is that there isn't an evaluative component to self-identity (i.e., judgments about the extent to which attributes are either good or bad); that's where self-esteem comes in (to be discussed shortly). Instead, self-identity is simply how we describe ourselves to others. There is evidence that overinvestment in one aspect of your self-identity can have certain risks, especially when faced with circumstances that threaten that part of you. For example, if you are an athlete who overidentifies with your physical ability, then you are more likely to struggle following a health crisis that limits your physical achievements. This excessive focus also means that you may neglect other areas in which you are capable, such as your relationships or other activities that interest you.

One gauge of the degree of investment you have in a crisis is your emotional reactions at the time the crisis strikes and in the days and weeks after. As I have noted before, a strong emotional reaction after a crisis is normal and expected, but if your emotional response is incapacitating and persists for days or longer, you are likely overinvested. Consider what you think and how you feel when a crisis arises. Do you feel disabling stress, anxiety, or fear? Are you negative, uncertain, or worried? Do you sweat, does your heart pound, do you feel short of breath, or are your muscles tight and shaky? Do you feel as if you want to flee the situation right away? Finally, and most importantly, do these reactions persist beyond the immediate aftermath of a crisis? All of these red flags are caused by a threat you perceive as devastating to your self-identity, and the cause of that threat reaction is an overinvestment in the crisis that lies before you.

"In the social jungle of human existence, there is no feeling of being alive without a sense of identity."—Erik Erikson, noted psychologist [2]

Too Zone

In general, too much of anything is not a good thing. When *too* is related to a crisis, it can be one of the most dangerous words. If your self-identity becomes overly tied to a crisis, you enter what I call the "Too Zone." Of course you need to care about a crisis, but you shouldn't care too much. A crisis is inherently important (otherwise, it probably isn't a crisis), but you don't want it to become too important to you.

When you enter the Too Zone, your connection to the crisis holds too much of your self-identity, and as a result, what starts out as a serious situation that must be addressed shifts to a potentially devastating occurrence that throws you for a loop. Not surprisingly, your reactions when you are in the Too Zone are neither pleasant nor helpful. The crisis seems overwhelming. You're unable to think clearly. You become absorbed in everything that can go wrong. Your confidence and motivation deteriorate because you don't believe that you can overcome the crisis.

Life or Death

When you are overly invested in a crisis, it feels like life or death. Consider this disturbing scenario: an armed robber stops you on a dark street and threatens to shoot you if you don't give him your wallet. How will you feel? Probably terrified. And how effective will your efforts to resolve this crisis be? In all likelihood, not at all because your primordial instincts, emotions, and reactions will take over, which may be entirely self-defeating. Of course, when you're faced with most modern-day crises, it's less likely that your physical life will be threatened. But, if you are overly invested in a crisis, it can feel as if someone is threatening to kill another part of you, namely, your self-identity. Certainly, crises must be taken seriously, and admittedly, some crises are literally life-or-death situations. Ironically, however, responding as if a crisis is life or death, whether literally or figuratively, will not further your cause of surmounting it.

Self-Esteem

Self-identity involves the perceptions that you hold about yourself, while self-esteem is how you evaluate yourself in relation to those perceptions. Self-esteem can be positive or negative and can be seen as your overall sense of self-worth or value as a person. Additionally, self-esteem has an emotional component in which certain feelings impact your evaluations (e.g., pride or shame). Questions that can help you understand your self-esteem include

- Am I a competent person?
- Do I have confidence in my capabilities?
- Do I like and respect myself?
- Do I feel valued by others?

There are several reasons why self-esteem is so important when experiencing a crisis. First, high self-esteem is grounded in love and security, which can be reassuring during a time when you may not be feeling loved or supported and your life has become less stable and secure. Also, research has shown that people with low self-esteem tend to see themselves as less capable, have difficulty maintaining relationships, and are more likely to engage in negative thinking and self-defeating behavior. These common traits become more pervasive with increased stress and have the potential to cause significant harm during a crisis. In contrast, those with high self-esteem tend to view themselves as being competent, take responsibility for their lives, exhibit more confidence, are more likely to connect with others, and are more resilient in the face of challenges. As you can imagine, these traits are very beneficial in facing the difficulties of a crisis head-on.

You want to be constantly vigilant when it comes to the impact your self-esteem has on your response to a crisis. Of course you want to do everything you can to ensure that you develop and maintain healthy self-esteem before a crisis strikes, but there are a number of factors that can make this challenging. These variables include external and internal influences, such as people around you (e.g., family, friends, co-workers), unconsciously held messages that you have received throughout your life (e.g., need to be perfect, pressure to succeed, failure is bad), and other influences that are beyond your control (e.g., inborn temperament). Some low self-esteem warning signs to have on your radar, especially during a crisis, include

- Wanting to avoid difficult or challenging situations
- Wanting to stay in your comfort zone
- Being averse to taking risks
- Experiencing debilitating anxiety

- Giving up easily
- Being highly self-critical
- Feeling out of control
- Making excuses and blaming others

Given these red flags, low self-esteem in a crisis may result in thoughts like "I really can't handle this!" Awareness of these signs can help you mitigate them. So if you see the warning signs of low self-esteem in yourself, don't take them as indictments of your inability to deal with a crisis. Rather, see them as calls to action to help you better manage your red flags and shift your self-esteem in a more positive direction.

> "You are the sum total of everything you've ever seen, heard, eaten, smelled, been told, forgot—it's all there. Everything influences each of us, and because of that I try to make sure that my experiences are positive."—Maya Angelou, American poet, singer, and civil rights activist[3]

Goals

As human beings, we are motivated by goals. One of our greatest sources of satisfaction is setting, striving toward, and achieving deeply felt goals. Our goals aren't just objectives we want to accomplish; they are meaningful attainments that reflect our values, attitudes, aspirations, hopes, and dreams. Since they reveal so much about who we are and what we want in our lives, we often can become very invested in them.

Unfortunately, crises don't usually play nice with our goals. In fact, they are often immense obstacles that block the path to our goals. When we are so invested in our goals and they are thwarted by a crisis in our lives, our reactions can be strong and negative. We can feel frustration, anger, hopelessness, and despair. The more a crisis has the potential to interfere with the pursuit of your life goals, the more threatening the crisis will be to your self-identity and the more likely an emotional reaction will be harmful rather than helpful.

Investment

In order to devote the necessary time, effort, and energy to overcome a crisis, you absolutely must be invested in a crisis when it confronts you. That said, as noted previously, a crisis that poses a high threat to your self-identity, self-esteem, and goals can lead to overinvesting in rectifying the crisis, which often results in self-defeating behavior and a poor resolution to the crisis. Therefore, it's imperative that you maintain a healthy level of investment when a crisis arises. Developing awareness about your level of investment in a crisis will allow you to prevent your emotional reaction from getting in the way of a constructive response. With increased awareness, you can take active steps to reduce your investment to a healthy level and pursue a path to a positive resolution of the crisis.

Balance Your Self-Identity

If you are only invested in a few areas of your life, then a crisis in one of these important aspects of your self-identity can feel like a significant threat. It may be easier to understand how self-identity impacts people by first thinking about life as similar the stock market. It is very risky to invest all of your savings in one or two stocks because there is a chance that those stocks will go south and you'll lose most or all of your money. Conversely, if you invest your savings in a diversified and balanced portfolio, you may lose some money with some of your investments, but you're less likely to lose all of them. While the losses will be unfortunate, they won't be ruinous.

In terms of self-identity, consider the following example. Let's say you are a lawyer immersed in your career. You have worked hard for your accomplishments and often evaluate your success by your productivity and successes at work. It's safe to say that you align your self-identity closely with your career. Then, your spouse suddenly becomes ill and is unable to work due to a serious illness. Subsequently, you have increased responsibilities at home, assist with health-care needs, and ensure the bills are paid. As you face the crisis of your spouse's health decline and manage the stress you feel from your additional responsibilities outside of work, the time away from the office starts impacting the quality of your work and ability to be productive. Now there's another crisis brewing as you begin to experience a threat to your self-identity.

On the other hand, if you better balance your self-identity so that it is comprised of your career as a lawyer, your role as a spouse, your desire to help others, and your ability to problem-solve difficult situations, you will better manage your spouse's health crisis because you view your identity as consisting of multiple contributors, which allows you to respond more fluidly to the crisis. Further, since your self-identity isn't solely based on your career, the intensity of the threat to your self-identity is diminished and the potential for a self-identity crisis is eliminated. As a result, you won't feel a crippling impact because you will have other sources of meaning, satisfaction, and joy to fall back on.

> "Balance is not something you find; it's something you create."—Jana Kingsford, motivational speaker[4]

A balanced self-identity can play a valuable role in your response to a crisis at several levels. First, a balanced self-identity means that you will not place your happiness or well-being on the line when you face a crisis. Yes, a crisis is upsetting in many ways and you will experience many unpleasant emotions. Yet, a balanced self-identity allows you to maintain your "psychic integrity" despite the tumult of a crisis.

Second, you will be able to keep the crisis in perspective because a crisis is not usually an existential threat to who you are as a person. Third, a balanced self-identity enables you to see a crisis in a more positive light. You will be more optimistic, less fearful, and more clear-headed as you approach the crisis. More importantly, a balanced self-identity won't incur the psychological, emotional, and physical costs that an imbalanced self-identity can have on your life in the midst of a crisis.

A balanced self-identity is best created by ensuring that you embrace healthy values that will support your efforts in a crisis (see chapter 4). Having a self-identity pie with many slices allows you to spare one piece without sacrificing the whole pie, both psychologically and emotionally. So, even when a crisis devours a few pieces of your self-identity pie, there are slices that remain intact for your "nourishment." This balanced investment of your self-identity reduces the negative aspects of the crisis, such as anger, exasperation, and weariness. It also fosters prolonged engagement and commitment to the sometimes long and arduous process of overcoming a crisis.

Another way to maintain a balanced self-identity is to set goals for the resolution of aspects of a crisis that you can control. As I have discussed throughout this book, many of today's crises are outside of our control, which can lead to feelings of helplessness and frustration. When you establish goals you can control, you feel empowered, build confidence in your ability to surmount the crisis, and focus on aspects of the crisis that you can actually impact, thus making success more attainable.

"People with goals succeed because they know where they're going."—
Earl Nightingale, motivational speaker[5]

Finally, if you consider your overall self-identity "pie," you can also create balance by ensuring that no one slice is too big, thus preventing this piece from becoming the dominant influence in your life. You can do this in two ways. First, you can recognize other important areas of your self-identity that you tend not to give much attention to. For example, perhaps you value being a supportive boss or a loving parent and can gain appreciation for those roles in your life. In doing so, you invest more in previously uninvested parts of yourself, which results in a substantial decline in your investment in a crisis.

Second, you can actively create new sources of self-identity by seeking out new roles in your life. Some examples include pursuing a hobby you've been interested in for a while, reconnecting with old friends, or giving back to your community. No matter how you develop a more balanced self-identity, you shrink the piece of the pie a crisis potentially contaminates. As a result, your investment and its negative impact on your response to the crisis are reduced.

Let Go

At the heart of overinvestment is attachment. As Buddhists will tell you, when we are overly invested in something, we allow ourselves to become inextricably connected to it and can stubbornly hang on when letting go may be a much better course of action. There is no doubt that when you care deeply about something and a crisis disrupts it, the sense of loss can be painful. To reduce that pain, we often cling more tightly to what we have lost in the hope that we can get it back. This attachment can be to our savings, a marriage, our health, or the home in which we live.

The reality is that most crises are not life-or-death situations. Even though your quality of life may not be the same as it was prior to a crisis, you will survive regardless of how the crisis turns out. Of course, you may be disappointed, sad, hurt, angry, and frustrated; you may think that life is unfair or even that life is over for you. Usually, it isn't. Assuming you decide to put your life back together again, you will move past the crisis and, in time, your life will continue. And, hopefully, you will look back on the crisis with 20/20 hindsight and see pain, inspiration, setbacks, and successes. More importantly, hopefully, you will recognize the many life lessons you learned that prepared you to embrace your new life and pursue new dreams, regardless of how different your journey may be now.

If you can truly let go of your overinvestment, you will have a game-changing epiphany. You will feel liberated from fear and able to pursue the resolution of the crisis with vigor and without hesitation. As you approach the crisis, you will feel motivated, confident, relaxed, and focused. You will feel prepared physically, emotionally, and mentally. You will be excited for what lies ahead, rather than afraid. And, with a healthy amount of investment in the crisis, you set yourself up to have a better chance of overcoming the crisis and achieving the goals you set for yourself.

> "If I were to suggest to other people what they 'should' do if they're going through a tragedy. . . . I would say you must start with accepting the fact that the change happened."—Michael Hingson, blind author[6]

Ways commonly used to let go of attachments include the following:

- Accept the crisis without attempting to explain, rationalize, or blame (it is what it is)
- Acknowledge how you're feeling (e.g., frustration, sadness, anger)
- Identify what you're holding on to (e.g., a past relationship, a perception of yourself)
- Understand your reluctance to let go of what's been lost (why the need to hang on to it?)
- Challenge your attachments (what value do they provide to you?)
- Place the crisis in the context of your broader life (it is part of your life, not life itself)
- Focus on the present (what can you do now?)
- Focus on what you can control (let go of the uncontrollables)
- Connect with people you care deeply about (you'll benefit from the support)
- Journal or talk to people about your feelings (let your emotions out)
- Help others (it provides a brief respite from the crisis)
- Express gratitude for good parts of your life (this generates positive thoughts and emotions that counteract the bad ones)
- Keep the crisis in perspective (most things will pass)

"Sometimes we have to let go of what's killing us, even if it's killing us to let go."—Unknown [7]

Don't Make the Crisis Your Life

A crisis can be overwhelming and all encompassing. A crisis can haunt your every waking moment, when you are working, eating, socializing, exercising; you can't escape it. It can absorb your thoughts, emotions, energy, and time like a black hole absorbs matter. A crisis can *become* your life!

The problem is that when a crisis becomes your life, you are automatically overinvested in it because there is nothing more important to invest in than your life. To prevent a crisis from overtaking your life, you must first take a step back and recognize that it may currently be an urgent part of your life, but it isn't your whole life. Then, identify the other parts of your life that are still important to you (e.g., family, work, exercise, or faith). For example, a divorce is one of the most personally painful experiences someone can have. It can be seen as a personal failure and have immense ramifications on many other aspects of your life, including parenting and finances. A divorce can plunge you into a very deep and dark place. Though you certainly must allow yourself to grieve for the dissolution of your marriage, if you can step back from the anguish of the divorce and put it in perspective within the totality of your life, you may find that it is more manageable than you might initially think. For example, you can focus on the satisfaction that you get from your career. You can recognize the family and friends whom you love and who love you. You can relish the relationships you have with your children. And you can stay involved in avocations and other activities that bring you joy.

You may actually find it useful to schedule when to address the crisis during the day, much as you do your work hours and family time. Not only does this remind you that a crisis is only a part of your life, but it also helps you compartmentalize the crisis. There is a time to focus on the crisis and there is a time to live your life. When you're in the crisis, be completely in it. When you're in your life, be totally immersed in it and allow yourself to be temporarily distanced from the crisis.

Bolster Your Self-Esteem

When a crisis strikes, you can't instantly build positive self-esteem. Whether high or low, self-esteem evolves from years of experiences. Bolstering it is a process that requires self-understanding, conscious awareness, committed effort, and patience. There are no quick or easy ways to build (or rebuild) your self-esteem. At the same time, it is possible to bolster your self-esteem in the short term to help you cope more effectively with a crisis. A few simple strategies can give your self-esteem a shot in the arm.

Feel the love. As noted earlier in this chapter, a key component of self-esteem is feeling loved. So, it makes sense that a great way to lift your self-esteem is to reach out to people who love you and allow yourself to feel their caring and support. Also, express your love openly and often to them. Not only does this further your connection, but your love will be reciprocated many times over. Then, take that love and use it to build up your confidence and feel good about yourself. In turn, this will help raise your belief that you can successfully overcome the crisis with which you are confronted.

Support your sense of competence. One of the most difficult aspects of a crisis is doubting you have what it takes to surmount it. As we know, another important part of self-esteem and overcoming a crisis is feeling competent and confident in your capabilities. There are several ways you can support your sense of competence.

First, make a list of the strengths you bring to the crisis. These assets may be general (e.g., "I'm a competent person") or involve specific skills you have related to the crisis (e.g., "I understand financial issues"). Competence may also involve personal attributes you possess that will help you navigate the crisis, such as being relentless, detail oriented, and good at solving problems. This exercise pushes against negative views you might be having about your competence (low self-esteem) and helps create a positive feeling about your competence with which you can approach the crisis.

Second, think back to past crises you've managed and identify what enabled you to do so. Ask yourself how you approached those situations, what posed a potential threat to your ability to successfully navigate those challenges, and what helped you to overcome them. This strategy is not based on feel-good affirmations, as these are easy to reject when under the weight of a crisis. Recounting past crises and your response to them offers you tangible evidence that you are competent and have the capabilities to get through another crisis.

Third, you can solicit feedback from trusted family, friends, and coworkers about your competence. It's one thing to tell yourself that you're capable, but you may not believe what you say; hearing it from others is reassuring. More importantly, if you hear it enough from people you trust, the message might just sink in.

Fourth, make a plan. Regardless of your level of self-esteem, a crisis is threatening to your competence because it is overwhelming and would feel as such for anyone. When you set reasonable goals and make a detailed plan, you take the enormity of a crisis and break it down into manageable pieces that will make you feel more capable of addressing it (more details on making a plan in chapter 9).

Lastly, you can reinforce your sense of competence by praising yourself for your efforts and successes in combating the crisis. Praise your commitment, determination, and efforts; your curiosity and ingenuity; your openness to viewing the crisis from a positive perspective; and especially, the little victories you accrue on your journey through the crisis.

One of the most powerful ways to boost your self-esteem is to see the successful consequences of your actions. So, when you accomplish a "win" as you confront a crisis, don't chalk it up to luck or convenience; praise yourself and the success you've created. Additionally, tell others about your efforts and accomplishments, and allow them to praise you as well. All this praise is fuel you'll need to repel the crisis.

Focus on what you can control. Particularly with contemporary crises that are indirect, intangible, and often delayed, there is so much outside of your control. Another helpful way to bolster your self-esteem is to focus on those aspects of a crisis you have control over. One way of doing this is to follow this process:

1. Break down the crisis you are facing into as many of its components as you can, including likely causes and possible effects.
2. Take a sheet of paper and divide it into two columns.
3. At the top of the left column, write "Controllable," and at the top of the right column, write "Uncontrollable."
4. Assess each cause and effect to be either controllable or uncontrollable.
5. Place the items into their respective columns on the sheet of paper.

6. Cut the sheet in half.
7. Throw away the "Uncontrollables" half.
8. Tape the "Controllables" piece somewhere you can see it and refer to it regularly as you tackle the crisis.

"People not only gain understanding through reflection, they evaluate and alter their own thinking based on their behavior."—Albert Bandura, Canadian-American psychologist [8]

Adjust Your Goals

A crisis may very well cause the pursuit of your goals to grind to a painful halt as your time, focus, effort, and energy are diverted away from the goals and onto the immediacy of the crisis. This necessity can be a huge source of frustration and dismay. As previously noted, a crisis can be a threat to the goals that you hold most dear and ones in which you are heavily invested. Because of this, a crisis can cause you to feel that you have to put your life on hold when you would prefer to be full steam ahead in striving toward your goals. Rather than have your life goals act as an anchor against which you must fight in your efforts to respond to a crisis, harness that energy and apply it to goals related to resolving the crisis.

Put your goals in a broader context. When a crisis strikes, you will only feel stymied and aggravated if you continue to focus on your goals, or more accurately, your inability to pursue them. To prevent yourself from being engulfed by these feelings, you will need to back away from your goals so you can see them in the broader context of your life. In doing so, you will be able to put your goals into perspective, which will better serve you in responding to the crisis at hand. You will come to see your goals as only one part of the landscape of your life rather than the central part. This new perspective will make it easier to accept what is more immediately important (the crisis) and make peace with what isn't (your life goals). The result is that your investment in your life goals will temporarily decline to a manageable level that allows you to refocus your energies onto the more pressing matter of the crisis.

Redirect to your crisis goals. After putting your goals in a broader context, you can redirect your goal-setting passion and skills from your life goals to goals you need to set to overcome the crisis. By shifting your investment from your life goals to the crisis at hand, you ensure that you make a wholehearted commitment to achieving your crisis goals. Not only will this help resolve the crisis; it also provides similar meaning, satisfaction, and joy as fulfilling your life goals, thus making it more palatable to temporarily set aside your life goals. It also allows you to return to pursuing your life goals as soon as possible.

EXPECTATIONS VERSUS GOALS

When we are confronted by a crisis, we quickly develop certain perceptions about it. For some of us, our perceptions are positive and hopeful. For others, they are negative and pessimistic. The way we view the crisis informs the expectations we set related to the crisis and how it will turn out, either in our favor or quite the opposite. In either case, we then invest ourselves in these expectations, which often turns into overinvestment because the crisis is so important to us. In turn, our overinvestment interferes with how we respond. As you will learn shortly, expectations are often the "kiss of death" when it comes to getting what you want in a crisis. Expectations carry so much psychological and emotional baggage that they usually do far more harm than good.

> "It's not the situation, but whether we react (negative) or respond (positive) to the situation that's important."—Zig Ziglar, business guru[9]

Expectations

A dictionary definition of expectations is "a strong belief that something will happen in the future . . . a belief that someone will or should achieve something." When a crisis arises, it's natural to show hope by establishing an expectation that the crisis will pass and the consequences will not be dire. At first glance, setting this expectation may seem like a pretty good idea because it suggests confidence that the expectation can be fulfilled. Such expectations may have been reasonable during primitive times as crises were clear and resolution was immediate. However, for today's crises, these expectations can feel more like a burden that may actually prevent you from having the positive resolution you want.

Let's first explore the meaning and implications of expectations in light of a crisis. First, expectations have a sense of certainty, an assumption that you will get a particular result (e.g., "I expect this crisis to resolve itself!"). Unfortunately, as anyone who has ever experienced a crisis knows, there is little certainty in contemporary crises as so much is unknowable, unpredictable, and uncontrollable. As a result, expectations are often turned on their head.

Second, with the sense of inevitability that comes from having certain expectations, one can feel that the expectation has already been fulfilled. To better illustrate this concept, go back to when you were, say, eight years old. Your birthday is coming up in a few months and there is a toy that you want really bad. You tell your parents in no uncertain terms that you want this toy for your birthday. In doing so, you create the expectation that you will get the present. For the months leading up to your birthday, you think about the gift, see it, feel it, touch it, and play with it. In your mind, you already have it. Your birthday arrives and you open your presents only to find that you didn't get the gift you had expected. How do you feel? Devastated! Why do you feel so badly? Not because you didn't get the present; you would have only felt disappointed by that. Instead, you feel beyond terrible because in your mind and heart you already had the present, and your parents ripped it out of your hands! Therein lies one of the dangers of expectations.

Third, an implicit threat lies hidden in every expectation, almost as if there is an invisible "or else" at the end of any expectation. For example, "I expect to succeed . . . or else I will be terribly embarrassed." Sometimes the "or else" may not be clear, but having an expectation puts you in the position of feeling you absolutely must fulfill it or something bad will happen. As a result, expectations create stress and pressure at a time when you feel enough of both from the crisis itself.

Fourth, expectations are all-or-nothing propositions; there is no gray area around them. You either fulfill the expectation and succeed or you don't and you fail. This means there is only a small opportunity to succeed and a very large chance of failure.

Finally, expectations have a complicated relationship with emotions. When I ask people about expectations, their reactions are pretty much the same. They frown, grimace, and get uncomfortable. They say things like, "I hate it when people expect things from me," or "When I build up expectations about something, I feel like I'm setting myself up for failure."

Expectations take a big emotional toll on us, particularly during a crisis when the volume on our emotional life is already turned way up. They produce emotional reactions that feel bad and usually interfere with a positive response to a crisis. Positive expectations (i.e., anticipating a good outcome) can create pressure to fulfill the expectations and fear that you won't, which creates a threat reaction that hurts your efforts to respond to the crisis. Conversely, negative expectations— "I'm doomed!"—create a self-fulfilling prophecy that impairs your confidence and motivation to confront the crisis. Both types of expectations limit your efforts to resolve the crisis as they can produce a cautious mindset fueled by fear, stress, poor confidence, and an inability to focus.

> "Expectation is the root of all heartache."—William Shakespeare, English playwright [10]

Six Phrases That Create Expectations (and Pressure)

I often hear six cringe-worthy phrases from people when they're experiencing a crisis—cringe-worthy because they are big red flags of expectations:

1. I must . . .
2. I have to . . .
3. I need to . . .
4. I should . . .
5. I better . . .
6. I gotta . . .

Try saying these six phrases out loud and see how you feel. Just saying them causes me to tense up and feel the weight of expectations on my shoulders. They exemplify a crisis mentality with an unhealthy dose of desperation thrown in because there is no room for error. What makes these phrases so unpleasant is that they all are followed by an implicit threat. For example, "I must resolve this crisis . . . or my life is over." The specific threat you feel is determined by the meaning you attach to not being able to fulfill your expectations. Regardless of the threat, it feels bad and it prevents you from having a positive response to a crisis.

If you become aware that you are using any of these six phrases, you can replace them with much more beneficial alternatives, such as

1. I would like to . . .
2. It is my goal to . . .
3. I am working hard to . . .
4. I am directing all of my energy to . . .

5. I am excited to . . .
6. I am hopeful that . . .

Now, try saying these six phrases and see how you feel. When I say them, I feel positive, empowered, and motivated. These are clearly different reactions compared to the preceding six phrases. The second set of phrases illustrates the power of an opportunity mindset.

> "*Pressure* is a word that is misused in our vocabulary. When you start thinking of pressure, it's because you've started to think of failure."
> —Tommy Lasorda, World Series–winning manager[11]

Goals

I hope I've convinced you that expectations will do you no good as you attempt to resolve a crisis. But let's be realistic. Your efforts at overcoming the crisis may be Herculean and worthy of admiration, but if you don't actually surmount it, then there is little benefit to your efforts. So my challenge is to give you a better alternative than expectations for you to continue to aim for a desired outcome related to a crisis. My solution is to have you focus on goals, not expectations. On the surface, goals and expectations may seem similar, but they are vastly different animals. Let's explore some of the differences that separate goals from expectations.

The Power of Goals

Goal setting is actually wired into us. It has helped us survive and thrive since we were cave people 250,000 years ago. Goals have been responsible for many of the great developments that have gotten us to where we are today in contemporary society. Setting, working toward, and achieving goals is rewarding to us. As a result, we feel pride, inspiration, and excitement in putting forth the effort and seeing our effort reach fruition.

Unlike expectations and their air of certainty, goals are about the possibility of accomplishment as long as you stay positive and committed and give your best effort. Another great thing about goals is that they aren't black and white like expectations; rather they are about degree of attainment. Not every goal can be achieved, but there will almost always be improvement toward a goal and that progress defines success. There is little chance of failure and great opportunity for success if you give your best effort. When I ask people about goals, they react very differently than they do when asked about expectations. Their faces perk up and they say things like, "It means I decide to do something and I want to work really hard to do it."

Here's an example to illustrate the difference between an expectation and a goal. As I discussed earlier, the Great Recession of the late 2000s had a devastating impact on many people's financial lives. Let's say you had an investment portfolio of $500,000 before the financial crisis struck, and your nest egg for your retirement plummeted to $200,000 in its immediate aftermath. After the initial shock of this dramatic decline, you create an expectation of returning your portfolio to its initial half-million-dollar level within two years. After two years, your portfolio rose to $400,000. You failed to meet your expectation and feel deep disappointment that you fell short. By contrast, if a return to your previous level was your goal, then you still feel pretty good because you see a significant improvement and upward trajectory in your portfolio, even though your goal wasn't fully realized.

The emotional experience of goals is also very different from that of expectations. When you set goals, you feel motivated and excited to strive toward them. You see them as challenges to pursue rather than threats to avoid. If you succeed in achieving your goal, you feel elated. While you certainly feel some disappointment if you fail to meet your goal, you also feel some pride in knowing that you gave it your all and you remain hopeful that you can achieve the goal in the future. So if you're going to set something related to results, set goals and not expectations.

From Outcome to Process

There's another step you must take to increase your chances of success even more in overcoming a crisis. Once you have established goals for the crisis-related outcome you want, it's time to immediately shift from outcome goals to process goals for what you need to do to achieve your outcome goals. For example, let's say you sustain a serious leg injury in a car crash. You set a goal of being able to walk normally within one year. With that outcome goal established, you then set specific process goals for your physical therapy that your medical team believe will enable you to achieve that outcome goal. You have now successfully shifted your focus from the outcome to the process.

"Setting a goal is not the main thing. It is deciding how you will go about achieving it and staying with that plan. Once you have the What, decide on the How, and stick with that plan until you achieve your goal."—Tom Landry, Super Bowl–winning football coach [12]

There are several key elements about process goals that distinguish them from outcome goals. First, if you achieve the process goals, you are very likely to achieve the outcome goals you set for yourself. This is because you have broken down your outcome goal into manageable goals that increase the likelihood that you will give a sustained and consistent effort in pursuit of those goals. Second, process goals are entirely within your control, which means that you have the power to accomplish them. This isn't always true of outcome goals. You can only exert some degree of control over the outcome by giving your best effort in pursuit of your process goals. In other words, when you achieve your process goals, you are more likely to achieve your outcome goals (in chapter 9, I will describe a goal-setting program that you can implement).

"The great mistake is to anticipate the outcome of the engagement; you ought not to be thinking of whether it ends in victory or defeat. Let nature take its course."—Bruce Lee, martial arts legend [13]

SHORT TERM VERSUS LONG GAME

In the aftermath of a crisis, we're wired to focus on its short-term consequences. Back when we were cave people, crises were immediate and required an urgent response. Back then, concentrating on the threat directly before us was essential for our survival. Unfortunately, this narrow and in-the-moment focus doesn't serve us well for many of our current crises because they are often complex and unfold well into the future, with no instantaneous response that will resolve them.

Short Term

The short-term impact of a crisis is unsettling psychologically and emotionally, and causes significant disruption in our lives. It's easy to be consumed by the shock of the experience and react much as our primitive ancestors did. Additionally, if we are overly focused on the immediate repercussions and react instinctively, we don't take the time to consider its long-term implications or explore the different options of how to respond that may produce a more desirable outcome.

Let me expand on the earlier stock market metaphor to further illustrate the problems with a short-term investment following a crisis. Day traders are investors who "play" the stock market, meaning they engage in frequent and short-term trading looking for immediate returns on their investments. Traders try to understand a stock and time the market accurately so that after they buy the stock, its price goes up and they can sell it for a profit. All of this occurs within a matter of a day, hours, or even minutes. Sounds like a winning formula for making a lot of money in a short time, doesn't it? Except that it isn't. Research has shown that 80 percent of day traders lose money and only 1 percent are reliably profitable because of the uncertainty and unpredictability of market forces and the lack of information that could lead to good trading decisions—not to mention traders' egos, cognitive biases, and emotions, which distort thinking and interfere with their ability to think rationally.

When it comes to responding to a crisis, this same approach will have a similar success rate with even more dire consequences. Focusing on short-term concerns and looking for short-term solutions may produce immediate benefits without regard to long-term ramifications of the crisis. As an example, lets return to the Great Recession. Following the financial collapse that led to the Great Recession, many people withdrew money from their investment portfolio to prevent further losses. Doing so protected them against additional losses in a depressed and volatile stock market. At the same time, it ignored the historical fact that the stock market always returns to and surpasses its pre-crisis level. Such knee-jerk reactions are more reflexive than reflective, meaning they are often driven by the amygdala and its accompanying primitive instincts, emotions, and reactions.

Moreover, a singular focus on short-term gains ignores long-term considerations related to the causes and effects of a crisis. The net result of a short-term investment during a crisis is to perhaps ease its immediate consequences while unintentionally creating the possibility of more severe and longer-lasting consequences in the future. In contrast, deliberate responses are made by our cerebral cortex and benefit from its ability to gather and synthesize solid information and weigh both the immediate and long-term effects of our actions. Based on this measured thought process, we are able to make more sound judgments.

Long Game

There is no doubt that some attention must be paid to the short-term impact of a crisis on your life. There may very well be steps you can take to mitigate the immediate effects of the crisis. The downside is that when you are driven by short-term needs without consideration of the future impact of your actions, you develop an expectation of finding an immediate and successful solution to the crisis, which can lead to over-investment and disappointment.

Let me return once more to the stock market metaphor to help demonstrate the power of the "long game" in approaching a crisis. If you look at one bad day on the stock market, you will see, for example, a drop of three hundred points on the Dow Jones Industrial Average or an extended market decline, such as in 2000–2002 when the Nasdaq Composite dropped 78 percent. Based on this information, you would likely conclude that investing in the stock market is a really bad idea. Further, if you already have money in the stock market, you might want to pull your money out right away. Similarly, if a crisis strikes, your natural tendency is to act immediately and try to resolve it as quickly as possible. As I have said many times throughout this book, what worked as a cave person probably won't work in the twenty-first century. When you react immediately, you are relying on a short-term perspective, limited information, and a primitive response that will likely result in a poor response and unwanted outcome to the crisis.

Now, if you step back from that stock market chart and look at it over the last nearly one hundred years, you see a jagged line with many ups and downs (including some long, dramatic declines such as 1966–1982). More importantly, you distance yourself from the bad days, weeks, months, or even years and can see that the jagged line progresses steadily upward. From this long-term perspective, putting your money in the stock market—and keeping it there during down swings—is a very good investment.

Similarly, you want to step back from the immediacy and intensity of a crisis in much the same way. When you think of a long-term perspective on a crisis, you give yourself the time to shift the power from your amygdala to your cerebral cortex, thus avoiding rash and ill-advised reactions. You give yourself time to gather relevant informa-tion and the necessary resources. You allow yourself to engage in a deep and expansive analysis of the crisis. In the end, you enable your-self to take everything you've processed and turn it into a well-thought-out and detailed plan for addressing the crisis in the most effective way possible.

I want you to take a few important lessons away from this chapter about confronting a crisis. First, let go of overinvestment and setting expectations for immediate action and results. Second, determine your long-term needs and use them to set goals. Third, develop a plan that takes into consideration your long-term needs and goals and is aimed at surmounting the crisis. Finally, don't be quick to judge your progress toward resolving the crisis simply based on how things have been going recently. Remind yourself that the stock market has its ups and downs, but overall it is heading in the right direction. Similarly, look at the general direction of your efforts to combat the crisis over an extended period. This emphasis on the long game will keep you motivated, positive, and calm even on your worst days of a crisis. In turn, this approach will increase your chances of reaching a satisfactory resolution.

Chapter Six

Attitudes

You Gotta Believe!

Attitudes are so important to how you react to crises. They act as the filter through which you look at, understand, interpret, feel about, evaluate, decide on, and respond to a crisis. An attitude is defined as "a settled way of thinking or feeling about someone or something, typically one that is reflected in a person's behavior." According to the "ABC model," attitudes are comprised of three components. First, there is the *affective* (A) component, which involves the emotions you experience related to the attitude (e.g., fear). Second, the *behavioral* (B) component encompasses how the attitude impacts your response to the crisis (e.g., avoidance). Third, the *cognitive* (C) component is comprised of your thoughts about the crisis (e.g., "I can't overcome this crisis!").

As you can see, your attitude toward a crisis has a wide-ranging impact on what you think, how you feel, and how you react. For example, Sam loses his corporate job due to downsizing. His attitude toward the job loss will largely determine how he responds. If his attitude is negative ("In this economy, I'll never find a job I want."), his emotional reaction to the situation will likely include anxiety, doubt, and worry (crisis mentality). As a result, Sam will probably delay or avoid looking for a new job. Conversely, if he thinks, "This is as a chance to reevaluate my professional life and find work that better aligns with my values," then he is more likely to approach his job loss with excitement, inspiration, and determination (opportunity mindset). Subsequently,

Sam will be more likely to embrace the challenge of finding a new job and he may even find one that he likes better.

When faced with a crisis, your attitudes can serve as either a weapon that hinders your efforts or a tool to boost your efforts. Attitudes as weapons are negative, critical, stress inducing, and distracting. Attitudes as tools are positive, supportive, calming, and focusing.

A challenge with attitudes is that they can be either conscious or unconscious. By conscious, I mean that you are aware of your attitudes, you know where they came from, they are readily available to think about, and they are relatively easy to change. Conscious attitudes develop through experience, introspection, and deliberate choice. For example, based on how conflict has impacted your life and your observations of how others positively and negatively manage conflict, you may develop an appreciative attitude toward conflict and choose to see it as an opportunity for growth. In contrast, unconscious attitudes are murkier. You may not know how they developed, they aren't easy to access, and as a result, they are more difficult to change. For example, as a child you may have seen your father avoid conflict, which led you to develop an avoidant attitude toward conflict. Your goal is to ensure that you consciously choose attitudes about a crisis that will support your efforts to overcome it. You accomplish this objective with several steps:

1. Become aware of your own attitudes toward a crisis and whether they help or hurt you.
2. Identify attitudes that will help you overcome the crisis.
3. If you find a discrepancy between the attitudes you hold and those that will best serve you in a crisis, you should examine how the unhelpful attitudes developed, acknowledge the benefits of the healthier attitudes, and gradually shift your attitudes in a more productive direction.

There are three attitude forks in the road. There are many attitudes that will influence how you respond to a crisis. For example, your attitude about discomfort, determination, adaptability, confidence, stress, and many more. And with each attitude, you have the choice to take the good road or the bad road. I have identified three broad-based attitude forks in the road that I deem most fundamental to overcoming a crisis. Taking the good road with these three attitudes will act as the foundation for more specific attitudes you can adopt to help you confront the crisis with a positive and productive orientation.

"Attitude is a little thing that makes a big difference."—Winston Churchill, former British prime minister [1]

VICTIM VERSUS MASTER

Since the fight-or-flight reaction has been ingrained in our genes for hundreds of thousands of years, it's easy to be consumed by a crisis mentality and become a victim of our own inner experience. Your thinking, emotions, and reactions can make you feel like you are being swept down a rushing river in a canoe without a paddle and with no way to resist the current. This primordial psychology and physiology, driven by your amygdala, is immediate and so visceral that it can overwhelm and victimize you.

At the same time, we are fortunate that our cerebral cortex developed and gives us the capacity to exercise conscious control over our thinking, emotions, and reactions. It acts as a master by interrupting our primitive instincts and enabling us to make deliberate choices about how we react to crises. Your ability to master these intense and deeply entrenched reactions will give you one more way to resist the gravitational pull of the crisis mentality and leverage an opportunity mindset in the face of large and small crises.

"You may not control all the events that happen to you, but you can decide not to be reduced by them."—Maya Angelou, American poet, singer, and civil rights activist [2]

Victim

Crises indicate that something has occurred that threatens our status quo. Moreover, many aspects of crises today are out of our control. Common examples include car accidents, illnesses, and natural disasters. This lack of control leads us to feel helpless and more vulnerable to fall into the role of a victim.

Although there are objective aspects of crises that we have no control over, we do have control over our attitude. In other words, you can control your attitude toward the crisis. To respond well, you must have a positive attitude from which you can operate. This means your attitude ultimately dictates whether you experience the crisis as a master or a victim. Here are some things that can lead you straight to victimhood.

> "I am not what happened to me. I am what I choose to become."
> —Emma Watson, British actress and activist [3]

Focusing on the Externals of a Crisis

When a crisis strikes, we are wired to focus intently on its external causes, the goal of which is to ensure that we pay enough attention to resolve the crisis and ensure our survival. That approach worked when crises tended to be more immediate and "in your face" (think saber-toothed tiger or rival tribesperson). Because today's crises are often at a distance, delayed, and beyond our explicit control, focusing on external causes can produce a sense of victimization. Instead of leading to a sense of agency and action that is needed to surpass the crisis, external focus may actually encourage a sense of victimhood because it takes away from the attention that needs to be on the elements of the crisis over which you do have control. The most notable element is our attitude.

> "One way to boost our willpower and focus is to manage our distractions instead of letting them manage us."—Daniel Goleman, author and science journalist [4]

Having a Pity Party

As discussed in chapter 2, crises generate a tsunami of truly unpleasant emotions, one of which is self-pity. When life doesn't go as you want, it's easy to fall into a "Woe is me" mentality and to have a pity party in an attempt to avoid taking responsibility for the cause or resolution of the overwhelming situation at hand. Usually this response produces a lot of sympathy, which feels good but doesn't have any practical value in addressing a crisis.

> "No one can make you feel inferior without your permission."
> —Eleanor Roosevelt, former first lady and American diplomat and activist [5]

Focusing on the Forest

Crises these days are so multifaceted that they can be overwhelming. There is so much to identify, understand, synthesize, decide, and act upon (the trees) that you simply feel unprepared to do it all. Often the natural reaction when this happens is to do nothing and fall into victimhood. Of course, crises don't go away because you want them to, just like you don't find your way out of the forest by looking at each individual tree. While this narrow focus may provide some temporary relief, the end result is that you don't find your way out.

> "You cannot escape the responsibility of tomorrow by evading it today."—Abraham Lincoln, sixteenth US president [6]

Not Recognizing Your Capabilities

At the heart of victimhood is the belief that you aren't capable of overcoming the magnitude of challenges a crisis presents to you. Holding this belief can make you feel like you're standing at the base of Mt. Everest without any climbing experience or the alpine gear necessary to reach the summit.

Master

People who respond to crises with aplomb and calm—whether a soldier saving a comrade, a boy standing up to bullies, a CEO trying to save her company, or a president trying to save the country—are often considered to be a special breed, quite unlike us normal human beings. We see them as people who don't experience crises the way the rest of us do; they have intestinal fortitude or nerves of steel or the ability to let things slide off them. It's as if they're somehow endowed with superpowers that we mortals simply don't have and aren't capable of ever possessing.

Though these seemingly extraordinary people are certainly worthy of great admiration for their remarkable acts of courage and determination, putting these heroes up on a pedestal gives them too much credit and ourselves too little. As I have observed previously, our primitive instincts are reactions that we are physically incapable of completely divorcing ourselves from. In addition, from our cells to our outward appearance, human beings are surprisingly alike. The reality is that quite often we all feel similarly, but with varying degrees of intensity depending on our inborn temperaments and life experiences. The seemingly battle-hardened warriors of whom we stand in awe actually experience fear, frustration, anger, and despair just like the rest of us. The difference is not the absence of an emotional reaction, but the ability to respond positively to crises in the face of those intense feelings.

What we attribute to these stalwarts as being exceptional is better explained as ordinary people who do extraordinary things because they were prepared to do them. For example, police officers, trauma surgeons, and soldiers weren't born into those careers. Rather, they trained to do their jobs, which informed who they became and what they were (and are) able to accomplish. They have learned to master their emotional reactions when confronted by a crisis rather than falling victim to them. You are equally capable of responding to crises with an opportunity mindset if you develop attitudes similar to those seemingly remarkable people whom we hold in such high esteem.

What holds many people back from gaining this mastery is their belief that our reactions are set in stone at birth and, as a result, are not amenable to change. As I discussed earlier, the temperament we were born with has an influence on our reactions to a crisis. At the same time, genetics are not destiny, which means that biology isn't the only influence on our reaction to a crisis; our experiences also have an important impact. In fact, our responses, as I suggest throughout *How to Survive and Thrive*, are not a single immutable personality trait at all. Instead, they are a constellation of attitudes, beliefs, resources, and skills that develop with experience and deliberate effort and allow us to change how crises impact our lives.

> "Being challenged in life is inevitable, being defeated is optional."
> —Roger Crawford, first athlete to play a Division I sport with a severe disability[7]

Prepare Yourself

Mastery of a crisis begins before it even occurs and well before you experience its associated emotional reactions. Much like you train for a marathon to prepare yourself for the rigors of the 26.2-mile distance, you can also train and prepare yourself for the challenges of a crisis:

1. Gain a clear understanding of the situations you experience as crises.
2. Identify the thoughts, emotions, and reactions that result.

3. Develop strategies to gain control of those reactions before they occur.

If you can accomplish these three steps, then you will be ready when a crisis arises and you will be better able to respond to it in a positive and constructive way.

> "A goal without a plan in just a wish."—Antoine de Saint-Exupery, French aviator and author[8]

Know the Situation

The situation in which the crisis occurs plays a role in your reaction to it. Think about the experience of being diagnosed with a serious illness, the loss of your financial nest egg, or a divorce. Each of these circumstances is likely associated with different thoughts and feelings. Being able to see the situation in which the crisis occurs allows you to identify your most likely reactions and the strengths you have at your disposal. In doing so, you are better able to predict and head off those ineffective reactions, encourage yourself to take on the role of master rather than victim, and respond in a productive way.

Know Your Thoughts

We have thoughts about everything. It's important to be aware of how you tend to think about things when under stress as your initial thoughts can often determine the direction your reactions take after a crisis hits. Consider the following thoughts: "There's nothing I can do about this," or "I'm just not going to let this happen." Obviously, each of these thoughts will produce very different thoughts, emotions, and reactions. If you know the typical thoughts you have when confronted by a crisis, you can anticipate and prevent unhealthy thinking from dictating your response.

Know Your Emotions

We tend to respond to stressful situations in characteristic ways. Some of us react with upset and tears, others get angry and yell, still others react with fear and attempts to avoid the crisis altogether, and the rare few stay as "cool as a cucumber." Being able to recognize your own pattern of emotions in reaction to a crisis allows you to foresee and preempt those emotions if they interfere with your ability to respond productively to the crisis.

> "People may hear your words, but they feel your attitude."—John C. Maxwell, American author and speaker[9]

Identify Your Strengths

It is essential that you identify your strengths when faced with a crisis. Focusing on the assets you bring to a stressful situation counteracts the feelings of helplessness that can lead to victimhood. Whether they're general capabilities or a skill set specific to the crisis, reconnecting with the strengths you bring to bear gives you a boost of confidence and motivation that will help you more easily assume the role of master.

Focus on the Trees

As noted, when a crisis hits, it is easy to become overwhelmed by the enormity of the forest you find yourself in. In this case, to cut the crisis down to size (pun intended) and make it more manageable, it is best to shift your focus from the expansiveness of the forest down to the specifics of the trees. In other words, identify key elements of the crisis and direct your attention and energy onto those areas. As the crisis continues, you can move from tree to tree until the crisis is resolved.

> "Someone's sitting in the shade today because someone planted a tree a long time ago."—Warren Buffett, business magnate and philanthropist[10]

Have a Plan

It is very difficult to alter your reactions to a crisis in the moment because the force of your instincts and emotions is immediate. But you can stop, mitigate, or alter that reaction if you have a plan in place before the crisis arises. For example, think back to elementary school when fire drills were conducted to prepare students and teachers for how to respond safely when the fire alarm sounds. If these drills weren't completed on a regular basis, imagine the chaos that would ensue if a fire were to break out. Students would be terrified, teachers would be trying to remain calm and think, and kids might get lost without a preplanned way to keep track of them. Understanding the context in which crises may occur and the typical thoughts and emotions you have in response allows you to devise a plan that includes a challenge response, an optimistic mindset, and constructive actions that are readily accessible when a crisis strikes.

> "Failing to plan is planning to fail."—Alan Lakein, time-management author[11]

Take the Good Road

At the heart of being a master is knowing the perceptions you hold about yourself and the crisis, and the emotions you feel, and using that information to choose how you will respond to the situation. As I discussed in the introduction, how you learn to respond to a crisis is a *simple, but not easy, choice.* If you have two options—experiencing unhealthy emotions and taking unproductive action that leads to a poor outcome *or* experiencing healthy emotions and taking productive action that leads to a positive outcome—the choice is simple in that you will certainly choose the latter option. That said, while it is a simple choice, it is not an easy one to make because millions of years of evolution and deeply ingrained habits born of your temperament and life experiences can compel you to react in ways that prevent you from responding well to the crisis.

Take Bethany Hamilton, the professional surfer who lost her arm after being attacked by a shark. By focusing on her strengths as an individual and taking her recovery one step at a time, she was able to see the trees rather than becoming consumed by the enormity of the forest. As a result, in a short time, she returned to competitive surfing with remarkable success.

Learning to make the simple, but not easy, choice when confronted with a crisis involves recognizing the forks in the road where you avoid going down the bad road that leads to becoming a victim and choose to take the good road that allows you to master the crisis. The great thing about making this simple, but not easy, choice when facing a crisis is that it is self-rewarding: when you make the simple but not easy choice, you feel good, you do good, and the outcome will more likely be good as well.

> "Self-control is strength. Right thought is mastery. Calmness is power."—James Allen, nineteenth-century British writer[12]

Mastery in Action

Despite the visceral role your reactions play in your efforts to meet the challenges you face in crises, you probably haven't thought too much about how to deal with those reactions in a practical way. It's more likely that you react and then hope your reaction doesn't do too much harm. Such an approach leads you to become a victim of the crisis itself, as well as your own primitive reactions. To avoid this, your goal is to gain mastery of the crisis by responding positively to those initial reactions, thereby shifting from a crisis mentality to an opportunity mindset.

"Yesterday is not ours to recover, but tomorrow is ours to win or lose."—Lyndon B. Johnson, thirty-sixth US president[13]

Step Back

When your instincts first get triggered by a crisis, instead of reacting to them, take a step back. Temporarily separating yourself from the crisis creates psychological and emotional distance that eases the grip your instincts have on you. Additionally, that distance allows you to let go of the physical stress associated with the crisis. Loosening this mental and physical hold allows your cerebral cortex to reassert itself over the caveman brain that is the source of your initial, and unproductive, reactions.

"Sometimes you need to take a step back to move forward."—Erika Taylor, author[14]

Take a Break

Next, if the crisis doesn't require an immediate response, take a break and do something that is completely unrelated and relaxing, puts you in a good mood, and clears your "emotional chalkboard." Activities that can help relieve a crisis's physical and psychological burden include having something to eat, listening to music, getting some exercise, or socializing.

If the crisis requires your urgent attention, a few deep breaths may be all the break you can manage. That brief respite alone can help you relax your body and clear your mind. In addition, it lessens the uncomfortable physical symptoms that can come with a crisis, generates pleasant feelings, and makes you feel more comfortable, confident, and in control. All of these benefits will counteract unproductive reactions and prepare you to respond to the crisis constructively.

> "You can discover more about a person in an hour of play than in a year of conversation."—Plato, classical Greek philosopher [15]

Express Yourself

The ethos of the American mind includes the belief that people who overcome a crisis are tough and unemotional, almost like the US version of the English expression "keep a stiff upper lip." Yet, the body of research exploring the most productive ways to respond to adversity and stress (which crises have in spades) contradicts this view. The findings indicate that emotional expression (i.e., talking about your feelings rather than bottling them up) is associated with increased adaptation and growth. So, whether you're experiencing fear, frustration, anger, despair, or any other emotion, share them with others. You'll feel better from having an emotional release and feel support from those with whom you share. Plus, the opportunity to process your emotions with a trusted friend will put you in a better space from which to tackle the crisis.

> "Live life as though nobody is watching, and express yourself as though everyone is listening."—Nelson Mandela, South African political leader [16]

Identify the Problem

Once your immediate reactions have been mitigated, you are ready to confront the crisis head-on with a calm and clear mind. In this receptive state, you can focus on understanding the crisis by first identifying the specific problems that are causing it. With an awareness of the cause of the crisis, you are in a better position to find a successful solution.

Think Small

Many crises today, such as the Great Recession, are simply too big and too overwhelming for you to completely comprehend, much less control. Crises of this ilk are precisely the kind that can easily engulf you with destructive reactions that interfere with your ability to overcome them. Focusing on these oversized crises will exacerbate the natural psychological, emotional, and physical reactions you are going to experience. With these sorts of crises, your best chance is to identify those aspects that are within your control. Then, you can break down the bigger crisis into smaller, more manageable problems toward which you can direct your energy and find solutions. For example, think back to the Great Recession. Although you probably didn't have the ability to influence economic policy, you were able to revisit the distribution of your investments and choose to create a more diverse portfolio.

"The journey of a thousand miles begins with a single step."—Lao Tzu, Chinese general and philosopher [17]

Discretion Is the Better Part of Valor

Crises can't always be resolved immediately, particularly modern-day ones. Thus, continued efforts in the short-term pursuit of their resolution would be futile and inevitably descend into a crisis mentality. The barriers to overcoming a crisis may just be too great to surmount in that moment or on that day. You may need more information, more analysis, or more help before moving forward.

You have two beneficial options here. First, you can change your goals related to the crisis to ones that can be achieved in the short term. For example, let's say you're afraid because the company you work for may have to file for Chapter 11 bankruptcy. You probably can't have much direct impact on that decision, but you can make sure that your department is running at top speed with all its work in order. You may also begin to explore other job opportunities. The second option is to take a break. There are going to be days when you just aren't making progress toward resolving a crisis. On these days, continuing to try unsuccessfully to address the crisis will only serve to amplify the threat reaction. Trying to force the issue will actually hurt your efforts in the long run. In this case, it may be wise to push "pause" and fight another day. In doing so, you can recharge your emotional batteries and return the next day with a refreshed attitude, a renewed vigor, and a rededicated commitment to overcoming the crisis.

"Know your enemy and know yourself and you can fight a hundred battles without disaster."—Sun Tzu, Chinese general and philosopher [18]

RENT VERSUS OWN

There's a metaphor I use to help people understand why ownership lies at the heart of how you approach a crisis: which do you treat better, a car you rent or a car you own? Clearly, you take better care of the car you own. Why? Because it's yours; you've invested in it financially and emotionally. You want the car you own to perform its best and last a long time, so you take care of it by having regular checkups and tune-ups. You get it washed, vacuumed, and polished so it looks good.

There's an expression that relates here: "Pride of ownership." You're proud of owning your car, so you put time and effort into its care and maintenance. Just as the engine of your car propels you toward your destination, ownership of a crisis is the engine that drives you toward its resolution. There is a big difference in how you approach a crisis when you don't take ownership of it or the outcome, compared to when you take full ownership of both.

> "Until you take ownership for your life, you will always be chasing happiness."—Sean Stephenson, motivational speaker [19]

Rent

Taking ownership of a crisis is hard to do. In some cases, a crisis may feel too insurmountable to own. In other cases, it may be too threatening to accept ownership of a crisis because you may equate ownership with being responsible for it. Or, you don't believe that you have the capabilities or the resources to take ownership. Sometimes, it's just easier to assume the role of victim and let other people take ownership of the crisis and resolve it for you. A lack of ownership shows itself in

- Blaming others for a crisis
- Making excuses to deflect responsibility away from you
- Avoiding the crisis
- Lack of initiative in responding to a crisis
- Poor effort expended toward finding a resolution
- Little resilience in the face of the challenges presented by a crisis

> "When you blame and criticize others, you are avoiding some truth about yourself."—Deepak Chopra, author and public speaker [20]

Own

Ownership means you believe the successful outcome of a crisis is up to you. A successful outcome requires your initiative, your strength, your determination, and your perseverance. Often in a crisis you need support from others, but you understand that success is on your shoulders and there are no guarantees. There are many degrees of ownership of a crisis, ranging from none to complete ownership. When you don't take ownership, there's little chance of having an impact on the resolution; you must simply pray to the all-mighty gods that things will turn out OK and fall victim to whatever ensues. In contrast, the more ownership you accept, the more power you have over how a crisis affects you. And, while accepting total ownership doesn't ensure a positive outcome, you'll give yourself the best chance of overcoming a crisis. Ownership in response to a crisis is expressed in several ways:

- You take the challenge that the crisis presents to you seriously.
- You fully embrace an opportunity mindset because you believe it is the only possible starting place for resolution of a crisis.
- You are thoroughly engaged in every aspect of the crisis, leaving no stone unturned and no detail ignored.
- You do the very best you can in everything; this is a fundamental value that directs your approach to the crisis, regardless of the odds for a positive outcome.
- You see the crisis through a positive lens, as an experience from which you can learn and grow.
- You take pride in everything you do because you know that the journey can be rewarding even when the outcome may not end up being the one you want.

After reading these criteria of ownership, ask yourself: do I own my crisis? If you're still unsure, here are a few more questions to help you find out:

- Do you take responsibility for everything you have control over that impacts the crisis?
- Are you proactive in looking for solutions to the crisis?
- Do you give your best effort consistently?
- Do you persevere in the face of the many challenges you are confronted with by the crisis?

If you answered yes to these questions, you take ownership of the crisis with which you are presented. If not, you can find steps in the next section to help you gain ownership.

First, let me illustrate the importance of ownership in a crisis situation. Imagine you are miles from safety in the expansive Grand Canyon and find yourself trapped between a rock and a hard place, literally. Aron Ralston found himself in this predicament when a boulder crushed his arm during a canyoneering accident. He was trapped for more than five days. He freed himself from this horrific circumstance by, remarkably, amputating his own arm with a jackknife. After surviving this life-threatening situation, Ralston continued engaging in outdoor pursuits and many bucket list items with the help of a prosthetic arm. Even though it wasn't his fault that a boulder fell on him, Ralston owned the traumatic reality in which he found himself and took it upon himself to ensure his survival. He may have lost his arm, but he could very well have lost his life.

I hope I've convinced you that ownership is essential for successfully prevailing over a crisis; you must *own your crisis*. It certainly sounds good in theory, doesn't it? It's one thing to think about ownership and it's an entirely different thing to actually gain, and maintain, ownership every day that a crisis dominates your life. So, at a practical level, what does it mean to own your crisis?

> "If you own this story you get to write the ending."—Brené Brown, research professor[21]

Own Your Mind

A key theme of this chapter is that the greatest ally you have in response to a crisis is your mind. If you are your own worst enemy, you have no chance. Owning your mind means your thoughts, emotions, and reactions are on your side and work to your benefit. If you can own your mind, you eliminate the crisis mentality, which is often the greatest obstacle when facing a crisis. Moreover, by owning your mind, you create in yourself an opportunity mindset that reframes the crisis as a challenge, which ultimately sets the stage for a positive and determined response to the crisis.

> "This I believe: that the free, exploring mind of the individual human is the most valuable thing in the world."—John Steinbeck, Nobel Prize–winning author[22]

Own Your Understanding of the Crisis

To gain full ownership of the crisis, you must have a clear understanding of all its facets and complexities. This knowledge includes its causes, its effect on you, what you need to know about the crisis, whom you can enlist to help, and anything else that will take you toward a successful resolution. I encourage you to be relentless in exploring the crisis far and wide by asking questions and researching topics. Be open to suggestions and opinions ranging from conventional to outside the box to truly "out there," because desperate times may require desperate measures.

Own the "Controllables"

As I have noted before, there are a lot of things related to a crisis that you can't control, such as your age, other people, getting old, natural disasters, corporate malfeasance, and world poverty. At the same time, there is often much in a crisis that you can control, including yourself, your knowledge, resources, access to information, and much more. Because the odds in a crisis are often stacked against you, you must ensure that you marshal every "controllable" you can and use it to your advantage.

> "If opportunity doesn't knock, build a door."—Milton Berle, American actor[23]

Own the Details

The old saying "the devil is in the details" is used to highlight that little things are important, and when they are overlooked, problems arise. In other words, details can be the difference between success and failure in any endeavor, including a crisis.

When faced with a crisis, start by examining the basic facts to develop a general understanding of what it presents in your life. But don't stop there, because it is not the broad strokes that make a masterpiece. As you begin to address a crisis, you want to uncover and pay attention to its details. This can make a real difference in how you respond to it.

At its broadest level, the idea of owning the little things involves making sure that the crisis takes priority in your life. This involves ensuring that you are making choices that best serve the goals related to the resolution of the crisis. These decisions aren't always easy, particularly when a crisis first presents itself, because our natural tendency is to flee from it in the form of denial and avoidance. Additionally, chances are that your life is already busy balancing your career, family, and other activities. As a result, you may not feel that you have the time and energy to devote to exploring a crisis's details.

Still not convinced about the importance of details? In 1999, a spacecraft team and a flight team at NASA were attempting to put a spacecraft in orbit around Mars. On the day it was sent into orbit, the spacecraft overshot the target distance and disintegrated on the spot. During the investigation into what caused the mishap, it was discovered that NASA's software made the calculations based off of metric units (Newton seconds), but the thrusters on the orbiter were using English units (foot-pound seconds). The result of not correcting this detail? The $125 million orbiter burned in Mars's atmosphere.

There are also little things related to the demands of a crisis that can have a big impact. The fact is that a lot of what you do as you pursue resolution of a crisis is boring, tedious, exhausting, and sometimes painful. Examples might include reviewing your health records, financial statements, insurance policies, and a plethora of rules and laws. It can be easy to convince yourself the little things don't matter that much, and it won't hurt you to address them halfheartedly or not at all. The reality is that the details do matter and doing them tepidly or skipping them all together hurts your chances of overcoming the crisis.

"The difference between something good and something great is the attention to detail."—Charles Swindoll, Christian author [24]

Own Your Plan

Once you've collected, collated, synthesized, and analyzed all relevant information; gathered all useful resources; and considered all available options, it's time to make firm decisions about the road toward a desirable resolution to the crisis. Once you've made your decisions and formulated a plan of action, it's time to own the plan. This phase of dealing with a crisis is the most difficult. Execution of a plan to surmount a crisis can wear you down as it co-opts your time and focus, drains your motivation and energy, and results in a lukewarm effort, missed opportunities, and less-than-ideal outcomes. Yet, this is the most important step because it is "where the rubber meets the road." In other words, this is the final determinant of the ultimate impact the crisis has on you.

OUTCOME VERSUS PROCESS

Let's start by defining *outcome attitude* and *process attitude*. An outcome attitude focuses on the end result of a situation. In contrast, if you focus on what you need to do to produce the desired outcome, then you have a process attitude. There are a lot of misconceptions about the role of outcomes in overcoming a crisis. Of course, the end game is to produce a "victory" in the face of a crisis, whether it's recouping losses from a financial crash, recovering from a serious illness, finding a new job, or adjusting to parenthood. At the same time, the key question is how do I go about getting that desired outcome? Ironically, the answer is not what you may think.

I often ask people whether an outcome or process attitude will lead to a better outcome. Much to my surprise, many say an outcome attitude is better because it keeps their "eye on the prize" and pushes them to toward the result they want. I would suggest, however, that this outcome attitude actually hurts the progress toward a successful resolution, rather than helping it.

"Hold the vision, trust the process."—Unknown [25]

Outcome

Let me explain what I see as the paradox of an outcome attitude. As I just noted, many people think you need to focus on the results you want in order to reach them. Ironically, having an outcome attitude actually reduces the chances you will achieve the outcome you want in a crisis. Here's why: First, overcoming a crisis is usually a long and sometimes painful journey. If you're focused on the outcome and not the process, then you will lose sight of what you need to accomplish to progress to the crisis's conclusion and produce the desired outcome. Second, the primitive instincts, emotions, and reactions that often lead to an undesired outcome are triggered by the fear of a bad outcome. More specifically, these emotions react to the crisis, hurting you deeply in some way. The bottom line is that when you focus on the outcome, you are far less likely to get the outcome you want.

That's not to say that there isn't a time and place for checking on the outcome as you progress through the process of addressing a crisis. Reminding yourself of the positive resolution toward which you're striving can inspire and motivate you and keep you focused on doing what you need to do. Also, realistically, the outcome in a crisis can be an evolving target that shifts as you, the situation, or the world around you changes. You can use the morphing of the crisis to inform you on what you might need to do differently in your plan and its execution.

Here are two suggestions to help you shift your focus away from the outcome and onto the process. First, avoid thinking about the outcome. In an ideal world, I would like you to have an almost entirely process-driven attitude and just check in on your desired outcome occasionally as a point of reference. Taking a peek at the outcome also ensures that you're continuing to head in the right direction since the outcome can change.

Second, ask others around you to avoid talking about the outcome. The fact is there is no point. Once you've taken the steps to determine where you want to go when you're hit by a crisis, you know the desired outcome. You also know when you're making progress, and you definitely know when you're not. If you're like most of us, when important people in your life assume an outcome attitude and constantly talk about the end game, you can't help but to be swept up in that talk, too.

Here's where the real world collides with the ideal world that I wish existed: in the real world, results do matter. It's not likely that you can just expunge the outcome from your mind, particularly when confronted by a crisis in which it seems like the outcome is all that really matters. As someone experiencing a crisis, you are playing a high-stakes game in which you have set big goals for yourself, often directed toward a specific and difficult-to-achieve outcome. The odds are frequently stacked against you.

I can't expect you to not think about the end game in a crisis. In fact, let's assume that you are going to think about the desired outcome a lot, which makes sense to a degree because it gives you hope. At the same time, remember that thinking too much about the results, especially at times when you need a laser focus on the process, actually hurts your chances of success. So, your challenge is what to do when your mind becomes preoccupied with the outcome.

There are several reasons why your mind fixates on outcomes. First, you may have always been obsessed with results in all aspects of your life, so an outcome attitude has become a deeply ingrained habit of your mind. Over time, this way of thinking has become hardwired into your brain's neurophysiology. Second, the people around you—whether family and friends, or resources, such as physicians, financial planners, or attorneys—may continue to communicate messages about results. For example, how often do you hear from well-meaning people, "I just know you'll be cured" or "Your house [that was destroyed by the wildfire] will be rebuilt before you know it." It's difficult to think differently when you're constantly bombarded by messages from others about the outcome they want. Third, in the face of a crisis, you want that good outcome badly, because to not get it could be traumatic or tragic. Finally, we live in an outcome-based world: academic success is measured by grades, athletic success is measured by wins, and corporate success is measured by revenue. We are surrounded by inherent messages that the outcome is what matters, which makes it easy to lose sight of the process. Let's see what we might be missing.

> "Success usually comes to those who are too busy to be looking for it."—Henry David Thoreau, essayist and philosopher [26]

Process

With a process attitude, you increase your chances of getting the outcome you want. The process is what you need to do to resolve the crisis. If you focus on the process, what are you most likely going to do? Precisely what needs to be done, because that's where you are focused. And if you do that, you're more likely to achieve the outcome in the crisis you wanted in the first place.

A move from an outcome attitude to a process attitude in response to a crisis may require that you make a fundamental change in how you think about results. In doing so, you alter the way the end game impacts how you think, feel, and respond to a crisis, regardless of whether the outcome ends up being positive or negative. Making this shift from outcome attitude to process attitude is just like retraining a bad habit you've engaged in for years. It involves commitment, effort, persistence, and patience. Here is a process you can follow to help you move from an outcome attitude to a process attitude.

Understand Outcome and Process Attitudes

You must first understand why you are making this shift. As I hope I have convinced you, an outcome attitude hurts your efforts to overcome a crisis in many ways: how you think about it, the emotions you experience, the decisions you make, and how you respond. In contrast, a process attitude will directly help your efforts to achieve your crisis goals by producing purposeful thinking, emotions, decisions, and reactions that encourage intentional and focused efforts. If you really believe in these differences, it will provide you with a clear rationale and a strong incentive to make this shift from an outcome attitude to a process attitude.

> "It is our attitude at the beginning of a difficult task which, more than anything else, will affect its successful outcome."—William James, philosopher and psychologist[27]

Recognize Outcome Attitude Moments

Your outcome attitude will probably arise most often in common situations such as when

- A crisis first emerges
- The magnitude of the crisis hits you
- You recognize the consequences
- You feel overwhelmed, stressed, or upset about the crisis

These times are those forks in the road that I discussed in the introduction. You can't take a different road if you don't see the fork. You should have your mental radar on when you are approaching those situations in which your outcome attitude is most likely to get activated. With this recognition, you'll be in a position to make the positive shift from outcome attitude to process attitude.

After making what seemed like a decision driven by his own ego rather than what was best for the company, Apple cofounder Steve Jobs was asked to walk away from the company he helped build. At a speech he gave at Stanford University many years later, Jobs referred to his departure from Apple as one of the greatest things that could have happened to him because the lack of pressure to perform allowed for the time and energy to be creative.

> "There are no ordinary moments."—Dan Millman, American author[28]

Pink Elephants and Blue Hippos

It would be great if I could simply tell you to not think about the potential outcomes of a crisis and you would stop your outcome attitude, but that just isn't how it works. In fact, the more I tell you to not think about the outcome, the more you are going to think about the outcome. Here's another way to look at it: I don't want you to think about a pink elephant. What did you just think about? The pink elephant, of course. If I keep repeating, "Don't think about a pink elephant," you will continue to think about that pink elephant. In fact, it will gain a hold in your mind that will be difficult to release. So, it's basically impossible to not think about something when you're told not to think about it. Instead, the solution is to think about something else because we are incapable of thinking about two things at once.

Let's try a variation of the pink elephant scenario. I want you to think about a blue hippo. What did you just think about? The blue hippo, obviously. What did you not think about? Gee, the pink elephant. Now, wasn't that easy? Of course, it's easier making the shift from pink elephant to blue hippo than from outcome attitude to process attitude, but the basic road is the same. When your outcome attitude begins to take control of your thinking, you must first recognize it and then consciously refocus onto a process attitude—that is, thinking something like, "What can I do to take steps toward resolving the crisis?" rather than, "I can't wait for this to be over."

Additionally, as I discussed earlier, part of the challenge of letting go of an outcome attitude and embracing a process attitude involves resisting the forces that exist in your world that keep you preoccupied with the outcome. To help with this, take time to identify the people (e.g., family and friends) and cultural forces (e.g., social media) that keep pulling you toward an outcome attitude. Your goal is to remove, limit, or ignore these messages. This is challenging because you can't change your family and friends, and realistically, you aren't likely to stop using social media.

There are, however, a few things you can do. First, ask the people closest to you and whom you see as key to your support system to stop talking about any possible outcomes of the crisis, whether good or bad. Explain to them why encouraging a process attitude will help you achieve the outcome you want more than a constant focus on outcomes. Second, realize that those closest to you who are talking about outcomes are making a well-intentioned effort to support you, even though it's misguided. With this in mind try to focus on the underlying message of what they're saying, how much they care about you, and their desire for you to get through this crisis unscathed, instead of paying attention to the overt messages about results. Third, if you feel like social media is more of a hindrance than a help, then do your best to stay away from social media that discusses your crisis, particularly if it is shared by many people. Continuing to follow crisis-related social media will only increase your absorption in the crisis and prevent you from maintaining control over your own thinking about it. The bottom line is that the more you can reduce the messages that reinforce your outcome attitude, the easier it will be to embrace a process attitude.

Like any sort of change, making this shift requires commitment, effort, time, perseverance, and patience. At first, it may be a real struggle because you will be pushing against deeply ingrained thinking and emotional habits, while continuing to hear unhelpful messages about the crisis from others. But, just like retraining a bad habit, the more you shift away from an outcome attitude and see the benefits of a process attitude, the easier it will become. In time, you will retrain your old, unproductive outcome attitude into a new, helpful process attitude that will serve you well as you continue your journey toward a positive resolution to the crisis.

> "When faced with a challenge, look for a way, not a way out."
> —David Weatherford, psychologist and author [29]

Stay in the Now

When a crisis arises in your life, it's easy to go down the road of bad times. If you dwell on what already happened with a crisis, you may become overwhelmed with hopelessness, doubt, and worry. You can get stuck on the road from the past and begin to enact the "woulda, coulda, shoulda" feedback loop that will only add insult to the injury of the crisis. This dark road of thinking will also take you down a painful road of emotions filled with disappointment, frustration, anger, and regret. Not only do these emotions make you feel bad, but they also hurt your motivation, confidence, and focus as you attempt to navigate the crisis. Carrying the past around on your shoulders directly interferes with the psychology and physiology you need to constructively address the crisis in the present.

Similarly, the future is no better place to dwell than the past when you're dealing with a crisis. Thinking about what might happen can range from dreaming of the ideal outcome to being immersed in the nightmare of the worst-case scenario. Whether you're focused on the positive or negative possibilities, the future brings the burden of expectation that acts as a weight on your shoulders when you need to be light and agile during a crisis. In these moments, an outcome attitude may take hold of you. Your focus will shift to the results you want, causing you to worry about achieving them and feel fear about the consequences of failure. The future distracts you from staying focused on what you're doing in the present and, like the past, creates a psychology and physiology that makes a successful future less likely.

An attitude that focuses on the present sets the stage for you to be as prepared as possible to confront a crisis head-on in the moment. Here's a simple question to ask yourself if you start to go down the roads of the past or future: What do I need to do *now* to respond positively to the crisis? This question is powerful for several reasons. First, it pulls your mind away from the past and future and directs it onto the present. Second, it encourages you to focus on what actions you can take in the present to resolve the crisis. Third, this action orientation will give you confidence and energize you because you are not carrying the weight of the past or future. You are also taking steps that you have control over and that will best prepare you to give your best effort in the present, which will result in the best possible outcome to the crisis.

> "You can't stop the waves, but you can learn how to surf."—Jon Kabat-Zinn, mindfulness expert[30]

Chapter Seven

Mindset

What Were You Thinking?

When you hear the word *mindset*, the first thing that may come to mind is Dr. Carol Dweck's wonderful work exploring the impact of a fixed versus growth mindset on achievement. As much as I appreciate Dr. Dweck's work, my conception of mindset is entirely different (though not in conflict in any way). Rather than viewing mindset as similar to attitude, I see mindset as one step closer to consciousness and everyday life. Attitudes guide your big-picture life in relation to how you perceive your world, the decisions you make, and the actions you take. By contrast, your mindset directs your day-to-day thinking, efforts, and actions. One helpful way to distinguish mindset from attitudes is to think about them as parts of a large organization (you). Your attitudes are your bosses who are several levels up the organizational chart and residing on the fiftieth floor. Your mindset is the supervisor to whom you report directly and is situated on the first floor.

> "Only those who will risk going too far can possibly find out how far one can go."—T. S. Eliot, American poet [1]

There are three mindset forks in the road. Your mindsets are filters through which information passes. They impact how you perceive a crisis, which determines your moment-to-moment responses to the crisis. Additionally, these filters act to synthesize the plethora of information you use to identify the different responses you could make and, ultimately, determine how you respond.

The importance of your mindset is elevated during a crisis. To help you understand the role of your mindset in seemingly threatening situations, I identify three mindsets that most directly guide your thinking, emotions, and reactions as a crisis unfolds and present three forks in the road that take you on very different journeys as you navigate a crisis: pessimism versus optimism, disrupted versus stable, and comfort versus risk.

PESSIMISM VERSUS OPTIMISM

One of the most distinctive and noticeable qualities in people is the degree to which they are pessimists or optimists. In other words, do they see their glasses as half empty or half full? Do they approach their lives with uncertainty and fear or hope and possibility? Do they see the world as full of threats or full of opportunities?

As I'm sure you can imagine, where you lie on the pessimism-optimism continuum will have a significant influence on whether you adopt a crisis mentality or an opportunity mindset, which informs the impact of the crisis on you and your response to it. Generally, pessimists tend to hold a crisis mentality because they view crises as threats to be avoided. In contrast, optimists more readily adopt an opportunity mindset because they see surmountable challenges they want to pursue rather than major roadblocks preventing them from getting where they want to go. So, are you a pessimist or an optimist? When faced with a crisis, do you

1. Tend to focus on what has gone wrong or can go wrong, or what you can do to make it right?
2. Want to run away or confront it head-on?
3. Feel mostly unpleasant (e.g., fear, frustration, anger, sadness) or pleasant (e.g., excitement, pride, inspiration) emotions?
4. Feel out of control and panicky or in control and comfortable?
5. Have negative or positive self-talk?
6. Feel dejected or motivated?
7. Experience anxiety or stay calm?
8. Question yourself or believe in your capabilities?

As you may suspect, if you leaned toward the negative side in your answers to these questions, you're most likely more of a pessimist. If you tended toward the positive side, you're likely more of an optimist. In either case, it's probably not a surprise because you're one or the other in most aspects of your life and likely always have been. That said, if you consider yourself a pessimist, then this should be a wake-up call for you. Although pessimism can have its place in a crisis, an optimistic mindset is generally more beneficial.

> "The optimist proclaims that we live in the best of all possible worlds: and the pessimist fears this is true"—James Cabell, American author [2]

Pessimism

Before we go any further in our discussion of the role pessimism can play in your response to a crisis, let's define it. Pessimism is "a tendency to see the worst aspect of things or believe that the worst will happen; a lack of hope or confidence in the future." Certainly not a feel-good way to go through life.

Ironically, we're probably wired to be pessimistic through evolution. Think of it this way: pessimistic cave people focused completely on the threat before them, worried about it, and did everything they could to avoid it, which increased their chances of survival. In contrast, optimistic cave people either minimized or ignored the threat ("Oh, that saber-toothed tiger isn't going to eat me"), making it more likely that they would be eaten.

Even with today's crises, some pessimism has its place. In fact, research has shown that pessimism isn't the bete noire (French for dark beast) that our positive-psychology-obsessed culture believes it to be. Pessimism can motivate you to avoid the worst-case scenario. If you find yourself in a desperate situation, you're going to do everything you can to get out of it. It keeps expectations low, which can mitigate disappointment when things don't turn out the way you want. Pessimism ensures that you don't get overconfident or complacent because failure is always lurking just around the corner. It helps you anticipate bad news, which allows you to start working through the emotions associated with undesirable outcomes before they happen. In other words, pessimism can lessen the devastation you might feel should bad news arrive. Moreover, in anticipation of the bad news, you may put supports or strategies into place that will help you respond constructively. For instance, you may schedule a lunch with your best friend on the day you're supposed hear whether you landed a new job or remain unemployed. In addition, during the days leading up to the announcement, you may even lay the groundwork for another round of job applications in the event that you don't get the job.

> "Don't worry about failures, worry about the chances you miss when you don't even try."—Jack Canfield, motivational speaker and author[3]

So, if pessimism is evolutionarily effective and can motivate proactive actions during a crisis, is it really that bad? Pessimism can be good in moderation, but let's be honest—the pessimism we often feel is not in moderation, especially in stressful situations. More often it's doom and gloom, which is a real problem when faced with a crisis. At the heart of pessimism is the feeling of despair ("the complete loss or absence of hope"). It's the belief that nothing you do will enable you to overcome the crisis in front of you. More than likely feelings of despair will demoralize you, particularly when confronted by a crisis that is unexpected and where the consequences are dire. That pessimism is in stark contrast to the pessimism research has found to be beneficial in some instances. The accompanying feelings of despair and dejection lead to a sense of learned helplessness. You perceive the crisis as being completely overwhelming and your capabilities are deemed insufficient to overcome the challenges that lay before you. Thus, you get caught in a vicious cycle: pessimism leads to negativity, despair, helplessness, and hopelessness, which puts you in a hole with no way to climb out. Plus, pessimism just plain feels bad. During a crisis, you already have enough bad feelings without adding more bad feelings.

The following are common signs of pessimism.

Worst-Case Scenario

When you focus on the worst-case scenario (otherwise known as catastrophizing) in a crisis, you set yourself up for failure by creating a situation that is negative and overpowering. The outcome of the scenario becomes virtually impossible to overcome. Starting with this defeatist mindset leads to negative thinking and emotions that will take you to the "dark side." Ultimately, you will fall victim to a crisis mentality.

> "You'll never find a rainbow if you're looking down."—Charlie Chaplin, American actor[4]

Black-and-White Thinking

When under the stress of a crisis, our primitive minds drive us to engage in black-and-white, or all-or-nothing, thinking. Viewing our choices as being in direct opposition with one another is our brain trying to make the situation as simple as possible, thereby making it easier and faster to make decisions. Our ancestors' choices were fairly simple: fight or flee. The problem is that the complexity of today's crises isn't usually amenable to either-or propositions. When you allow your ancient brain to focus on the two most extreme possibilities, you lose sight of the shades of gray and the many possible options that lay in between black and white, where the solution to the crisis will likely be found.

Overgeneralization

A crisis tends to be a singular event that stands out dramatically from the norm of your life. The powerful impact of a crisis can lead us to view it as an omen that foretells a future of more crises. For example, losing your job can be devastating for a number of reasons. The added pressure of being unemployed can lead to a pessimistic mindset about your abilities that ultimately leads you to conclude you'll never get another desirable job. This overgeneralization precludes you from focusing on the discrete event—the loss of your job. No matter how dire the impact might be, this pessimism creates an impassable mountain range where there had once been a challenging, yet eminently climbable, mountain to scale.

Seeing Only the Negatives

As I discussed earlier, focusing on the negative aspects of a crisis ensured our ancestors would concentrate on and resolve the threat that lay before them. Unfortunately, only seeing the negatives today causes you to see a crisis in its entirety through dark-colored lenses. This mindset highlights the negative aspects of the situation and renders the positive ones invisible or obscure. It also causes you to miss opportunities, overlook constructive options, and fail to see positive outcomes that might exist just below the surface of a crisis.

> "If you expect the worst, you'll never be disappointed."—Sarah Dessen, American writer[5]

Doomsaying

As a means of gaining some sense of control over a crisis, we attempt to predict the future. Unfortunately, the dark view of the world that inevitably accompanies a pessimistic mindset often leads to predictions of doom. Your predictions can become Nostradamus-like, predicting the end of civilization, or at least life as we know it. Some examples include "We're going to have a global economic meltdown" or "Our company will never survive." Yes, crises can be bad events, even catastrophic; however, they are rarely as terrible as our doomsaying would suggest. Even if the outcome ends up being awful, dark predictions early on will only make it more difficult to confront the crisis with opportunity mindset, which increases the chances of an undesirable outcome.

Wearing a Weight Vest

Imagine that you are about to run a marathon. You know what lies ahead will be challenging, but you feel prepared. Then someone hands you a fifty-pound weight vest and tells you that you have to wear it while you run. How will you feel? It's likely that your anxiety will heighten; you may feel confused and possibly angry. How will you run? Since you'll be carrying extra weight, you'll be heavy-footed, sluggish, and slow. In addition, your focus will shift to the weight vest, the disadvantage you feel, and the unfairness of the situation. When you assume a pessimistic mindset in a crisis, you don a metaphorical weight vest that bogs you down and shifts your focus from an opportunity mindset to a crisis mentality.

In a pessimistic mindset, the negativity acts as the weight vest that permeates every aspect of your response to a crisis. With the weight of pessimism on your shoulders, you will be more likely to approach everything about the crisis from a position of weakness that sets you up for failure. Your thinking is filled with doubt, worry, and uncertainty. Your emotions are unpleasant and unhelpful; they include fear, anxiety, frustration, anger, and despair. You will unknowingly engage in self-sabotage by not giving your best and giving up quickly. The almost-certain result of this shroud of pessimism is an ongoing experience of unpleasant emotions and a disappointing outcome to the crisis.

"Pessimism never won any battle."—Dwight Eisenhower, thirty-fourth US president[6]

Optimism

An optimistic mindset views the world through a lens that's at the opposite end from pessimism on the continuum. Optimism is "a disposition or tendency to look on the more favorable side of events or conditions and to expect the most favorable outcome . . . confidence about the future or the successful outcome of something." Optimism creates possibilities and breeds confidence in your capabilities. It instills in you a belief that what you want can come true. It inspires you and fuels the fire that drives you to give your fullest efforts in pursuit of the most positive resolution to the crisis. In sum, optimism helps you shift from a crisis mentality to an opportunity mindset.

Being optimistic doesn't mean that you are Pollyannaish, wear rose-colored glasses, or approach a crisis blithely. That optimism, what I call "magical optimism," can be detrimental. It can lead you to deny the gravity of the crisis, underestimate its seriousness, and misjudge the challenges it presents to you. The outcome of magical optimism is rarely the fairy-tale ending to the crisis you had imagined.

You can be optimistic about your capabilities and the possibilities when a crisis strikes, but you can't deny the challenges you face. To do so would doom you to failure. As such, I encourage you to adopt "realistic optimism," which means that you believe in your capabilities, see a successful outcome as being possible, and are willing to do what is necessary to meet the challenges of a crisis. At the same time, you realistically acknowledge the roadblocks a crisis erects for you and accurately evaluate your chances of having a successful resolution.

Realistic optimism is a recipe with two ingredients:

1. A large dollop of optimism that creates a positive orientation toward a crisis and gives you hope and confidence
2. A smidgen of pessimism to ground the optimism in the reality of the crisis, which gives you added motivation to work hard toward a positive resolution, enables you to moderate your expectations, and prepares you emotionally if the outcome is disappointing

What anchors realistic optimism is the fundamental belief that things will turn out OK in the end, and if they don't, in most cases, we'll still survive. In sum, optimism can create a self-fulfilling prophecy by encouraging us to do what is necessary to achieve our goals related to a crisis.

The story of the two travelers illustrates this well. There was a traveler who was walking from a village in the mountains to a village in the valley. As he walked along, he saw a monk working in a field and stopped to talk to him. He asked, "I am on my way to the village in the valley. Can you tell me anything about it?" The monk asked where he came from and the traveler told him the village in the mountains. The monk asked what the village was like. The traveler answered, "Oh, it was awful. No one spoke my language, I had to sleep on a dirt floor in one of the homes, they fed me some kind of yak soup, and the weather was so cold!" The monk nodded his head. "Well then, I think that you will find the village in the valley much the same." The traveler grumbled and moved on. A few hours later, a second traveler came by the monk and asked him about the village in the valley where he was headed. "Where did you come from?" the monk asked. "The village in the mountains," answered the traveler. "What was the village like?" the monk asked. "Oh, it was great! We did not speak the same language, so we had to use hand signals and the such. One of the villagers was kind enough to let me sleep on their floor so I could stay warm, the food was hearty, and the weather was like I had never seen before," exclaimed the traveler. The monk nodded. "Then, I think you will find the village in the valley much the same."

Optimism creates an entirely different set of thoughts, emotions, and reactions compared to pessimism. Optimism makes us feel more confident, which can help us to dig in when faced with challenges, and it drives us to persist when the odds seem stacked against us. Optimism can act as a defense against the anxiety that often comes with the uncertainty of a crisis, and it can keep our spirits up when our situation appears desperate.

A large body of research has demonstrated the immense value of being optimistic. Optimists report less depression and anxiety, have better relationships, are physically healthier, and live longer than pessimists. Importantly, they are more resilient when faced with stress and life's challenges. People who have an optimistic outlook on their lives are able to cope more effectively with a crisis because they don't blame themselves for their misfortune, they view the situation as temporary, and they expect good things to happen in the future.

Having Hope

At the heart of optimism is a very powerful belief: hope. Why is hope so powerful? In a crisis, hope is the wellspring from which all other good things emerge. What is hope? It is the basic belief that good things will happen. Hope is the antithesis of despair, which drives pessimism in several ways. Where despair causes us to dwell on the past, hope directs our gaze to the future. Despair is about opportunities that were lost, while hope is about opportunities to be gained. We feel despair for our lack of agency in our lives, for what we aren't capable of doing. We feel hope for our sense of agency, for what we can do.

> "We must accept finite disappointment, but never lose infinite hope."—
> Martin Luther King Jr., civil rights leader [7]

To see the power of hope, close your eyes and imagine the feeling of having no hope. What emotions arise in you? Fear, anxiety, sadness, despair? A decidedly noxious constellation of feelings, to be sure. It can feel as if a dark cloud is hovering over you—that's hopelessness. Now, fill yourself with hope and tell me what emotions emanate through you. Inspiration, happiness, excitement, determination? That dark cloud lifts and the sun shines in your soul.

Hope isn't just a pleasant feeling; it is empowering and gives us confidence that if we try, then we can succeed. Hope gives us the motivation to pursue possibilities and opportunities. Hope drives us to work hard and persist even in the face of obstacles, setbacks, and failure. Why? Because believing something is possible creates energy that can be directed toward achieving it. Even during the darkest times, there is almost always hope. The trick is finding it and feeling it.

So, now that you see the benefits of being an optimist, you want to be one, right? You might say that you've always been pessimistic and believe that you were born that way. You're not entirely wrong; there is evidence that where you lie along the pessimism-optimism continuum is partially determined at birth because about 25 percent can be explained by your genes. While you may feel defeated that your pessimism is partially genetic, another way of looking at this statistic is through an optimistic lens: if 25 percent of your pessimism is genetic, then 75 percent of your mindset is not. In fact, the bigger chunk is due to your life experiences. Fortunately, if your life experiences can make you a pessimist, that means they can also make you an optimist.

Hopefully (pun intended) I've convinced you of the value of being an optimist and that you really do have the opportunity to become more optimistic. So now, the next question is, What can I do to be more optimistic? The rest of this section will cover some strategies that have been found to be effective in increasing optimism.

Keep Your Perspective

So, you've been hit by a crisis and that sucks. In this moment, it's difficult to recognize that every life has its ups and downs, its setbacks and failures, but it's important to remind yourself of this fact so you don't become fixated on the despair of the crisis. One way to do this is to take a step back and place the crisis in the context of your overall life. By creating this distance, the situation appears smaller, less over-whelming, and more manageable. In this way, you can see the crisis as a part of your life, not your life.

> "If you want to be happy, do not dwell in the past, do not worry about the future, focus on living fully in the moment."—Roy T. Bennett, American politician and writer[8]

Focus on the Specific Event

Do your best to not blow the crisis out of proportion. Remind yourself that this crisis is one unfortunate event in an otherwise relatively undra-matic and good life. Instead of being a portent of more bad things to come, recognize that a crisis is an unfortunate event that is statistically unlikely to happen again.

Remove the Weight Vest

The great thing about the weight vest that I discussed earlier is that you have the power to take it off, regardless of the reason you put it on in the first place. The burden of a pessimistic mindset rests within you. Pessimism is all in your mind; it's in the way you look at yourself and how you view the crisis. Your goal is to take the weight vest off, so you will feel unburdened. Newly lightened, you will be able to throw your-self wholeheartedly into the crisis with no doubt, worry, or hesitation. Instead, you will feel more optimistic and exude commitment, confi-dence, and courage. How will you feel and perform with that weight vest taken off? Light, free, strong, and ready to tackle the crisis head-on.

Hang Out with Optimistic People

At some point in our lives, we've all been around "downer" people. It's one thing to be in the presence of someone who's being negative, but think about consistently being exposed to that mindset by a lot of people. What usually happens? In my experience, I've noticed that their pessimism is contagious, and I become more pessimistic myself. Why is that? Because humans are social creatures. By default, this means we are influenced by those around us and tend to adopt the dominant messages we receive. Thankfully, if pessimists are infectious, then so are optimists. If you hang out with optimistic people, their messages will be positive, and you can't help but feel more optimistic yourself. Therefore, when a crisis strikes, it's important to identify and seek out optimistic people who will send you positive and hopeful messages.

Find Optimism Outside Yourself

Beyond just hanging out with optimistic people, you can also "catch" optimism by seeking out stories of others who have experienced and overcome crises in their own lives. Whether from books, articles, YouTube videos, TED talks, or other media, learning about how others prevailed over a crisis offers you hope and inspiration. Seek out both similar and different crises from your own. In addition to increasing your optimism, exposure to others' successes offers practical strategies to help you conquer your own crisis.

Seek Solutions

Pessimists are really good at seeing the problems a crisis presents. While it's important to recognize the problems, dwelling on them can take you to a dark place. Instead, as soon as you identify the problems you must face and the obstacles you must overcome in the crisis, shift your gaze and your attitude toward finding solutions. This optimistic orientation makes it more likely that you'll overcome the challenges and feel more positive and less stressed.

Look for Progress

Pessimists are also really good at looking at the obstacles in their path and seeing how far they have to go to surmount a crisis. This focus can be daunting and discouraging, given that today's crises can be long lasting. Instead of focusing on how far you have to go, pay attention to the incremental gains you are making every day toward resolving the crisis. These signs of progress reinforce your efforts, bolster your feelings of hope, and give fuel to a more optimistic view of a decidedly difficult experience.

> "Failure is success in progress."—Albert Einstein, German theoretical physicist[9]

Set Yourself Up for Success

It's easy to feel pessimistic when a crisis hits and you have no idea how to overcome it. In turn, it's a lot easier to be optimistic when you have your ducks in a row, have a plan, and determine a process for successfully responding to a crisis. As such, you want to establish a clear path forward as quickly as possible when a crisis unfolds. This path should be one that you believe will set you up for a successful resolution of the crisis.

Take Care of Yourself

One thing for sure about a crisis: it is psychologically and emotionally stressful. It is extremely difficult to think and feel optimistically when your body is communicating pessimism from feeling worn down, exhausted, or sick. To get your body feeling optimistic, you need to take care of it. Specifically, this means getting enough sleep, eating a healthy diet, going easy on the alcohol, avoiding drugs, and exercising regularly. Admittedly, this can be difficult when you're experiencing a crisis. In times of stress we often prefer to curl up in front of the TV and eat a pint of ice cream (or whatever your vice of choice). To resist these urges, you should schedule healthy living into your day by developing an exercise routine, preparing meals at home, and practicing good sleep hygiene (eat dinner a few hours before bedtime, don't watch TV or use technology in bed, regulate your sleep schedule). In addition, you should enlist the support of family and friends to help pull you out of the funk you will inevitably feel as you confront a crisis.

Challenge Your Pessimism

When a crisis strikes, it's easy to get sucked into the black hole of pessimism; there is perverse comfort in wallowing in the pain that a crisis delivers. That said, becoming a victim of your pessimism feels bad and is decidedly counterproductive. Instead, when you begin to go to the dark side of a crisis, challenge your pessimism. Ask yourself whether your thoughts are realistic or helpful in terms of reaching your goals. Remind yourself that such negativity does you no good. Then, identify alternatives to your pessimistic thinking that are both optimistic and realistic. For example, instead of dwelling on the problems presented by the crisis that are usually outside your control, highlight what you can control and begin to formulate a plan of action.

> "One can have no smaller or greater mastery than mastery of oneself."—Leonardo da Vinci, Italian Renaissance artist and scientist [10]

Be Grateful

One of the most robust findings in the study of happiness and well-being is that thinking about and expressing gratitude makes people feel happier. It's certainly difficult to feel gratitude when you feel there is little to be grateful for, which is often how a crisis leaves us. Yet, if you broaden your focus outside of the crisis, you will likely find much to be thankful for, such as the people who support you or the activities that give you a respite from the crisis. Taking a few moments to feel and express gratitude internally or to others is a practical way to free yourself from the clutches of pessimism.

DISRUPTED VERSUS STABLE

There is one thing you can count on with a crisis: it never sleeps. There are no breaks, no naps, and no vacations. A crisis is always on and always wreaking havoc on your life. Whether you are spending time with your family, working, exercising, sleeping, or what have you, a crisis marches inexorably forward, upending your life. In other words, a crisis is persistently, frustratingly, and sometimes painfully stable.

Similarly, your pre-crisis life is also stable. From your bedtime to when you wake up to mealtimes to your work schedule, it all creates a consistent rhythm and flow to your daily life. Being able to rely on that stability enables you to be productive and efficient. Emotionally and cognitively, it allows you to worry less, feel less stress, and be more comfortable because you know what you'll be doing tomorrow and in the days to come. You probably don't even realize the powerful impact that stability plays in your everyday life, until a crisis strikes. One of the most insidious aspects of a crisis is that it disrupts your routine and expectations. Its disruption is persistent and adds another roadblock to the already daunting task of overcoming the crisis you face.

Disrupted

Think about everything in your life that makes it run so smoothly: sleep, meals, work, relationships, hobbies, and physical, cultural, or religious activities; the list goes on. Now, think about that stability disappearing. Whatever habits, routines, and patterns you have are thrown for a loop. The familiarity, predictability, and control that gives you confidence and comfort is no longer there in the ways you rely on. Even before you actually have to address the challenges a crisis presents to you, you are already at a disadvantage by having the crisis throw a wrench in the machinery of your life.

Stable

When faced with a crisis, your goal is to reestablish stability in your life as soon as possible. Clearly, that is easier said than done. And, realistically, it may not be completely possible depending on the nature of the crisis. In some cases, you may have to find stability within the instability. That is, wherever possible, establish small beachheads of stability within your disrupted life. There are several key areas in which to prioritize restoring stability.

Live a Stable Life

When a crisis occurs, one of your first responses should be to reset as many of your daily habits, routines, and patterns as possible. This response is especially important because the crisis will likely cause you to feel that your life is out of control, which can cause you to feel disoriented and stressed. When you reestablish some degree of normalcy in your life, you regain a semblance of control because you are, in fact, taking control of your daily life. Returning stability in your life will make you feel more comfortable and provide you with a secure base from which you can respond positively to the crisis.

Here is a list of key aspects of daily life that give it stability. Do the best you can to return to your previous habits, routines, and patterns in these areas:

- Sleep

- Meals
- Work
- Exercise
- Relationships
- Hobbies
- Activities

Have a Stable Mind

Having a stable mind is another essential piece of the stability puzzle. In fact, everything we have covered thus far in *How to Survive and Thrive* has been devoted to helping you create a stable mind that produces stable responses to crises. The entirety of your internal life—including your instincts, emotions, reactions, values, investment, attitudes, and thoughts—coalesces into a stable mind that will increase your chances of having a successful outcome of a crisis.

You gain stability of mind by understanding the different internal factors that influence your responses to a crisis. Then you can identify the roles each factor plays and make a commitment to consistently use those mental resources to combat the crisis. You can further support a stable mind by actively avoiding the bad roads and choosing to take the good roads I describe in each chapter.

> "In the midst of movement and chaos, keep stillness inside of you."
> —Deepak Chopra, New Age author [11]

Make a Stable Effort

Once you've developed a plan to overcome a crisis (to be discussed later), your best chance of success is to implement it with stable effort. This means you must consistently put in the required time it will take for your plan to succeed. Additionally, your effort must be reliably purposeful, focused, and determined. This means doing everything you need to do to address the crisis as fully and as well as you can with the utmost quality. This isn't easy because pushing against a crisis is hard work. It's not fun and it can get old fast. Yet, because a crisis is sure to expend effort to mess up your life, you need to respond in kind. As the saying goes, you "fight fire with fire," and applied here, the best way to fight a crisis is to "fight instability with stability."

COMFORT VERSUS RISK

As humans, we are wired for comfort. In primordial times, comfort was equated with survival. Whether it was fear, exhaustion, or pain, any discomfort triggered our primitive brain to ensure that we acted to return to comfort. Not surprisingly then, it's natural for us to seek out safety, security, and comfort when confronted with the uncertainty and threat of a crisis in modern times. This is our attempt to regain a sense of equilibrium and minimize the impact of the crisis on us.

> "It's only after you've stepped outside your comfort zone that you begin to change, grow, and transform."—Roy T. Bennett, American politician and writer [12]

Yet, no matter how instinctive a reaction it might be, is seeking comfort in the face of a modern-day crisis really the best way to respond? If my arguments in part I holds any water, it's not likely. Whereas returning to the status quo was the goal during our cave-person days, today's crises rarely allow us to return to normalcy in the short term.

I'm not suggesting that you take irresponsible risks that have a better chance of increasing the severity of the crisis. Instead, it is important to take appropriate risks that may improve the outcome of the crisis. These risks are important because crises cause you to confront a situation that is out of the norm and outside of your comfort zone. Therefore, seeking comfort by staying within the norms of your regular life may very well be ineffective in finding a resolution.

Comfort

We all seek comfort because, well, it's comfortable and it feels good. Comfort tells us that we are safe and secure. We find comfort both within and outside of ourselves. As I noted earlier, we do what we can to make our lives as stable as possible. Externally, we seek to create a life that is familiar, predictable, and controllable. We establish daily habits and routines, spend time with the same people, and engage in activities that provide us with maximum comfort. Internally, we do our best to maintain a psychological and emotional equilibrium that fosters our comfort. We think agreeable thoughts, do things to generate enjoyable emotions, eat aptly named "comfort food," and do meditation, yoga, and different types of exercise that promote physical relaxation. In this stability, we find comfort.

Yet, too much comfort creates inertia, stagnation, and inflexibility. Our ability to think on our feet and be agile declines. With excessive comfort, we become attached to pleasant thoughts and emotions and lose touch with our ability to respond positively to the unpleasant internal machinations that are an inevitable part of life. We also lose our ability to be resilient and to adjust to the ever-changing world of the twenty-first century. Developing new skills, thinking flexibly, and adjusting to circumstances requires growth. In order to grow, you must do things differently. This means you must get out of your comfort zone. Therefore, without discomfort, there can be no growth. In addition, avoiding discomfort leaves you ill equipped for the massive discomfort you will feel when a crisis strikes.

"Pearls don't lie on the shoreline. If you want one, you must dive for it."—Chinese proverb [13]

Despite the urging of millions of years of evolution, I would suggest that acting (or not acting) to stay comfortable is not a productive aspiration because crises are naturally disruptive and uncomfortable. Although some degree of stability can be regained during a crisis, the reality is that complete comfort during a crisis is neither possible nor advisable. As the saying goes, "Desperate times call for desperate measures," and in the case of a crisis, those measures mean having the willingness to make yourself uncomfortable and take suitable risks.

Risk

Let me preface this discussion of risk by saying that I am not suggesting that you take ill-advised risks. These include things like gambling with your retirement money in the hope of getting snake eyes, or quitting your job when you have no prospects for finding a new job and no rainy-day fund. I also don't mean taking risks for which you are unprepared, you have little chance of success, or where the consequences of failure are dire. That's not taking risks; that's being stupid.

The dictionary defines risk as "a situation in which you expose yourself to danger." Back in primitive times, our ancestors were at physical risk from rival tribes, predatory animals, starvation, and disease simply because they were alive. In the twenty-first century, the risks we take are usually less physically risky, unless we choose to participate in activities that have inherent thrills, such as skiing, mountain biking, or bungy jumping. Clearly, some level of risk is essential for success in almost every aspect of life. A few examples include attempting to win an Olympic gold medal, starting a tech company, or telling someone "I love you." If you don't take risks, you won't improve, grow, or accomplish your goals. And taking some risks is often necessary to achieve a satisfactory resolution to a crisis.

> "Life is inherently risky. There is only one big risk you should avoid at all costs, and that is the risk of doing nothing."—Denis Waitley, motivation speaker and writer[14]

To Risk or Not to Risk

Hopefully, I have convinced you of the necessity of taking reasonable risks in response to a crisis. When your world has been rocked by a crisis, deciding to take risks is a simple, but not easy, choice. It's a simple choice because most of us would rather take risks and give ourselves a chance of a positive resolution to a crisis over playing it safe (and comfortable) and leaving the outcome to chance. At the same time, it's not an easy choice because taking risks introduces us to the possibility of failure. As we know, no one likes to fail, particularly when so much is on the line in a crisis. It's also not easy because there are a variety of powerful psychological and emotional forces that hold you back from taking risks. Here are some of them:

- Fear of failure (you won't take a risk if you're afraid to fail)
- Fear of blame (you feel at fault for the crisis)
- Helplessness (you feel that you have no control over the crisis)
- Lack of confidence (you don't believe you are capable of taking the risk)
- Doubt (you don't believe that the risks will be rewarded)

At the heart of risk taking is the willingness to accept that it may not turn out as you hope, but the consequences of inaction are more likely to be worse than those of action. Additionally, risk taking involves recognizing that you rarely end up worse off than where you started, even though a risk might not pay off. Also, the nature of risks involves a possibility of failure. At the same time, risk taking increases your chances of success. If you can truly accept the potential of failure while clearly seeing the potential benefits, there's no reason not to take risks because there is rarely success with inaction.

Now, before we dive more deeply into how risk taking can help you overcome a crisis, let me reframe it in a way that you may find more palatable. When we use the word *risk*, our tendency is to focus on its negative aspects and what can go wrong. In risk taking, what I really think you are doing is *opportunity taking*. This means you see the prospect of something good happening and you're willing to embrace that opportunity.

In fact, herein lies a significant distinction between a crisis mentality and an opportunity mindset. In the former, the emphasis is on what can go wrong and be lost, while in the latter, the attention is on what can go right and be gained. Despite this change in orientation toward a risk, I will continue to call it risk taking because opportunity taking is unfamiliar and a bit awkward. Plus, now that you have this new perspective, you'll be able to make the change mentally without having to see the words *opportunity taking*.

"It's better to make errors of commission than errors of omission."
—Unknown

Risk Taking Is a Lifestyle Choice

Risk taking is as much a lifestyle choice as it is a skill. The chances are that it will be more difficult to take risks when a crisis hits if you weren't a risk taker in your pre-crisis life. With this in mind, it's easy to see how it's actually healthy to practice risk taking in your life before a crisis arises. If you can make taking risks a part of who you are, then risk taking in response to a crisis will be much easier to do. You can experiment with taking small-scale risks in your work, with your family and friends, and in your avocations. They don't have to be big risks with significant upsides or downsides, like a major life change; rather, any risks will help you gain experience in taking risks. For example, you could ask someone out on a date if you are single, try a new hobby, or travel to a part of the world you haven't visited before. Frequent practice in risk taking increases your willingness, confidence, and comfort to do so in the future, particularly when faced with a crisis.

"He who is not courageous enough to take risks will accomplish nothing in life."—Muhammad Ali, boxing legend [15]

How to Take Risks

Risk taking isn't something you should do as a knee-jerk reaction, and it shouldn't be spontaneous, when you're emotional, or when you're in a hurry. Risks you take under those conditions are usually driven by your primitive instincts, emotions, and reactions and rarely end well because they tend to be misguided when confronting modern-day crises. Again, those risks may have worked in response to an immediate and urgent crisis in ancient times, but today's crises are seldom resolved in such a cut-and-dried way.

Given a crisis will be of some significance in your life and that any action you take will have consequences, taking risks should occur at the end of a very intentional process. Risks should be taken after careful analysis, thoughtful deliberation, and conscious decision making. They are a purposeful end to a calculated means. Any risks should be a well-thought-out part of your plan for combating the crisis you face.

To that end, you can follow a ten-step procedure to help you arrive at a risk worth taking in response to a crisis:

1. Gather all relevant information
2. Identify all options
3. List the benefits and costs of each option
4. Assess your capabilities and readiness
5. Weigh the likelihood of success
6. Consider the consequences of failure
7. Ask whether you are willing and capable of accepting those consequences
8. Get feedback from others
9. Make a decision
10. Commit fully to the decision

Of course, you don't want to constantly take risks during a crisis; that would simply add unnecessary stress and discomfort to an already distressing experience. Depending on the immediacy and severity of the crisis, its probable course, and the degree of control you have over its events, there is a time and place for taking risks and for remaining prudent.

> "Don't be too timid and squeamish about your actions. All life is an experiment. The more experiments you make the better."—Ralph Waldo Emerson, American poet[16]

No Time Like the Present to Take Risks

It never feels like the right time to take risks, particularly when a crisis occurs. As I noted previously, there are risks to taking risks and those risks may not be rewarded right away. In other words, risks can take time to reach fruition, and you may experience short-term setbacks along the way.

Additionally, you may struggle at first after taking a risk. Your confidence may suffer and you may question whether risk taking is the right path. You might say to yourself, "Gosh, maybe I should just play it safe during these tough times." The problem is that the safety that may have worked when your life was normal may very well not work in a crisis because crises aren't normal in any way, shape, or form.

As the noted educator Margaret Spellings once said, "If all you ever do is all you've ever done, then all you'll ever get is all you've ever got."[17] When it comes to a crisis, you don't want to get all you've ever got. Rather, your efforts shouldn't be devoted to where you are now in the crisis, but to where you want to be at its conclusion.

> "That is where it all begins. Everything starts here, today."—David Nicholls, English novelist[18]

Assess Threat versus Challenge

As I've discussed, the real risk of taking risks is that they may not be rewarded. The magnitude of the crisis and severity of its potential consequences can lead you to be overly focused on the costs and consequences of those risks. This fixation increases the chances that you will remain in a crisis mentality and even rely on the threat instinct (described in chapter 1), which drives you to protect yourself from the threat of the risk's failure. As a result, you become risk averse and are less likely to take the risks that may facilitate a positive resolution to the crisis. Moreover, even if you do get yourself to take a risk that you deem reasonable and necessary, it may not pay off because you are unlikely to commit fully to it when you're feeling threatened.

When you assume a psychology of opportunity, you see taking appropriate risks as a challenge to pursue, not a threat to avoid. With this challenge response, you will be receptive to taking risks. This approach allows you to commit fully to your choice and increases the chances that your risk taking pays off.

Finally, you may still think that taking risks in a crisis is risky. But the reality is that not taking risks can be equally risky. In your effort to resolve a crisis, doing the safe and comfortable thing may not get you where you want to go. Similarly, there is no certainty if you take risks; however, crises are so far outside the norm of daily life that acting as you typically would will likely not be effective. In fact, you often give yourself a lot better chance of overcoming the crisis when you take risks and step outside of the stability and comfort of what's familiar. So, when you look at it that way, taking risks in a crisis isn't as risky as you might think!

> "Twenty years from now you will be more disappointed by the things that you didn't do than by the ones you did do. So throw off the bowlines. Sail away from the safe harbor. Catch the trade winds in your sails. Explore. Dream. Discover."—Mark Twain, American author [19]

Take a Leap of Faith

Taking risks is an uncertain endeavor. First, you don't know whether you will actually be able to take the risks you need to take to get a desired outcome. You also don't know whether those risks will bear fruit, even with the best of intentions, thoughtful planning, and significant effort. No one, not even your family, friends, or experts related to the crisis, can foresee what will happen to you if you take a risk. There is going to be fear of the unknown: can you take the risk and will it pay off? Therefore, any risk you take must be a leap of faith because it is uncertain. A leap of faith involves taking action when there is little assurance or certainty that the desired outcome will occur. The leap of faith begins with the conviction that only by getting out of your comfort zone and taking risks will you have any chance of positively resolving a crisis. While this can be somewhat exciting, it can also be quite scary.

To help you fully understand the challenge of taking a leap of faith in a crisis, let me use an analogy from the film *Indiana Jones and the Last Crusade*. Indiana Jones is in search of the Holy Grail and is following a map that leads him along a treacherous path. Near the end of his journey, Jones comes to a seemingly bottomless chasm across from which is the doorway to the Holy Grail. There is no apparent bridge across the abyss, yet the map shows a picture of a man stepping into the void and a message telling him to take a leap of faith. Mustering his courage and choosing to take an immense risk, Jones takes that leap of faith—he jumps!—and finds that there is an invisible bridge that he can walk across to seize the Holy Grail. Against the direst of consequences if he was wrong (plummeting to his death!), Jones had the faith to choose the risky path that led him to the successful conclusion of his quest. Similarly, you must have the strength of your conviction and belief in the value of taking risks to take a leap of faith and discover your Holy Grail, a positive resolution to your crisis.

The leap of faith begins with an acknowledgment of the severity of the crisis and its potential consequences. You must then determine that inaction or a safe path forward is far riskier. The next step is to have faith that you can effect the necessary change in response to the crisis. The leap of faith involves having a basic confidence in yourself and your capabilities. You must also have the belief that good things will happen if you take judicious risks. It's important to recognize that some misgivings are a normal part of the process; you can never be 100 percent certain that things will work out the way you want. If there weren't doubts, then it wouldn't require a leap of faith.

Further, it's paramount that you understand that this leap of faith is not blind faith. Rather, you take the time to respond to the crisis through risks that are informed by a lifetime of experience, knowledge, and skills, as well as extensive resources, such as family, friends, and other forms of support, that you can use to bolster your efforts.

"Leap and the net will appear."—John Burroughs, American naturalist[20]

Chapter Eight

Mental Muscles

Feelin' Strong!

When you look at part II, Your Cerebral Cortex, you see the different levels of influence that our evolved brain exerts on our lives and, more specific to our purpose, the role it has in how we respond to crises. Through the previous chapters you've seen the level of influence moving from a more broad-based and diffuse impact to the much more immediate influence on our day-to-day lives. Metaphorically speaking, we started at fifty thousand feet and have moved to the ground level. Now chapter 8, Mental Muscles, brings the focus to the influence that takes place in the trenches, the most direct impact on your ability to engage and sustain your efforts as you combat a crisis.

Confronting a crisis takes strength, physical and mental. Physical strength is important because crises take a toll on your body. They can wear you down, exhaust you, and can even cause both illness and injury. In addition, crises can tax your mind, so you must also have mental strength. Each chapter of *How to Survive and Thrive* offers you ways to find the psychological fortitude necessary to overcome a crisis. It's one thing to have the overall strength to face down a crisis. It is an entirely different experience to have the day-to-day and moment-to-moment endurance to resist an adversary that is invisible yet can seem superpowered and invincible.

I see the cerebral cortex as comprised of mental "muscles" that can be strong, weak, or injured. Like physical muscles, if your mental muscles are weak, then you won't able to use them to their fullest capabilities. And you won't be able to exert maximum force against the substantial resistance that the crisis brings. Additionally, a crisis can cause your mental muscles to incur an "injury." This happens when some aspect of your psychological or emotional musculature sustains damage that makes it even more difficult to push back against a crisis. For example, a crisis can injure your confidence muscle or determination muscle. Your best bet is to enter the fray of a crisis with your mental muscles as strong as possible, so you will have the best chance to flex those muscles to overcome the crisis.

Your goal is to strengthen your mental muscles to prevent injury and to allow yourself to respond with overwhelming force in the face of a crisis. In order to do so, you want to have an "exercise regimen" that you can follow to keep your mental muscles healthy and strong.

> "I am not what happened to me, I am what I choose to become."
> —Carl Jung, founder of analytical psychology [1]

There are three mental muscle forks in the road. In this chapter, I introduce three mental muscles I believe are most essential to marshalling a vigorous defense against a crisis. With these three mental muscles, I present forks in the road; as long as you take the good road at each fork, you will have the means to strengthen those mental muscles both before and during a crisis. Those strong mental muscles will enable you to exert your opportunity mindset and give you the immediate strength you need when a crisis hits and the stamina to keep fighting if the crisis goes on for longer than anticipated.

DOUBT VERSUS CONFIDENCE

So much of your ability to respond positively to a crisis depends on whether you believe you can respond positively to the crisis and whether you believe your efforts will be sufficient to meet the challenges you face. If you doubt your capabilities against such a formidable opponent as a crisis, you aren't likely to overcome it. In contrast, if you have confidence that you will overcome the crisis, you will give a strong and sustained effort that will more likely produce the desired outcome.

Doubt

There are many reasons why you may doubt you can prevail over a crisis. If you lack confidence in your general abilities as a person and don't have a strong sense of agency or the feeling that you have control over your life, then you will likely feel ineffective in the face of a crisis. In addition, you may have experienced crises in the past and were unable to surmount them, thus providing evidence of your incapability. Moreover, if you don't have knowledge or expertise in the specific area in which the crisis occurs—for example, natural disaster, personal safety, or technology—you will feel that you don't have the tools to fix the problems that the crisis creates. Finally, doubt can also arise from your immediate experiences as a crisis envelops you. Anything that counters your belief in your ability to achieve your crisis goals will hurt your confidence.

> "The only limit to our realization of tomorrow will be our doubts of today. Let us move forward with strong and active faith."—Franklin D. Roosevelt, thirty-second US president [2]

Negativity

If you have doubt, you aren't going to believe in yourself, which can result in a self-fulfilling prophecy. As Henry Ford once said, "Whether you think you can, or think you can't—you're right." Having doubts leads to a lot of negative self-talk or negative talk to others, which reinforces your doubt. As you experience a crisis, you may be thinking, "I just can't do this" or "This crisis is just too much for me to handle." Or you may tell a friend, "I'm not ready for this" or "I don't have a chance." Not surprisingly, this negativity sets you up for failure because you've become your own worst enemy. When you turn against yourself in the midst of a crisis, you give yourself little chance of a positive outcome.

Stress

If you have considerable self-doubt, you will likely experience an inordinate amount of stress as the crisis emerges and continues unabated. As I discussed in part I, Your Amygdala, that stress is an innate reaction to a perceived threat. If you doubt your ability to overcome a crisis, then you will certainly see the situation as a massive threat. As with other reactions related to doubt, experiencing high stress creates a self-fulfilling prophecy because its negative psychological and physical effects make it more difficult to respond in a positive and intentional way. The highly unpleasant physical symptoms of stress (e.g., racing heart, shortness of breath, muscle tension) send a message to your brain that confirms your doubt and triggers a flight reaction. Fleeing obviously prevents you from doing what you need to do to respond constructively to the crisis.

> "It's not the load that breaks you down, it's the way you carry it."
> —Lena Horne, American singer and actress [3]

Lack of Effort

Doubt, and the accompanying stress, sets off your flight response, which may manifest as diminished effort or complete surrender (to be discussed further in the subsequent section). From your doubtful perspective, there's no point of trying when you know you will fail. This toxic stew of doubt causes you to lose determination and creates a vicious cycle of ever-increasing doubt, low effort, and ongoing failure. Entering this cycle basically means that you have zero chance of marshalling a reasonable response to the crisis.

Poor Results

The greatest cause of doubt is failure. Failure can mean making mistakes as you confront a crisis, such as, delaying a report of harassment at work or not filing an insurance claim immediately after an earthquake. Missteps can cause you to lose faith in your ability and become tentative, cautious, or overwhelmed. Failure can also mean you put in the effort, but fail to achieve the results you want. Nothing increases doubt during a crisis more than failure because it provides evidence that any confidence you may have is unjustified.

Confidence

Confidence lies at the other end of the continuum from doubt. Instead of uncertainty, there is trust. Rather than negativity, there is positivity. In place of stress, there is energy. The definition of confidence is having a strong belief in your ability to overcome challenges and produce the outcome you want. Confidence may be the single most important mental factor when facing a crisis because you can have all the abilities in the world, but if you don't believe that you do, then you won't use them fully to resolve the crisis. For example, you may have the emotional capabilities to be a father, but if you don't have faith in those abilities, then you will struggle to assume the role of caregiver when your first child is born.

To respond positively to a crisis, you must develop and maintain a deep, lasting, and resilient confidence in your ability to respond positively. This confidence will keep you positive, motivated, relaxed, and focused, especially in times of stress. With confidence, you can stay positive even in the face of struggles. You won't be doubting yourself or feeling uncertain when obstacles come into your path. Confidence also encourages you to face the difficulties of a crisis head-on.

> "Self-confidence is the first requisite of great undertakings."—Samuel Johnson, eighteenth-century English author[4]

A common misconception that many people have is that confidence is something inborn or that you will never have confidence if you don't have it at an early age. In reality, confidence is a muscle that can be strengthened, much like your biceps and quadriceps. Just like any other muscle, confidence can be developed through exercise, that is, by exerting focus, effort, and repetition to strengthen it.

Confidence Challenge

It's easy to stay confident when your life is free of stress, conflict, or crisis. The real test of confidence is how you respond when things aren't going your way. I call this the Confidence Challenge because it shows if you are able to maintain belief in yourself even when a crisis is throwing everything it has at you. Let me be clear, everyone struggles during a crisis. The key is to not get caught up in the negativity and to stay confident through the ups and downs until you've successfully overcome the crisis. There are several keys to mastering the Confidence Challenge.

- Adopt an opportunity mindset rather than a crisis mentality.
- Develop the attitude that crises are challenges to be sought out, not threats to avoid.
- Believe that some crises in life are inevitable and that you can overcome them.
- Be well prepared to meet the challenges of a crisis.

- Stay positive and motivated in the face of the difficulties.
- Focus on what you need to do to overcome the challenges.
- Accept that you may experience failure when faced with a crisis.
- Most importantly, never, ever give up!

> "If you have no confidence in self, you are twice defeated in the race of life."—Marcus Garvey, twentieth-century political leader and journalist[5]

Strengthening Your Confidence Muscle

Ultimately, the goal of having confidence is to develop a strong and resilient belief in your ability to overcome a crisis whenever one arises in your life. I have identified seven exercises you can use to create a virtuous cycle that will strengthen your confidence even as you confront a crisis. Each exercise alone can enhance your confidence, but using them all together allows your confidence to grow significantly stronger more quickly.

Preparation Breeds Confidence

Preparation is the foundation of confidence. This includes doing everything you need to do to ensure that you are ready to take on the crisis; for example, gathering relevant information, seeking the necessary resources, making appropriate decisions, and taking a deliberate course of action. If you have developed these areas as fully as you can before and shortly after a crisis hits, then you will gain faith from preparation and be able to respond to a crisis with your fullest commitment and effort. The more of these areas you fully address in your preparation, the more confidence you will breed in yourself. My goal for you is that when you are faced with a crisis, you can say, "I'm as prepared as I can be to tackle this crisis head-on."

> "One important key to success is self-confidence. An important key to self-confidence is preparation."—Arthur Ashe, tennis legend[6]

Mental Tools Reinforce Confidence

I encourage you to create a mental "toolbox" that includes everything you need to resolve a crisis. This toolbox is composed of all the internal and external resources I've discussed throughout *How to Survive and Thrive*. You can use these mental tools in two ways. First, you can "fine-tune" yourself, making subtle adjustments to get the most out of your efforts. For instance, use breathing to relax and focus or positive self-talk to stay confident in the face of setbacks. Second, make sure the tools in your mental toolbox are readily available when you have breakdowns in your response and need to fix a problem amid a crisis. This is similar to having a spare tire, tire iron, and jack in your car in case you get a flat tire while driving. For example, you might get scared during a crisis and go to the dark side in your thinking. In this moment, it's important that you have an internal (e.g., taking a break) or external (e.g., trusted support) tool at your disposal. Mental tools for your mental toolbox can include the following:

- Inspirational thoughts and images to bolster your determination
- Positive self-talk to fortify your confidence
- Stress control (e.g., breathing) to combat confidence-depleting anxiety
- Keywords that maintain your focus and help you avoid distractions
- Emotional-control techniques (e.g., meditation, exercise) to calm yourself when the pressure of the crisis weighs on you

This book is filled with a wealth of mental tools you can use to fix many "flat tires," but there are others that work as well.

Support Bolsters Confidence

It's difficult to successfully make it through a crisis on your own. Everyone who has ever experienced a crisis had people in their lives supporting them. There will be times when things are just not going well, and it helps to have people you can turn to for encouragement, such as family, friends, and professionals. Your confidence will wax and wane depending on various factors, including your emotions, how long you've been dealing with the crisis, and the success of your recent efforts to respond to the crisis. That's why you want people in your life who have unwavering confidence in you and on whom you can count to give you a "booster shot" of reassurance when needed. For example, have a close friend or sibling say, "I know you can do it" or "Hang in there. Things will turn around!"

Support is so important to building, maintaining, and regaining confidence when a crisis occurs. You should actively seek out and build a network of people who can support you in different ways. You need technical support from people who are experts in your type of crisis, for example, a medical team who can offer support related to a physical ailment. Emotional support will mostly come from family and friends, particularly when a crisis first arises.

> "If you have people that totally support you and have your back, I feel like you have all the confidence in the world, and you believe that you can do things that most people can't achieve."—Nicholas Cage, actor [7]

Success Validates Confidence

All of the previous steps in building confidence will go for naught if you don't have "wins" as you combat a crisis. Success validates the belief you have developed in your ability; it demonstrates that your confidence is well founded. Success further strengthens your confidence, making it more resilient in the face of new challenges. Success rewards your efforts to build confidence, while encouraging you to continue to work hard and persist in resolving the crisis.

Successes during a crisis can be defined in different ways. It may be a victory of gathering useful information and gaining a better understanding of a crisis. It can involve learning new strategies for responding. Success may also entail finding additional resources or support that can help you respond constructively to a crisis. Finally, success can mean making progress toward your desired outcome.

Use Positive Self-Talk

Positive self-talk is one of the most powerful mental exercises you have at your disposal to immediately build confidence. What you say to yourself as you progress through a crisis matters because your thoughts impact your emotions and your responses to challenges. Yet negativity is almost unavoidable in a crisis. Usually there is not a lot to be positive about, or at least that's the way it seems. As a crisis hits you full force, you might say to yourself, "I feel helpless!" "This crisis is overwhelming!" or some variation thereof. That negativity can deplete your energy and hinder efforts that should be directed at the crisis.

If your self-talk is positive, your thoughts and feelings will be positive. Instead of saying, "I don't have a chance today," try saying, "I'm going to deal with this crisis the best I can today." That will get you positive and fired up. By using positive self-talk, you'll be your own best ally. You will show yourself that even if the crisis is doing everything it can to beat you, you aren't going to beat yourself.

Positive self-talk helps in many ways. It increases your determination to persist in the face of obstacles, setbacks, and failures. You're more relaxed and focused because you believe you have what it takes to stand up to a crisis. Your emotions reflect positive self-talk with feelings of excitement and inspiration. You also feel less vulnerable to the disappointments you periodically experience in a crisis.

Positive self-talk is a simple, but not easy, strategy. It's simple because the idea of replacing your negative self-talk with positive statements is straightforward. However, it's not easy to do. By its very nature, a crisis can readily pull your self-talk to a very negative place. To prepare to combat this pull toward negativity, train yourself for positive self-talk by following these steps:

1. Identify situations when you tend to become negative, especially in a crisis. Perhaps it's when you can't find important information about the crisis, you can't get the help you need, or you're not making progress toward resolution.
2. Figure out exactly why you become negative in these situations. Common reasons include stress, fatigue, frustration, and despair.
3. Monitor what you say to yourself. I've found that people in a crisis tend to rely on certain "favorite" negative phrases. For example, "Gosh, I stupid," "I'm such a loser," and "What's the point of even trying."
4. Choose some positive statements to use in place of your usual negative self-talk. By doing this exercise *before* you face a crisis, you'll be ready to access the statements and have a better chance of deploying them when you're pulled toward negativity.
5. Constantly remind yourself to be positive. Since you've already identified the situations in which you tend to become negative, you're better prepared to recognize when stressful situations are approaching. This will help you focus on what you want to say rather than allowing your knee-jerk negativity to jump in.
6. Be patient and persistent. At first, you will probably fall off the wagon and slip back to your old, negative ways. Recognizing the slip and accepting that it is part of the process allows you to shift to being positive. With time and persistence, you'll see a gradual shift away from negativity and toward positive self-talk. Until one day you realize that you just went through a crisis situation and you stayed positive.

"Brain wave tests prove that when we use positive words, our 'feel good' hormones flow. Positive self-talk releases endorphins and serotonin in our brain, which then flow throughout our body, making us feel good. These neurotransmitters stop flowing when we use negative words."—Ruth Fishel, mindfulness expert [8]

Balance the Scales

In an ideal world, I would love to eliminate all negatives and have you only feel and express positives. Unfortunately, this is the real world and anyone who suffers a crisis will go to the dark side on occasion. In dealing with this reality, you should start by balancing the scales. If you're going to be negative when you experience setbacks, you should also be positive when you make progress. The immediate goal is to slowly decrease the negatives and increase the positives.

This step of tipping the scales toward positives is very important. Recent research found that negative experiences such as negative self-talk, negative body language, and negative emotions carry more psychological weight than positive experiences. In fact, it takes twelve positive experiences to equal one negative experience. Ultimately, you want to tip the scale heavily in the positive direction. Sure, you're going to say some negative things periodically. That's just part of being human. But when you tip the scales in the positive direction, you will find you are far more positive, you have much more confidence, and most importantly, you are your best ally during a crisis.

"There are always two voices sounding in our ears: the voice of fear and the voice of confidence. One is the clamor of the senses, the other is the whispering of the higher self."—Charles B. Newcomb, nineteenth-century philosopher [9]

Use Negative Self-Talk Positively

Even though I always emphasize being positive, the fact is you can't always be so in a crisis. Things don't always go your way, and the harsh reality is that resolving a crisis is an uphill battle with many roadblocks and setbacks. So, some negative self-talk is not only unavoidable but can actually be beneficial.

There are two types of negative self-talk: "give-up" negative self-talk and "fire-up" negative self-talk. Give-up negative self-talk involves feelings of loss, hopelessness, and helplessness. For example, thinking, "It's over. I can't do this." You dwell on everything that is going wrong. This self-talk hurts your confidence and determination, and takes your focus away from confronting the crisis head-on. There is never a time or place in a crisis for give-up negative self-talk for one simple reason: when you give up, the crisis wins.

In contrast, fired-up negative self-talk involves feelings of anger and being psyched up. For example, you may say, "I'm not getting where I need to go. I hate this!" You look to do better in the future because you hate how things have been going. Fired-up negative self-talk triggers your instinctive fight response and increases your determination to change course when the crisis is racking up victories. Fired-up negative self-talk can be a positive way to turn your response to a crisis around.

If you're going to be negative, then make sure you use fired-up negative self-talk, but don't use it too much. Negative self-talk and negative emotions burn a lot of energy that should be used to overcome the crisis. Plus, it doesn't feel very good to be angry all of the time.

"A negative thinker sees a difficulty in every opportunity. A positive thinker sees an opportunity in every difficulty."—Zig Ziglar, motivational speaker [10]

SURRENDER VERSUS DETERMINATION

As I have alluded to previously, a crisis is like a very high and treacherous mountain that confronts you on the road of life. Some parts of your route are easy, others are demanding, and still others can seem downright impassable. It is in the moments when you feel that the mountain of a crisis is just too high to climb that your determination is tested.

When faced with the daunting challenges of a crisis, your drive, motivation, and perseverance lie on a continuum ranging from surrender to determination. Not only are crises difficult because their challenges can be severe, but they often last an appreciable amount of time, which can wear you down, physically, psychologically, and emotionally. In moments of extreme difficulty you will respond in one of three ways: digging in and pushing forward even harder, continuing with minimal effort, or surrendering altogether. It's important to know where you are along the continuum as it often dictates how you will respond throughout your journey from onset to resolution of a crisis.

Surrender

At the heart of surrender is the belief that you no longer have control of a situation. Given the suddenness and harsh nature of crises, it's not surprising a common response is a feeling of surrender. The task of responding to a crisis can seem so gargantuan that the possibility of a positive resolution can seem exceedingly unlikely. The magnitude of a crisis can quickly lead to a sense of helplessness, hopelessness, and futility. In simple terms, you feel defeated and you just want to give up.

Surrender is different than the fight, flight, or even freeze (the three Fs) reactions that have been evolutionarily ingrained into our brains for millions of years. The three Fs are about taking action to avert a threat to your life (yes, standing still is an action). In all three responses, your mind and body are powerfully activated. Psychological, neurological, and physical changes coalesce around your behavior aimed at accomplishing the goal of survival.

In contrast, surrender is the absence of action, an entirely different reaction altogether. It involves giving up any hope of survival. In contrast to the three Fs, you shut down psychologically, neurologically, and physically. And, not surprisingly, surrender produces the exact opposite effect on your behavior: whereas the three Fs involve seeking survival, surrender leads to figurative or literal death. Clearly, surrender doesn't play well in a crisis. The simple fact is that when you surrender to a crisis, you lose in almost all cases. Depending on the type of crisis, losing can be realized in different ways, whether financial ruin, divorce, loss of career, or death.

Determination

There are many aspects of a crisis that you can't control. The one thing you can control is how you respond. That means how much effort and resolve you put into finding a solution to the crisis is up to you. To ensure you do everything within your control, it's vital to leverage your determination. Determination is defined as "the quality that you show when you have decided to do something and you will not let anything stop you; the ability to continue trying to do something, even if it is difficult." To prevail over a crisis, you must be determined to begin the process of resolving it, and you must be resolute until you've achieved a satisfactory outcome. Determination is the foundation of everything you do in response to a crisis. Without your determination to commit the necessary time, effort, and energy, your chances of finding success are very unlikely.

There are several reasons that determination is essential in a crisis. First, as I discussed in chapter 7, successfully resolving a crisis involves putting in consistent effort in every affected area of your life, which requires you to be determined. Second, determination dictates your willingness to continue to work hard in the face of fatigue, monotony, and setbacks. Determination involves an unwavering resolve to do what is necessary to overcome the crisis. It means continuing to push back against the crisis in the face of challenges and failures. It involves an ongoing commitment to fight the good fight until the crisis has been vanquished or its impact minimized.

> "All the adversity I've had in my life, all the troubles and obstacles, have strengthened me. You may not realize it when it happens, but a kick in the teeth may be the best thing in the world for you."—Walt Disney, creator of Disneyland[11]

Exercising Your Determination Muscle

Just like the previous mental muscles we've covered, determination is a muscle that needs to be exercised if you want to use it to its fullest against a crisis. To that end, here are several exercises to make your determination as strong as it can be.

Focus on Your Long-Term Goals

To surmount a crisis, you have to devote a lot of time and effort while facing difficult challenges along the way. As noted earlier, there will be times when the crisis wears you down and your determination starts to wane. When you feel this way, it helps to focus on your long-term goals related to the crisis. Imagine exactly what you want to accomplish. Tell yourself that the only way you'll be able to reach your goals is to continue to work hard and confront the challenges head-on and with your fullest commitment. It can also help to remind yourself why you're working so hard: for your children, your future, your safety, your life. Thinking about others who are impacted if you don't push forward can help increase your determination.

Focusing on your long-term goals hones your determination in several ways. First, when you feel overwhelmed and beaten down by a crisis, your mind and body are yelling to surrender. If you listen, then you will ease up or give up. By focusing on your long-term goals, you remind yourself, "No, we can't stop because my long-term goals are really important, too, so keep going!" In other words, you're giving yourself a reason to keep pushing forward in the face of the immediate desire to surrender.

Second, simply by focusing on your long-term goals, you take your mind off the frustration, doubt, fatigue, and pain you may be feeling as you face a short-term challenge. In doing so, all of the negatives become a little less intense and a little more tolerable. Focusing on the big picture puts your immediate struggles into perspective.

Third, focusing on your long-term goals generates positive emotions, such as inspiration and pride. Feeling more positive can counter less-pleasant emotions like anger, disappointment, or despair. Moreover, research has shown that positive emotions actually reduce fatigue and pain. So, when you're struggling to stay determined as you battle the crisis, think of your long-term goal and tell yourself, "That's why I'm doing this!"

> "You must have long-term goals to keep you from being frustrated by short-term failures."—Brigadier General Charles C. Noble [12]

Have a Crisis Partner

It's difficult to stay determined and resolute all the time in a crisis, especially if you're doing so on your own. There will be some days when you just don't feel like facing the crisis. You may be tired, stressed out, overwhelmed, bored, and burned out, and you may just want to surrender, even if only for a short time. No matter how hard you push yourself, you simply can't work as hard as you can when someone else pushes you. That someone can be a parent, spouse, friend, someone who is experiencing a similar crisis, or some other significant person in your life.

Having a crisis partner helps you stay determined in several ways. First, as the saying goes, "two heads are better than one." You can use both of your minds to gain more knowledge, synthesize and analyze information, make decisions and plans, and ultimately, take constructive action in response to the crisis.

Second, when you have a crisis partner, you don't feel as if you have to climb that high mountain alone. Rather, you have someone to support you every step of the way (and you can support them). Knowing you have someone helping you push forward makes it just a little easier to keep climbing higher.

Third, a crisis partner holds you accountable. For example, it's one thing to face a crisis on your own and encounter something unpleasant that makes you want to ease up or quit. But it's going to be a lot harder to slow down or stop when you know your crisis partner is there waiting for you. You can be sure that he or she will be quite upset if you don't show up as expected. So, even if you're not feeling it that day, you'll be there and do what's necessary because your crisis partner is counting on you.

Use Determination Cues

A big part of staying determined in a crisis involves being reminded to stay determined. Another part is to generate positive emotions associated with your efforts and progress toward your goals. A great way to create those feelings is with determination cues such as inspirational phrases and photographs. These cues might be quotes, for example, "I hated every minute of training, but I said, 'Don't quit. Suffer now and live the rest of your life as a champion'" (said by boxing legend Muhammad Ali) and "You're never a loser until you quit trying" (said by former NFL coach Mike Ditka). A determination cue might also be a photo of someone who inspires you or someone who exhibits the qualities you aspire to possess. The key is that the quote or photo generates positive thoughts and emotions that translate into increasing or maintaining your determination, especially when overcoming the crisis gets especially difficult.

These days, you can find determination cues everywhere on the Internet: blogs, YouTube videos, or websites. You can even find cues focused on your particular crisis (you're not alone!); there are websites devoted to every specific crisis, as well as supportive communities of which you can become a part. If you come across a quote or a photo that inspires you, place it where you can see it regularly, such as in your bedroom, on your refrigerator door, or in your office. Look at it often and allow yourself to experience the thoughts and emotions it generates. These reminders, and the emotions associated with them, will inspire and motivate you to continue to work hard and persist in the face of the challenges of the crisis.

Set Goals

There are few things more rewarding and motivating than setting a goal, putting effort toward it, and achieving it. The sense of accomplishment and validation that results when you see the outcomes your efforts produce makes you feel good. It motivates you to work toward accomplishing future goals. As a bonus, in the process of reaching goals you get a lot done. Goal setting is especially important when a crisis arises. It's valuable to establish clear goals of what you want to accomplish and how you will achieve those goals to overcome the crisis. Well-articulated goals act as road signs that guide you toward your desired outcome. They act as benchmarks of the progress you are making as you push against the forces generated by a crisis. Goals also generate feelings of pride and inspiration that continue to propel you toward higher achievements. Seeing that your hard work is moving you forward and producing results should motivate you further to realize your goals (I will describe how to set goals in more detail later in this chapter).

Ask Daily Questions

I'm sure your life is busy, filled with many obligations and activities unrelated to a crisis: work, school, family, hobbies, and other commitments. Even when a crisis strikes, particularly one in which the effects aren't immediate or dramatic, it can be easy to get wrapped up in your daily life. Sometimes regular life gets so busy that you may forget about or lose track of what you need to do every day to stay on the path toward overcoming your crisis. One helpful way to keep your crisis efforts and goals in the forefront of your mind is to ask yourself two questions every day.

1. When you get up in the morning, ask, "What can I do today to resolve the crisis I'm facing?" This question starts off your day in a motivating way. It focuses you on continuing to address the crisis proactively and consistently. It also prompts you to identify specifically what you need to do each day to continue your progress toward ending the crisis.

2. Before you go to sleep, ask, "Did I do everything possible today to resolve the crisis?" This question holds you accountable for what you did or did not do that day. If you did everything possible, you'll feel fulfillment and pride in your efforts. If you

didn't do your best, you will be forced to confront that fact and will feel disappointment and regret. In either case, your answer to this question will set the stage for what you decide to do tomorrow.

These two questions will serve as daily reminders of your goals and will challenge you to be motivated to work toward them each day. I recommend that you write down these two questions and put them where you can see them every morning and every night.

> "You've got to get up every morning with determination if you're going to go to bed with satisfaction."—George Lorimer, author [13]

The Heart of Determination: Staying Motivated

The techniques I've just described are effective in increasing your short-term determination. They can get you through some of the immediate and short-term challenges of a crisis. But determination is not just about keeping at it day-to-day. It's also about staying motivated for as long as a crisis lasts. That could mean you're pushing for days, weeks, months, and even years before it is completely resolved. The reality is that there are no quick fixes or easy strategies for staying determined over the long haul. Ultimately, you need to find a reason to continue down the hard road of overcoming the crisis. Your determination must come from within. It's important to have a very deep and personal reason for wanting to continue to commit the time and effort toward resolving the crisis. When you get right down to it, you just have to want it really bad.

Determination: A Moment-to-Moment Choice

It's one thing to say that you are committed to overcoming a crisis. It's a different thing entirely to demonstrate your determination every day of your life. In fact, determination is a moment-to-moment choice. It involves many forks in the road that will dictate your final destination in the journey you are taking with a crisis. Examples of some decisions you may have to make are as follows:

- Should I learn more about the crisis?
- Should I seek out more resources?
- Should I go to bed early tonight?

- Should I try unproven approaches to the crisis?

There are many obstacles to determination in those moments. Many that I have already mentioned include exhaustion, tedium, the wish to avoid the crisis, the desire to do other things, and a multitude of distractions in your daily life. At each fork in the road, you must decide what is important to you. The determination you bring to the crisis, the motivation you have to achieve your goals related to the crisis, and the priority you place on those goals will encourage you to take the good road. However, competing forces in your life can act as a Siren's call for your attention, time, and energy and force you to take the bad road. At these forks in the road you will face each day, you must decide which road to take. These decisions will ultimately determine whether you overcome the crisis that now dominates your life.

> "You'll be surprised to know how far you can go from the point where you thought it was the end."—Unknown[14]

DISTRACTION VERSUS FOCUS

Focus may be the most underappreciated and misunderstood mental aspect that contributes to how we respond in a crisis. There are two important things you need to know about focus. First, most people think of focus as concentrating on one thing for a long time. Yes, at times, you do need to zero in all your attention on one task. For example, it would be important to sit down and review your investment statements from the past few years after you incur significant losses in a stock market collapse. At the same time, focus involves the ability to adjust outward (e.g., looking at printed information and listening to experts) and inward (e.g., identifying and analyzing different investment strategies moving forward) as the demands of a crisis may require. Being able to modify your focus will help you respond to the myriad of tasks required to overcome a crisis.

Second, focus is so important in a crisis because it's the gateway to effectively using all higher-order thinking: perception, memory, language, learning, understanding, creativity, reasoning, synthesis, analysis, problem solving, and decision making. Without the ability to focus effectively, you are more likely to revert back to your primitive brain of instincts, emotions, and knee-jerk reactions. Not consciously engaging our cerebral cortex prevents us from accessing our evolved forms of thinking that allow us to do what's necessary to overcome a modern-day crisis.

Simply put, focus involves paying attention to one or more things. Focus, in and of itself, is neither good nor bad; it's how you use focus that determines whether it helps or hurts you. In a crisis, good focus helps you understand and analyze the causes and effects, which then helps you respond to the crisis. In contrast, poor focus involves being distracted and paying attention to internal and external cues that take your attention away from the task at hand. There are two types of poor focus: interfering and irrelevant. Interfering poor focus directly hurts your efforts. It includes negative thoughts, such as doubt and worry, and negative emotions, such as fear or frustration. Irrelevant poor focus isn't harmful in itself, but simply distracts you from focusing on what you need to do in the moment to make progress in a crisis. For instance, attending to people around you or other responsibilities or even to internal cues like being hungry.

Value of Focus

Focus has several essential benefits in overcoming a crisis. First, you are far more *effective* in your efforts because you are consistently attending to what you need to accomplish on your journey toward a resolution. In other words, what you focus on, you do well. Second, you are more *efficient* in your efforts. You'll get more done in a shorter amount of time with more focus. Finally, you will be more *consistent* in your efforts because the more consistent your focus, the more consistently you'll put your energy toward overcoming the challenge at hand.

There are three goals to keep in mind as you strengthen your focus muscle. Goal number one: identify the internal and external variables that need your focus for you to perform well on the crisis-related task at hand. Goal number two: identify the internal and external distractions that prevent you from focusing effectively. Internal distractions may be negative thoughts, emotions, and physical sensations. External distractions may include noise, other people, and daily life demands. Goal number three: actively and consistently focus on the good things and remove or block out the distractions.

Foundation of a Strong Focus Muscle

As you can see, it is essential to develop control of your focus before and maintain it throughout a crisis to ensure that it helps your efforts. Keeping in mind the preceding three goals, your first step in establishing control of your focus is to gain an understanding of the general areas in which you should direct your focus. These broader areas act as the foundation for more specific exercises you can use to control your focus and accomplish your goals as you work to resolve a crisis.

A major problem many people have in a crisis is that they focus on things they can't control. This focus has no value because you can't change something if you don't have control over it. Focusing on the uncontrollables hurts your efforts for several reasons. First, it has a negative psychological, emotional, and physical impact on you. Feeling out of control hurts your confidence and determination because you feel helpless to do anything. Second, feeling out of control creates anxiety, which comes with emotional and physical discomfort. This discomfort exacerbates the feelings of loss of control because you now feel internally out of control. Third, focusing on things you can't control distracts you from what you need to focus on to address the crisis. The fact is, there's only one thing you can control: yourself. This includes your mind, your body, and your actions. If you focus on those things, you'll be more confident and relaxed, and you'll be better able to focus on what you need to do to overcome the crisis.

Outcome versus Process Focus

As I discussed in great detail in chapter 1, perhaps the greatest obstacle to good focus is being distracted by the outcome during a crisis. "Outcome focus" involves focusing on the crisis's potential impact on your life, usually it's the worst-case scenario. In contrast, a "process focus" means focusing on specific aspects of the crisis over which you have control and directing your energy toward those areas in attempting to resolve the crisis. For example, you gain new information from others or seek out additional resources. In my view, an outcome focus spells doom because it prevents you from focusing on the process, which is what you need to get beyond the crisis.

A mistake many people make is equating *thinking* with *focusing*. They believe that if they're thinking about something, like how to deal with a cyberattack, then they are also focusing on it. However, there is a big difference between thinking and focusing; one will help your efforts while the other will hurt them.

Thinking is connected to your investment in the crisis (see chapter 5), that is, the degree of its importance to you. Thinking is often about things that not only don't help your efforts, but actually interfere with them (e.g., negative thinking, worry, and anxiety). Thinking is critical, judgmental, comparative, and emotional. If you make a mistake or have a setback when you're in thinking mode, it can set off a vicious cycle of harmful thinking, emotions, and actions. Thinking interferes with your ability to focus. It detracts from what will help you address the crisis and causes you to lose determination and confidence, feel anxiety, and experience a deterioration in your efforts.

In contrast, focusing simply involves paying attention to relevant internal or external cues. This process is impartial, objective, unemotional, and detached from investment or judgment. If you make a mistake while you are focusing, you're able to accept it, you won't be overly disappointed by the failure, and you can shift your focus back onto your continuing efforts. In focus mode, you're able to use the failure as information to correct the problem, remain positive, and better focus in the future.

> "Stop overthinking, you're only creating problems that aren't there."—
> Unknown[15]

Focus Exercises

To strengthen your focus muscle, you can add several focus exercises to your mental muscle training regimen.

Have Clear Goals and Process

A simple reality of focusing is that you can't focus on something if you don't know where and on what to focus. So, the first step in developing focus in a crisis involves specifying what you hope to accomplish. Having a clear understanding of your goals allows you to determine on what you should specifically be focusing. That said, you can focus on various aspects of the crisis that need to be addressed. For instance, gathering information, learning more about the causes and effects, or other steps you need to take to resolve the crisis.

Once defined goals are established, you now have clarity in your focus. However, you can't simply repeat that goal in your mind as you move forward and expect it to come to fruition. The next step is to take your goals and create a plan to accomplish them. The process of accomplishing your goals is where you will actually put your focus during your crisis-related efforts. Take, for instance, the case of a teenager making the anxious transition from high school to college. Rather than thinking about moving away from home and anticipating the difficulty of the coming change, she might choose to focus on learning about the new experience by reading about the campus, reviewing the course catalog, talking to people she knows who went there, and making a list of all of the items she will need for her dorm room.

Identify and Limit Distractions

No matter how clear your focus goals and processes are, you won't be able to focus well if you're distracted by people or things in your internal and external environments. You want to scan the thoughts and emotions and the setting you're in that can clutter your mind. After recognizing the many distractions, identify the most prominent ones that prevent you from achieving and maintaining focus. Common external distractions in a crisis include family members when you're at home or the noise in a nearby coffee shop. Typical internal distractions include negative thoughts, irrelevant thoughts, unpleasant emotions, and physical anxiety. Once you have identified these distractions, you can develop strategies to limit them. For example, if you are distracted by your family while doing a job search after having been laid off, you can retreat to your office away from them. If you are feeling anxious about an upcoming job interview, you can listen to music and focus on your breathing to take your mind off your anxiety and lessen your internal distractions.

Relax

The stress you experience when you are confronted by a crisis can be a substantial obstacle to effective focus. Stress impacts your focus in several ways. To start with, it narrows your focus to the point that the thing causing the stress, in this case the crisis, dominates your energy. In addition, you develop tunnel vision to the extent that you start thinking about and become consumed by the enormity of the challenges presented by the crisis, rather than focusing on more important, controllable aspects of the crisis. Finally, stress produces uncomfortable physical changes, including muscle tension and a racing heart, that are further distractions.

Fortunately, when stress interferes with your ability to focus on the crisis, there are active steps you can take to relieve it. The following strategies have proven to be helpful in restoring a sense of calm in your body and focus in your mind:

• Deep breathing
• Muscle relaxation
• Massage
• Meditation
• Yoga
• Hot shower or bath
• Exercise
• Music

Use Reminders

An odd yet very effective exercise for helping you focus involves writing down and posting frequent reminders where you can see them regularly. Let me explain how this works. When in the midst of a crisis, it's easy to get so wrapped up in all that is going wrong (major distraction!) that you forget to focus on things that will help you in the moment. For example, you can become so obsessed with all the overwhelming demands in your life that come with impending parenthood that you forget to focus on what you need to do to prepare for the upcoming birth and all of the wonderful changes that will also occur. Due to the magnitude of becoming a parent, it can be difficult to have the wherewithal to break free of this unhealthy absorption and redirect your focus in a positive and constructive way. That's where the reminders can come in handy. When you are distracted by your doubts and worries about being a parent and you see written reminders (e.g., breathe, stay calm) or photos of the baby's ultrasound images posted around your house, you are reminded of what you should be focusing on. These prompts help you break free of thinking and regain focus on what will help you be better prepared for the birth. They will also help you feel happier and more excited about becoming a parent.

"The only way to discover our true potential is to clear out the clutter and focus on what matters."—Unknown[16]

Four Ps

To help you remember what we've covered in terms of focus, I have a rule that will enable you to identify the general areas of focus as you progress through a crisis. I call it the four Ps.

The first P is *positive*. You should focus on positive things that will help navigate the crisis and avoid negative things that will hurt it.

The second P is *process*. You should focus specifically on what you need to accomplish to conclude the crisis to your satisfaction, not on distractions. If you stay focused on what you need to do, you will do more and move steadily closer to putting the crisis behind you.

The third P is *present*. You should focus on what you need to do at this moment to achieve your crisis goals and, if needed, remind yourself that you can't change the past. You also shouldn't focus on the future because you can't directly change it any more than you can change the past. The only way to impact the future is to control the present. The only way to control the present is to focus on it.

The final P is *progress*. Particularly in your journey of resolving a crisis, the end game can seem so far away that it seems unreachable. If you feel this way, it's best to focus on the incremental progress you're making every day toward surmounting the crisis. In doing so, each step ahead is more doable and the end game seems achievable. Ultimately, with every step forward you move that much closer to the end of the crisis.

Part III

Your Evolution

Your journey through a crisis concludes in part III, Your Evolution. One goal of *How to Survive and Thrive* is to open your eyes to how we humans are wired to react to a crisis and how the amygdala no longer serves us in a world that is vastly different from the one in which it developed. Another goal is to show you how our brains have developed in a way that provides us the opportunity to overcome those innate tendencies and use all that the cerebral cortex has to offer as we confront contemporary crises.

The hope is that, like human beings as a species, you have gone through an evolution of your own as you've read *How to Survive and Thrive*. In this evolution, you have mitigated the impact of your amygdala and your primitive reactions and have allowed your cerebral cortex to gain dominance over what you think, how you feel, and the ways in which you respond to crises in your life. Whether you are a cave person on the Serengeti faced with a drought or a human being faced with a crisis unique to the twenty-first century, both are existential crises that put your life at risk. And as you reduce your primitive urges and leverage your evolved brain, you must, ultimately, ready yourself and take action to overcome the crisis. That preparation and action is the focus on part III.

Chapter 9 explores how you can best prepare yourself to tackle the challenges that a crisis presents. You must be clear-eyed and decisive, and have a plan for how you will respond to the crisis. Relying on the five steps you took in part II as you fully engaged your cerebral cortex, chapter 9 sets the stage for you to take the determined final steps toward the resolution of the crisis.

How to Survive and Thrive concludes with an epilogue, Lights, Camera. . . . This final step through a crisis comes from your journey through every previous step you've taken as you have evolved from your primitive self to your modern-day self. You not only have the capabilities to reduce your amygdala's influence on a crisis, but also possess the necessary attributes that emerge from your cerebral cortex to navigate and arrive at your journey's destination.

Chapter Nine

Preparation

Ready, Set . . .

Through the first two parts, I have been laying the foundation to help you face a crisis head-on when one arises. Hopefully, you have taken the good road in regard to your values, investment, attitude, mindset, and mental muscles, so you are in the right place mentally to confront a crisis with confidence, commitment, and courage. You are now at the final stage of preparation before you take action toward producing a satisfactory outcome to the crisis.

There are three preparation forks in the road. You certainly don't want to take on a crisis unless you are ready to take action that will result in the outcome you want. Chapter 9 offers you three preparation forks in the road that will determine your level of readiness to embark on a successful journey in resolving a crisis. Each time you take the good road, you put yourself in a position to take action that will be decisive and grounded in reality, with a clear direction and identifiable markers of progress.

> "Knowing is not enough; we must apply. Willing is not enough; we must do."—Johann Wolfgang von Goethe, German writer and statesman[1]

BLURRY VERSUS 20/20 VISION

Of course, action in and of itself isn't enough. Instead, you need to take intentional action that clearly leads to an acceptable resolution. Obviously, *clear* is not a word typically associated with a crisis. Rather, a crisis is more often associated with something like driving down a road in a thick fog, with many aspects of a crisis making the road ahead difficult to see. Additionally, you can only see a short way ahead of you in a dense fog, just as you can't see far into the future in a crisis. Navigating your life in a crisis, is even more difficult when it's unfamiliar to you, which tends to be the case with crises. The alien nature of the road makes it even more difficult to navigate to your destination safely. The result is that you must drive very cautiously and are at constant risk of crashing. Such a hesitant approach is no way to make it through a crisis intact.

Instead, you must see clearly every cause and effect, influence, and possible outcome for you to successfully navigate your way through a crisis. With this clarity, you will have the best possible understanding of the situation, which allows you to take appropriate action and determine the quickest way to get through the crisis with the greatest success.

> "Clarity of vision is the key to achieving your objectives."—Tom Steyer, investor and political activist[2]

Blurry Vision

Many features of a crisis make it difficult to see clearly, some of which are distractions that were discussed previously: overwhelming emotions and life separate from the crisis (e.g., family, friends, work). In addition, the crisis may be multifaceted or complex, making it difficult to see everything about it you need to see. One of the most important variables that can blur your vision involves various ways your thinking can become muddled.

Fantasy Thinking

Because of the massive threat a crisis poses, it's easy to fall victim to what I call *fantasy thinking*. Fantasy thinking involves seeing a crisis in a distorted way. It's an inaccurate view of a crisis that sets you up for failure because all of your decisions, actions, and additional thoughts are based on faulty impressions, appraisals, and assumptions.

Interestingly, this fantasy thinking can lead you to have two very different perspectives on a crisis, one positive and one negative. Positive fantasies can result in an underestimation of the severity or impact of the crisis. Whether you call it being hopeful, optimistic, or Pollyanna-ish, if you're out of touch with the reality of a crisis, these positive fantasies can lead you to take inadequate action or no action at all. "It's not that big a deal," "Things will turn out fine," and "Let's just hope for the best" are a few examples of positive fantasy thinking that can cause complacency and inaction.

Negative fantasy lies at the other end of this blurry-eyed continuum, yet it, too, can set you up for failure. Negative fantasies can cause you to catastrophize the crisis—think worst-case scenario—producing an overreaction or misguided response. "We're doomed," "My life is over," and "What can I do?" are several examples of negative fantasy thinking that cause panic or surrender.

> "The pessimist complains about the wind; the optimist expects it to change; the realist adjusts the sails."—William Arthur Ward, inspirational writer[3]

Tunnel Vision

When the fight-or-flight response is triggered, your focus narrows onto the specific threat. As noted earlier, this response worked in primitive times when the threat was obvious and immediate, but today this "tunnel vision" prevents you from

- Paying attention to the multifaceted nature of modern-day crises
- Processing, synthesizing, and analyzing the many components of a crisis
- Considering the diverse options available to you
- Developing responses to constructively address today's crises

Myopia

This blurred vision may also create in you a myopia, or nearsightedness. This precludes you from considering the long-term implications of the crisis as you won't be able to look beyond the near-term consequences. Again, all that mattered for our forbearers in a crisis was whether they could survive in the moment so this myopia was an asset, not a problem. Today's crises are a far different story. Let's return to the economic crisis of 2008. Myopia was exemplified in the first few months when many people withdrew a sizable portion of their investment portfolio from the stock market and deposited it in safer investment instruments or stuffed it under their mattresses. This happened despite the consensus that the market would eventually rebound (it did). Experts advised that immediately taking out money would actually result in a long-term loss rather than a gain, unless the money was needed in the short term (also true). In fact, research shows that those who get out of the market early during a downturn tend to get back in too late to gain the benefits of the economic resurgence.

So why did people do this? The crisis produced myopia that caused them to focus on the immediate threat of financial loss rather than the long-term advantages of patience.

Stagnant Thinking

When experiencing a crisis, most people revert to old ways of thinking, feeling, and responding. These old habits are driven by primitive instincts that don't allow time for deliberation and conscious decision making. They are also learned habits that are familiar, comfortable, and readily accessible. Back in prehistoric times, ancestors were faced with only a few types of crises (e.g., rival tribes, wild animals, starvation) so they could fall back on tried-and-true ways of responding: fight, freeze, or flight.

Not so with today's crises. As indicated in the introduction, there are many more kinds of calamities that can befall us these days. Crises are often new, they may present in different ways than previously experienced, or they are too complex to rely on established habits or patterns. In fact, the very nature of a modern-day crisis is that it turns your life upside down, almost like Bizarro World in the old Superman comics, where everything that is good on our Earth is bad on Bizarro Earth. This alternative version of Earth has come to represent anything that is strangely opposite to how things are supposed to work. Looking at the crisis in the same old ways produces stagnant thinking that is likely to be ineffective in finding a solution to the current predicament.

20/20 Vision

For you to have any chance of surmounting a crisis, you must have crystal-clear vision and think about everything needed to understand how to accurately respond. Having 20/20 vision ensures that you see the crisis in a realistic way and provides you with the depth and breadth of information necessary to think about and act on the crisis constructively.

> "It's a lack of clarity that creates chaos and frustration."—Steve Maraboli, speaker and author[4]

Be Clear-Eyed

It is essential for you to see the crisis realistically. You will only be capable of identifying the relevant causes, contributors, and impacts by viewing the crisis for what it is, not through your wishes or fears. Your ability to see the crisis with clear eyes and lucid thinking will permit you to accurately understand, evaluate, and analyze it. Subsequently, you can create and implement a course of action that gives you the best chance of overcoming the crisis.

You can ensure clear eyes by shining a light on the crisis in which you learn everything you can about it. This process involves gathering all relevant information and speaking to experts who can provide a depth of knowledge and experience that allows you to see the crisis within its context.

Be Wide-Eyed

To capture the complexity and details of today's crises, you also want to see them through a wide-angle lens. This perspective helps you to avoid the tunnel vision that causes you to focus on the specific threat and miss out on essential information that could help you respond to the crisis more effectively.

You can expand your vision of a crisis in several ways. First, become aware when you are experiencing tunnel vision so you can deliberately broaden your focus onto aspects of the crisis outside of its specific and immediate impact on you. Second, actively seek out information beyond what is readily available. Third, seek out others who can provide in-depth perspectives and information about the crisis that might not be readily available to you. Finally, you can be patient, allow the crisis to evolve, and see what new information comes to light. In all these cases, you gather knowledge, insights, and viewpoints that reach beyond what is immediately in front of you, thereby helping you to formulate the best possible response to the crisis.

> "You must look within for value but must look beyond for perspective."—Denis Waitley, motivational speaker and writer [5]

Be Farsighted

Having 20/20 vision in a crisis also helps you to see the crisis as it unfolds and avoid the myopia that can keep you stuck. When you maintain a perspective on the crisis that is both farsighted and nearsighted, you have a field of vision that provides you with the full spectrum of information and options you'll need to address the crisis. You will be able to look back to past lessons learned, look forward to the future to evaluate the landscape ahead, and integrate them to respond in the best way possible in the present. This vision encourages calm and deliberate decision making in response to the crisis (an opportunity mindset) while preventing a knee-jerk reaction (a crisis mentality) that produces short-term relief but does more harm than good in the long run.

In addition, this farsightedness offers you several specific benefits. It helps you to predict the future course of the crisis and to recognize the potential long-term impact on your life. Farsightedness also enables you to establish goals for how you want to navigate the crisis, the end result you want, and develop a plan for getting there.

> "The difficulty lies not so much in developing new ideas as in escaping from old ones."—John Maynard Keynes, economist [6]

Be Innovative

Because crises are rarely the same and there is no cookie-cutter approach to resolving them, rote ways of approaching a crisis will likely not work. Instead of falling back on stagnant thinking, you want to adopt an innovative approach to a crisis that unlocks fresh and creative ways of examining, understanding, evaluating, and responding to it. This groundbreaking perspective enables you to find answers and solutions that best address the unique challenges of a crisis. In sum, 20/20 vision offers you deep insights into a crisis that include

- Seeing clearly what was, what is, and what could be
- Determining what is impossible, possible, and probable
- Thinking outside the box when others are trapped inside
- Seeing solutions where others see problems
- Breaking down barriers that may interfere with thinking clearly
- Looking beyond what you have done in the past and finding new ways of approaching the crisis in a constructive way
- Providing you with a response to the crisis that results in a satisfactory resolution

UNCERTAINTY VERSUS DECISIVENESS

Uncertainty is an absolute kiss of death in a crisis. It causes hesitation at a time when action may be the best course to follow, and it interferes with full commitment to whichever road you choose. At the same time, knee-jerk decisiveness can be worse than uncertainty because ill-conceived decisions usually escalate today's complex crises. Uncertain or poorly thought-out decisions increase the crisis mentality that is waiting on the edge of your psyche, when an opportunity mindset is needed most.

> "If you aren't in the moment, you are either looking forward to uncertainty, or back to pain and regret."—Jim Carrey, comedian and actor [7]

Uncertainty

In primitive times, there was no time to hesitate, and uncertainty had serious consequences. There were four choices—fight, flee, freeze, or die—and you had to act fast. At the same time, it was easier to be decisive in the past because crises were more immediate, simple, and clear, with fewer options to consider.

Uncertainty in modern-day crises is a bit different. In fact, uncertainty is almost a given because most crises are unfamiliar, unpredictable, and uncontrollable. Their causes are frequently ambiguous, and the impact is equally unclear.

Our uncertainty comes from doubt, worry, or fear that is caused or exacerbated by having insufficient information, having limited time to act, or simply not knowing where we want to go or how we are going to get there. Plus, the available choices for how to respond can be numerous, complex, and unclear. Additionally, as I emphasized earlier in this chapter, uncertainty can be a significant obstacle to overcoming a crisis because there comes a time when processing, synthesizing, and analyzing must end and you simply must act.

> "In any moment of decision, the best thing you can do is the right thing. The worst thing you can do is nothing."—Theodore Roosevelt, twenty-sixth US president[8]

Decisiveness

There's nothing more important to the successful resolution of a crisis than decision making because your decisions dictate the direction you take at every stage of a crisis. Yet, decision making can end up being impacted by the frantic and chaotic nature of the crisis itself, which is no way to make decisions. Instead, the process should be structured and deliberate to arrive at the best possible decisions as you traverse a crisis. Without a clear and effective process, you may make some horrendous and potentially catastrophic decisions, which may only deepen the severity of the crisis.

Cognitive Biases

In my work, I have found that people have considerable confidence in their decision-making capabilities. I have also learned that their confidence is often misguided and sometimes based more in fantasy than reality. In fact, research has shown that decision making is rife with and harmed by "cognitive biases" that lead to inaccurate judgment, illogical interpretation, and perceptual distortion. As a result, making objective and rational decisions becomes incredibly difficult. Yet, in a crisis there is little time and attention devoted to creating a structure and process in a crisis that facilitates good decision making and mitigates factors that lead to poor decision making. Let me explain how cognitive biases can be a significant problem in a crisis.

The conventional wisdom in classical economics is that we humans are "rational actors." Under this assumption, we naturally make decisions and behave in ways that maximize advantages and practical value and minimize risks and costs. For generations, this theory drove economic policy despite daily anecdotal evidence that humans are anything but rational. One example is how we invest our money and the debt we accumulate through ill-thought-out purchases. Economists who embrace this assumption seem to live by the maxim, "If the facts don't fit the theory, throw out the facts," attributed, ironically enough, to Albert Einstein.

Any notion that we are in fact rational actors was blown out of the water by Dr. Daniel Kahneman, winner of the 2002 Nobel Prize for economics, and his late colleague Dr. Amos Tversky. Their ground-breaking findings on cognitive biases have unequivocally demonstrated that humans make decisions and act in ways that are anything but rational.

> "We're blind to our blindness. We have very little idea of how little we know. We're not designed to know how little we know."—Daniel Kahneman, Nobel Prize–winning psychologist[9]

Cognitive biases can be characterized as the tendency to make decisions and take action based on limited knowledge and/or processing of information. We may also act in self-interest, overconfidence, emotions, or attachment to past experience. Cognitive biases can result in

- Perceptual blindness or distortion (seeing things that aren't actually there)
- Illogical interpretation (being nonsensical)
- Inaccurate judgments (being just plain wrong)
- Irrationality (being out of touch with reality)
- Bad decisions (being dumb)

The outcomes of decisions that are influenced by cognitive biases can range from the mundane to the lasting to the catastrophic, such as buying an unflattering outfit, getting married to the wrong person, or going to war, respectively. It isn't a big leap to see how cognitive biases can be a serious roadblock to the successful resolution of a crisis.

Cognitive biases can be placed in two broad categories. *Information biases* that include not paying attention to or adequately thinking through relevant information and using heuristics (or information-processing shortcuts) to produce fast and efficient decisions while sacrificing accuracy. *Ego biases* include emotional motivations (e.g., fear, anger, or worry) and social influences (e.g., peer pressure, the desire for acceptance, and doubt that other people can be wrong). Hundreds of cognitive biases have been classified. The following list of eleven cognitive biases are the most harmful to decision making in a crisis.

Information biases include

- *Knee-jerk bias*: make fast and intuitive decisions when slow and deliberate decisions are necessary
- *Occam's razor*: assume the most obvious decision is the best decision
- *Silo effect*: use too narrow of an approach when making a decision
- *Confirmation*: focus on information that affirms your beliefs and assumptions
- *Inertia*: think, feel, and act in ways that are familiar, comfortable, predictable, and controllable
- *Myopia*: see and interpret the world through the narrow lens of your own experiences, baggage, beliefs, and assumptions

Ego biases include

- *Shock and awe*: believe that your intellectual firepower alone is enough to make complex decisions
- *Overconfidence*: have excessive confidence in your beliefs, knowledge, and abilities
- *Optimism*: remain overly optimistic, overestimating favorable outcomes and underestimating unfavorable outcomes
- *Force field*: think, feel, and act in ways that reduce a perceived threat, anxiety, or fear
- *Planning fallacy*: underestimate the time and costs needed to complete a task

Think about the bad decisions you have made over the years, both minor and disastrous. You will probably see the fingerprints of some of these cognitive biases all over the evidence of those decisions.

The good news is that there are four steps you can take to mitigate cognitive biases when decision making in response to a crisis:

1. Learn as much as you can about cognitive biases, identify the biases that are most likely to influence your decisions, and challenge them directly. Awareness is key to reducing the influence of cognitive biases on decision making. Simply knowing that cognitive biases exist and can distort your thinking will help lessen their impact.
2. When you are making important decisions about a crisis, ask for feedback from others who are less likely to be impacted by biases. Collaboration may be the most effective tool for mitigat-

ing cognitive biases. Quite simply, it is easier to see biases in others than in yourself.

3. Using your understanding of cognitive biases, ask yourself questions that shed light on the presence of biases and the best decisions that avoid their trap. Inquiry is fundamental to challenging the perceptions, judgments, and conclusions that can be marred by cognitive biases.

4. Establish a disciplined and consistent framework and process for making decisions. Doing so increases your chances of identifying cognitive biases before they hijack your decision making. Though brainstorming and free-wheeling discussions can be valuable in generating options, they also increase the chances for cognitive biases to contaminate the resulting decisions.

Daniel Kahneman recommends that you ask three questions to minimize the impact of cognitive biases when making decisions:

1. Is there any reason to suspect that my decision is based on self-interest, overconfidence, emotions, or attachment to past experiences?
2. Have I fallen in love with a particular decision?
3. Was there groupthink or were there dissenting opinions within the decision-making process?

These questions are important for both individual and collective reasons. Separately, question 1 is important because we are vulnerable in crisis situations and it's easy to fall prey to a solution that you just "feel" is right. Question 2 highlights the danger of decision making based on strong positive emotion. That love can cause you to embrace a decision even if it's not objectively the best course of action. Question 3 preemptively challenges you to seek out feedback from others. The problem of groupthink can be mitigated before you start making decisions by having people involved who will proactively offer opposing viewpoints and challenge your conventional wisdom. Collectively, these questions provide checks and balances for decision making in important, yet intense, situations.

In answering these questions, you must look closely at how each may be woven into your favored decision and separate them from its value. If your preferred decision doesn't stand up to scrutiny on its own merits, free of your cognitive bias, then it should be discarded. This balanced approach to responding to a crisis ensures that all aspects are taken into consideration before a decision is made. It also ensures that the decision has been thoroughly vetted for the presence and impact of cognitive biases, as well as the accuracy of information. This calculated approach to decision making also encourages the rejection of the crisis mentality and the ongoing use of an opportunity mindset. At the end of the day, it's only by filtering out your inherent cognitive biases that you can be confident that you're making the most reasoned and deliberate decision based on the best available information.

> "If there is time to reflect, slowing down is likely to be a good idea."—
> Daniel Kahneman, Nobel Prize–winning psychologist [10]

Decision-Making System

Like any process, decision making is most effective when it is structured and organized. A decision-making system provides you with a consistent framework while making decisions, allows for the evaluation of the quality of their outcomes, and enables subsequent adjustments as needed to improve future decisions. Such a rubric is so important for several reasons. In addition to having primitive forces driving you toward a fast decision, a crisis is

- Frenzied and messy nature
- Complex
- Impactful
- Emotionally laden
- Stressful

Imposing a scaffolded approach to the experience of a crisis will help mitigate the preceding forces, activate your cerebral cortex, and support you in transitioning from a crisis mentality to an opportunity mindset.

In my work, I have developed a system that guides you through making a decision while simultaneously allowing for check-ins at each stage of the process to ensure that cognitive biases have a negligible effect on the decisions. My decision-making model is comprised of five stages that progressively lead you through the process. Each stage contains a series of specific questions and a key recommendation that will help you avoid common cognitive-bias pitfalls at different points along the way to your decision.

"The framing of a problem is often far more essential than its solution."—Albert Einstein, German theoretical physicist [11]

Stage 1: Frame the Crisis. This stage involves a deep understanding of the fundamental issues related to your crisis and what type of decision needs to be made. Essential questions to ask include

1. What is the specific crisis?
2. What is some essential information associated with the crisis?
3. What has been considered or acted upon so far, including what has not been pursued?
4. What is a simple and clear statement that best describes the decision you want to have come out of it (i.e., "The decision to be made is . . .")?

A common pitfall in this initial stage of decision making is trying to make the decision on your own or not getting the right people involved. You can avoid this trap by identifying the areas of expertise needed in your situation and carefully selecting a group of people with an ideal combination of knowledge, skill sets, perspectives, and experiences who can provide a broad and deep perspective on the crisis and how to resolve it.

> "Life is not a solo act. It's a huge collaboration, and we all need to assemble around us the people who care about us and support us in times of strife."—Tim Gunn, fashion consultant and media personality [12]

Stage 2: Analyze the Crisis. Stage 2 involves conducting an extensive analysis of the crisis. This means delving into its many facets to ensure that you have all of the relevant information about the crisis. Be sure to do the following:

1. Explore the issue from different perspectives (e.g., using the diverse expertise of your decision-making team).
2. Ask what, why, when, who, where, and how questions so the crisis is fully revealed.
3. Highlight the information that everyone sees as most important to making a decision.

At this stage, one of the most common pitfalls is to assume that you have your arms fully wrapped around the crisis, cease collecting information too early, and end up making a hasty and ill-advised decision. The best way to mitigate this pitfall is to ensure that you are collecting all the relevant information that will contribute to a quality decision and continue exploring the crisis when you think you have done enough. This can be accomplished by asking your team members to leverage their knowledge and experience to bring forward any information they deem relevant. This allows potential decisions to germinate in everyone involved for a while. If you think you have finished gathering information, I recommend that you check back in with your decision-making team to ensure that there aren't additional considerations needed.

Stage 3: Make the Decision. This is where the rubber meets the road. It is time to take the disparate information, perspectives, and suggestions and formulate a set of decision options from which you will choose your final decision. Essential steps to take include the following:

1. Create a list of possible decisions that could be made.
2. Examine the possible outcomes, risks, rewards, and odds of each decision option (include best- and worst-case scenarios).
3. Gain consensus on the best decision.
4. Challenge the decision and see if cognitive biases or other flaws are present.
5. Make the decision.

Jumping to conclusions is the most likely pitfall in this stage. As you filter through possible decisions, each can look attractive and the time this process takes can start to wear on you. These variables may cause you to choose a decision prematurely. I recommend that you commit to a thorough consideration of each decision option before you return to the one you think is best.

Stage 4: Take Action. The fourth step is the scariest because it's time to act. Any decision you make is not guaranteed to be successful, and you will likely have some second-guessing. At this point, you must trust the process you went through to get to this point and take the "leap of faith" I described earlier. This is also the time when implementation of your decision becomes as important as the decision itself. As you likely know from experience, even the best decisions can fail if they are not put into action effectively. With this in mind, the following four questions will help guide the implementation and maximize the likelihood that the decision was, in fact, a good one.

1. What are the goals and plan for implementation of my decision?
2. Who has which roles and/or responsibilities in my plan?
3. What is the timetable for success and how will it be measured?
4. How will I hold myself and my team members accountable?

A common pitfall in this stage is to be unrealistic in your expectations of the outcome. As with most things in life and particularly in a crisis, decisions take time to root and blossom, and they don't always go as planned. I recommend that you be patient and allow the decision to slowly reveal its worth and be ready to make changes on the fly as the crisis progresses.

> "Have patience. All things are difficult before they become easy."—
> Saadi, medieval Persian poet [13]

Stage 5: Evaluation. The final stage is often overlooked. We often become so busy putting our decision into action that we forget to step back and evaluate its effectiveness at different points in its rollout. This ongoing feedback and analysis provides an evaluation during the process of implementing your decision and for the outcome. Key questions to ask include

1. What has worked and what hasn't so far?
2. Did I miss any information that would have led to a better decision?
3. Based on this analysis, what adjustments can be made in my decision making to improve its effectiveness in continuing to respond to the crisis?

Not surprisingly, the greatest pitfall is to not evaluate your decision at all. The fundamental lessons from the debrief are to identify what is working in the decision-making process so you can repeat it and identify what hasn't been working to avoid repeating it. For any crisis that has a long shelf life, you can continually use the process for the evolution of your decision as new information becomes available, the conditions of the crisis change, or progress or setbacks occur. I recommend that you evaluate your decision often and make adjustments as needed.

MADNESS VERSUS METHOD

Quite simply, a crisis causes a sort of madness by taking everything that was normal and throwing it for a loop. Not surprisingly then, madness is a recipe for disaster in response to a crisis. The only solution for this crisis-induced madness is creating a method of action that is imbued with clarity of purpose and direction. This framework provides clearly identified roles and responsibilities, articulated goals, and processes to address the challenges of the crisis.

Madness

Life changes dramatically when a crisis strikes. Much of what made your life familiar, comfortable, and controllable ceases to exist. A crisis can sow disorder in your mind and your life, generate disruptive emotions, upend long-standing life patterns and habits, cloud thinking and judgment, and cause panic. In this overwhelmed state, you are ill-equipped to view the crisis with clear vision, to make well-thought-out decisions, or to take action that is purposeful and focused.

Method

One of the most important tasks in response to a crisis is to create a method that will corral the madness and enable you to tackle the crisis in an organized and systematic way. The specific method you choose will be determined by the nature of the crisis. Your method is really a set of goals you establish for yourself that will progressively guide you to achieve a satisfactory resolution to the crisis you're facing.

To that end, goal setting is a simple and practical tool you can use to create a method for meeting the challenges of a crisis. For some very elemental reason, people respond to goals in a very deep and personal way. The experience of setting a goal, working toward a goal, and achieving a goal has a powerful emotional resonance that causes us to continue to strive even farther. Pride and inspiration play a central role in how goal setting impacts your ability to overcome a crisis. Pride leads you to put forth the effort in pursuit of your goals while inspiration follows achievement of a goal and encourages you to set your sights on the next goal.

Aside from the more profound influence goal setting has on turning the madness of a crisis into a method, it also helps you disconnect your amygdala and engage your cerebral cortex. The result is a shift from a crisis mentality to an opportunity mindset. Setting goals also has real, practical value because goals offer two essential benefits that allow your method to rise above the madness. First, goals provide the destination: where you want to go with a crisis. This endpoint is important because if you don't know where you want to go, you're not going to have the impetus to get moving from where you are now. Second, having a place you really want to go doesn't have a lot of value if you don't know how to get there. Goals provide the road map for getting to your destination in a crisis.

Keys to Effective Goal Setting

There has been an enormous amount of research that has studied how goal setting can be used most effectively. The acronym SMARTER represents the seven criteria found to get the most out of your goal setting (there are variations on what each letter in the acronym denotes, and I have chosen those that I find most useful).

Specific. Your goals should be specific to what you want to accomplish through the crisis. For example, if you had a heart attack due to an unhealthy lifestyle, you don't want to set a goal of "I want to live healthier" because it's too general. Instead, you want to identify what aspects of your lifestyle you want to improve. More specific goals are "I want to stop snacking between meals" and "I want to exercise four times a week." The more specific you can get, the more you can focus on what you need to do to improve that area.

Measurable. One of the most robust findings from the research on goal setting is that not having an adequate benchmark for success is quite ineffective. Instead of "do your best" goals, you want to give yourself a tangible measure toward which you can strive. Returning to the previous example of living a healthier life to prevent another heart attack, a measurable goal might be "I want to exercise four times a week for at least thirty minutes." This goal offers specific parameters around what you would need to do to help alleviate your health crisis and improve your fitness.

Accepted. Taking ownership of your crisis is essential for you to have any chance of putting it behind you. Ownership of your goals is no less important. Goals that are set by others will not inspire or motivate you fully because they come from outside of you. When goals aren't your own, you won't feel real buy-in to work toward them. Setting your own goals that you deeply believe in weaves them into the very fabric of your efforts. You will almost have no choice about whether you strive toward them because ownership compels you to give your very best effort in pursuit of your goals.

Realistic. You want to set goals that are realistic yet challenging. The fact is that there are a range of possible outcomes to a crisis, from complete failure to complete success with gradations in between. Depending on the type of crisis you experience, complete success may not be immediately possible, for example, getting a job with equal pay to the one you just lost. But you do want to aim as high as is reasonable given your situation because where you aim is often where you hit.

Think of it this way: If you set goals that are too low, they will have little motivational value because you know you can achieve them without much effort. Conversely, you don't want to set goals that are too high because you know you can't achieve them, which means you will have little incentive to put forth any effort. Instead, you want to set goals that are both realistic and challenging. Realistic means they are possible to achieve based on your capabilities. In terms of being challenging, your goals should lie just beyond what you think you can attain; then you will have to really extend yourself to have any chance of attaining them. You should aim to stretch yourself with each goal because that provocation is your greatest chance of succeeding.

> "One way to keep momentum going is to have constantly greater goals."—Michael Korda, English writer and novelist [14]

Time-limited. Open-ended goals aren't effective because there is no urgency behind them. The best goals have a time limit for their achievement, particularly in a crisis for which time is of the essence. This timeliness incentivizes you to begin right away and stick with your efforts to meet the self-imposed deadline or the one that has been imposed on you by the crisis. If your goals are challenging, you will feel especially motivated to put in the time and energy necessary to reach them by a deadline. For example, if you are running out of money and need to get a job soon, your timeline will be determined by the "drop-dead date" of your bank account, which will drive you to find a job as soon as possible.

Exciting. Your commitment to strive toward your goals during a crisis is partly driven by the emotions associated with those goals. As a result, you want to set goals that inspire and excite you. These emotions can be the deciding factor in whether you achieve your goals in the face of setbacks, failures, disappointment, fatigue, pain, and tedium. They can also help you counteract other emotions that are commonly associated with a crisis, such as fear, worry, frustration, anger, and despair. As you set goals for yourself, put them to the excitement test by asking yourself whether your goals generate strong and positive emotions in you. In the job crisis example, an exciting goal might be "I'm going to return to school so I can have a career I love."

Recorded. Another robust finding in the goal-setting research is that you are more likely to stay committed to your goals when you write them down on a piece of paper, rather than typing them into a computer or just thinking about them. The benefit appears to be due to several things. First, the physical act of writing your goals seems to somehow imprint them more deeply in your psyche. Second, writing them down makes the goals more tangible and real. Third, the explicitness of writing down your goals appears to create a greater sense of ownership and accountability that makes you feel more compelled to focus on and strive toward your goals. Fourth, writing helps you avoid a common mistake many people make when they complete their goal setting: filing the goals away and forgetting about them. Instead, take your written goals and put them up where you can see them regularly, like on your refrigerator or bathroom mirror. This constant reminder keeps your goals at the forefront of your mind, especially during a crisis. As a result, you stay focused on accomplishing them and have a better chance of ultimately putting the crisis behind you.

> "By recording your dreams and goals on paper, you set in motion the process of becoming the person you most want to be."—Mark Victor Hansen, motivational speaker and author [15]

In addition to the SMARTER criteria, there are several other guidelines that can be beneficial in goal setting and offer the maximum benefit as you work to overcome a crisis.

Focus on the Degree of Attainment

Even though setting goals has been studied for decades and we have a pretty clear picture of why, how, and when it works, goal setting is still an inexact science. What makes goal setting a less-than-precise endeavor is that it involves human beings, and in general, we are pretty unpredictable creatures. Moreover, responding successfully to a crisis is also an inexact science because crises are also capricious creatures. Most crises don't have a clearly defined prescription you can follow that assures the positive outcome you want. Due to these uncertainties, your focus when setting and striving for goals should be on your degree of attainment instead of absolute attainment. Let me explain.

Absolute attainment means accomplishing the goal in its entirety. For example, if your computer system has been hacked and your identity stolen, you can rectify the breach, but you can't guarantee that it will be completely and assuredly secured and your identity safeguarded. Given the inherent uncertainty of the situation, expecting absolute attainment is a recipe for failure as it leaves only a small window for accomplishing the goal and a very large window for falling short.

In contrast, degree of attainment emphasizes progress toward the goal. Returning to the security breach, if you have evidence that major threats to your computer system have been closed and there is no immediate indication that your identity has been used, you've done as much as possible for the moment. Then, you can use the information related to your improvement to modify the goal of future security accordingly, either by changing the goal outcome or simply extending the time needed to reach the goal.

Make Your Goals Public

Still another result commonly reported in the goal-setting research is that you are more likely to adhere to your goals if you make them public or share them with others. You might do this by showing them to your family or friends or even posting them on your social media for your followers to see. By doing so, you become accountable to everyone with whom you shared your goals. The upside to making a public declaration of your goals is that you will receive a lot of support and encouragement from those with whom you share. In addition to your personal ownership, this external accountability and optimism will motivate you to work even harder in pursuit of your goals.

Review Your Goals Regularly

As previously noted, it is difficult to establish precise goals that are achievable with certainty, particularly with a crisis. Consequently, it's important to view goal setting as a dynamic and ever-evolving process of creation, effort, review, adjustment, and recommitment. As such, you should make it a habit to review your goals frequently and compare them to your progress. It can also be helpful to review them with your support team, who can provide useful feedback you can use to make modifications that will further motivate you to pursue your crisis goals.

Types of Crisis Goals to Set

Goal setting in a crisis involves establishing a series of goals that start the big picture and get more specific and actionable as you strive to resolve a crisis. The different types of goals include

- *Long-term goals*: what you ultimately want to achieve related to the crisis (e.g., regain your health following a heart attack)
- *Outcome goals*: what you want to achieve in the near term (e.g., lose forty pounds and increase physical strength and stamina)
- *Process goals*: what you need to do to achieve the outcome goals (e.g., exercise and adopt healthier eating habits)
- *Lifestyle goals*: what you need to do in your general lifestyle to support the above goals (e.g., sleep and engage in a supportive social life)

Decide what you think are reasonable goals that will resolve the crisis you are experiencing using the SMARTER guidelines, as well as the other criteria I described. If you are unsure of what goals to set, I recommend that you sit down with your support team and prepare your goals collaboratively. Since your team knows you well, understands the crisis, and often has experience and perspective related to the crisis, they can help you set the best goals to overcome a crisis in a timely manner.

Epilogue

Lights, Camera . . .

Everything I've discussed in *How to Survive and Thrive* prepares you to tackle the crisis you face head-on and to replace a crisis mentality with an opportunity mindset. You have made a decision on what road you should take in response to the crisis and are committed to that road. Now it's time to take action! This can be scary because often there is no going back. What can make it even scarier is that there is no certainty that the road you choose will take you out of the crisis that has arisen. At the end of the day, you must take action because doing nothing guarantees that you will fail.

There are several important individual characteristics at the heart of taking appropriate action in response to a crisis. First, your willingness to move out of the rhythm and comfort of the life that existed before the crisis. Second, your openness to embrace, rather than resist, the changes that the crisis imposes on you. As the old Texas adage goes, "If all you ever do is all you've ever done, then all you'll ever get is all you ever got." And getting all you ever got isn't going to get you where you need to go in a crisis. And third, pursuing your crisis goals with conviction, resolve, and patience. Your ability to successfully resolve a crisis depends on you identifying goals early on, setting a clear path to those goals, and taking action in ways that will encourage their pursuit even in the face of adversity.

Being open to change makes your ability to take effective and purposeful action possible. While this may sound simple, when a crisis presents itself, the willingness to change is decidedly not easy. Remember, it's simple because all you have to do is decide to act based on a strategy that will facilitate action and a commitment to yourself to take action.

While that sounds all well and good, I've described many reasons why taking action is not easy. In fact, it is downright difficult. That's why many people don't take deliberate and committed action when it is needed most. As I highlighted in the two sections of this book, there are many obstacles that stand in the way of effective action in response to a crisis. In addition, taking action requires incredible commitment, time, energy, and effort.

Given these caveats, what is the point of accepting the monumental challenge of confronting a crisis head-on and taking action with determination, purpose, and resolve? The point is simple, yet profound: to find a desirable resolution that will release you from the life-sucking grip of the crisis. For some, the resolution might mean simply surviving. For others, it might be using the crisis as an opportunity—there's that word again!—to grow and thrive. Imagine being free from

- Fear
- Doubt
- Worry
- Frustration
- Anger
- Despair

The freedom that comes from tackling and putting a crisis behind you allows you the opportunity to find or reaffirm your capabilities, ignite your passions and drives, and harness the experience to make you a better person than you were before it took over your life. Some changes you may experience include

- Feeling more deeply
- Giving more freely
- Accepting more readily
- Hoping without reservation
- Choosing more wisely
- Engaging more completely

Once crisis has been resolved, regardless of whether it was to your satisfaction, you can achieve several essential goals. You will know that you did everything in your power to face and overcome the crisis with strength and dignity. At the end of your day, year, or life you can be sure that you will not have to experience the most frustrating of all emotions—regret. This also means you won't have to answer what may be the saddest question of all: "I wonder what could have been?"

There are no guarantees when it comes to a crisis because there is so much about a crisis that you can't control. Even with an opportunity mindset, there are no assurances that you achieve the outcome you want. Sadly, you may still lose your money, struggle in a life transition, have difficulty finding a new job, continue to be burdened with substance abuse, experience identity theft, get divorced, and, yes, even die. But those unfortunate outcomes are less likely to occur if you take control of one thing: yourself. Included within you are all of the areas that I shared with you in *How to Survive and Thrive*. If you can do that, your experience of the crisis will be far more manageable and relatively more enjoyable (at least as much as you can expect to feel during a crisis) even if things don't turn out the way you want. You will also look back on the crisis knowing that you "fought the good fight" and you did everything you could to respond effectively. And, although a crisis may or may not end the way you wanted it to, there is some consolation and even a modicum of pride in that.

Notes

INTRODUCTION

1. "Viktor E. Frankl Quotes," BrainyQuote, accessed August 21, 2018, https://www.brainyquote.com/quotes/viktor_e_frankl_160380.
2. "Ryszard Kapuscinski Quotes," PoemHunter.com, accessed August 21, 2018, https://www.poemhunter.com/ryszard-kapuscinski/quotations/.
3. "Richard M. Nixon Quotes," BrainyQuote, accessed August 21, 2018, https://www.brainyquote.com/authors/richard_m_nixon.
4. "Henry A. Kissinger Quotes," Successories.com, accessed August 21, 2018, https://www.successories.com/iquote/author/215/henry-a-kissinger-quotes/1.
5. "Maxwell Maltz," Top Results Academy, accessed August 21, 2018, https://topresultsacademy.com/authors/maxwell-maltz/#quotes.
6. "Robert Freeman Quote," Goodreads, accessed August 21, 2018, https://www.goodreads.com/quotes/63563-character-is-not-made-by-crisis-it-is-only-exhibited.
7. "Desperate Sayings," Sayings Point, accessed August 21, 2018, http://sayingspoint.com/desperate-sayings/.

YOUR AMYGDALA

1. "Books by and about Thomas Szasz," Quoteland.com, accessed August 11, 2018, http://www.quoteland.com/author/Thomas-Szasz-Quotes/8189/?pg=1.

199

1. INSTINCTS

1. "Marcus Tullius Cicero Quotes," BrainyQuote, accessed August 11, 2018, https://www.brainyquote.com/quotes/marcus_tullius_cicero_165874.
2. "Abraham Lincoln Quotes," BrainyQuote, accessed August 11, 2018, https://www.brainyquote.com/authors/abraham_lincoln.
3. "Queen Rania of Jordan Quotes," BrainyQuote, accessed August 11, 2018, https://www.brainyquote.com/authors/queen_rania_of_jordan.
4. "Ben Okri quotes," Goodreads, accessed August 11, 2018, https://www.goodreads.com/author/quotes/31425.Ben_Okri.
5. "Awareness Quotes," BrainyQuote, accessed August 11, 2018, https://www.brainyquote.com/topics/awareness.
6. "Acceptance Quotes," BrainyQuote, accessed August 11, 2018, https://www.brainyquote.com/topics/acceptance.
7. "Albert Einstein quotes," Goodreads, accessed August 11, 2018, https://www.goodreads.com/author/quotes/9810.Albert_Einstein.
8. R. Frost, "The Road Not Taken," Poets.org, accessed August 11, 2018, https://www.poets.org/poetsorg/poem/road-not-taken.
9. "Arnold Schwarzenegger Quotes," BrainyQuote, accessed August 11, 2018, https://www.brainyquote.com/quotes/arnold_schwarzenegger_166118.
10. "Venus Williams Quotes," BrainyQuote, accessed August 11, 2018, https://www.brainyquote.com/lists/authors/top_10_venus_williams_quotes.
11. "Rocky Quotes," BrainyQuote, accessed August 11, 2018, https://www.rottentomatoes.com/m/1017776_rocky/quotes.
12. J. Brown, "100 Dalai Lama Quotes That Will Change Your Life," Addicted 2 Success, accessed August 11, 2018, https://addicted2success.com/quotes/100-dalai-lama-quotes-that-will-change-your-life/.
13. W. E. Henley, "Invictus," Poets.org, accessed August 11, 2018, https://www.poets.org/poetsorg/poem/invictus.
14. "Rumi Quotes about Reflection," AZ Quotes, accessed August 11, 2018, https://www.azquotes.com/author/12768-Rumi/tag/reflection.
15. "Voltaire Quotes—Page 2," BrainyQuote, accessed August 11, 2018, https://www.brainyquote.com/authors/voltaire_2.

2. EMOTIONS

1. "Sport Psychology Quotes," Sport Psychology Quotes, accessed August 21, 2018, https://sportpsychquotes.wordpress.com/tag/emotionsfeelings/.
2. "Maya Angelou: Quotes," Goodreads, accessed August 21, 2018, https://www.goodreads.com/quotes/7593317-each-one-of-us-has-lived-through-some-devasta-tion-some.
3. "Randy Pausch: Quotes," Goodreads, accessed August 21, 2018, https://www.goodreads.com/quotes/43459-we-cannot-change-the-cards-we-are-dealt-just-how.
4. "Marianne Williamson Quotes," BrainyQuote, accessed August 21, 2018, https://www.brainyquote.com/quotes/marianne_williamson_635533.
5. "Ray A. Davis: Quotes," Goodreads, accessed August 21, 2018, https://www.goodreads.com/author/quotes/8200672.Ray_A_Davis.
6. "Nelson Mandela: Quotes," Goodreads, accessed August 21, 2018, https://www.goodreads.com/author/quotes/367338.Nelson_Mandela.

7. "Guy Kawasaki: Quotes," Goodreads, accessed August 21, 2018, https://www.goodreads.com/author/quotes/21269.Guy_Kawasaki.

8. "Mark Twain Quotes," BrainyQuote, accessed August 21, 2018, https://www.brainyquote.com/quotes/mark_twain_138540.

9. "Anger Quotes," BrainyQuote, accessed August 21, 2018, https://www.brainyquote.com/topics/anger.

10. "Anne Lamott: Quotes," Goodreads, accessed August 21, 2018, https://www.goodreads.com/quotes/6830146-almost-everything-will-work-again-if-you-unplug-it.

3. REACTIONS

1. "React Quotes," BrainyQuote, accessed August 13, 2018, https://www.brainyquote.com/quotes/epictetus_149126?src=t_react.

2. "Lou Holtz Quote," QuoteCities, accessed August 7, 2018, https://quotecites.com/quote/Lou_Holtz_1782.

3. "William Shakespeare Quotes," BrainyQuote, accessed August 13, 2018, https://www.brainyquote.com/quotes/william_shakespeare_109527.

4. "Laird Hamilton Quote," Quote Fancy, accessed December 10, 2018, https://quotefancy.com/quote/1552111/Laird-Hamilton-Make-sure-your-worst-enemy-doesn-t-live-between-your-two-ears.

5. "Dr. Norman Vincent Peale Quotes," BrainyQuote, accessed August 7, 2018, https://www.brainyquote.com/quotes/norman_vincent_peale_390722.

6. "Ovid Quote," Quote Fancy, accessed August 13, 2018, https://quotefancy.com/quote/883327/Ovid-Take-rest-a-field-that-has-rested-gives-a-bountiful-crop.

7. "Leonardo da Vinci Quote," Quote Fancy, accessed August 13, 2018, https://quotefancy.com/quote/26132/Leonardo-da-Vinci-Every-now-and-then-go-away-have-a-little-relaxation-for-when-you-come.

8. "Problems Quotes," BrainyQuote, accessed August 13, 2018, https://www.brainyquote.com/quotes/albert_einstein_121993?src=t_problems.

9. "Abraham Lincoln Quotes," BrainyQuote, accessed August 13, 2018, https://www.brainyquote.com/quotes/abraham_lincoln_109275.

10. "Helen Keller Quotes," BrainyQuote, accessed August 13, 2018, https://www.brainyquote.com/quotes/helen_keller_382259.

4. VALUES

1. "Roy E. Disney: Quotes," BrainyQuote, accessed December 10, 2018, https://www.brainyquote.com/quotes/roy_e_disney_183365.

2. "Remarks by the First Lady at Tuskegee University Commencement Address," the White House, accessed August 12, 2018, https://obamawhitehouse.archives.gov/the-press-office/2015/05/09/remarks-first-lady-tuskegee-university-commencement-address.

3. "Marsha Sinetar Quote," PassItOn.com, accessed December 10, 2018, https://www.passiton.com/inspirational-quotes/4079-lifes-ups-and-downs-provide-windows-of.

4. "Tony Stewart Quotes," AZ Quotes, accessed December 10, 2018, https://www.azquotes.com/quote/1024495.

5. "Parker J. Palmer: Quotes," Goodreads, accessed December 10, 2018, https://www.goodreads.com/quotes/762982-before-you-tell-your-life-what-you-intend-to-do.

6. D. Tweney, "Apple CEO Tim Cook Tells Graduates: Values and Justice Belong in the Workplace," accessed December 10, 2018, https://venturebeat.com/2015/05/17/apple-ceo-tim-cook-tells-graduates-values-and-justice-belong-in-the-workplace/.

7. C. Jung, *Carl Jung Letters* (Vol. 1) (Princeton, NJ: Princeton University Press, 1916).

8. "Japanese Proverb: Quotes," Goodreads, accessed December 16, 2018, https://www.goodreads.com/author/quotes/7917117.Japanese_Proverb.

9. "Dr. Seuss Quote," Quote Fancy, accessed December 10, 2018, https://quotefancy.com/quote/74/Dr-Seuss-You-have-brains-in-your-head-You-have-feet-in-your-shoes-You-can-steer-yourself.

5. INVESTMENT

1. "Wayne Dyer Quote," Fearless Motivation, accessed May 8, 2018, https://www.fearlessmotivation.com/2016/05/23/change-the-way-you-look-at-things-and-the-things-you-look-at-change/.

2. "Erik Erikson Quotes," BrainyQuote, accessed May 8, 2018, https://www.brainyquote.com/quotes/erik_erikson_600792.

3. "13 of Maya Angelou's Best Quotes," *USA Today*, accessed May 8, 2018, https://www.usatoday.com/story/news/nation-now/2014/05/28/maya-angelou-quotes/9663257/
.

4. "Jana Kingsford Quote," JanaKingsford.com, accessed May 8, 2018, http://www.janakingsford.com/startchanging/5-6/.

5. "Goal Quotes," BrainyQuote, accessed May 8, 2018, https://www.brainyquote.com/quotes/earl_nightingale_383343?src=t_goals.

6. M. Hingson, *Thunder Dog: The True Story of a Blind Man, His Guide Dog, and the Triumph of Trust* (Nashville: Thomas Nelson, 2012, p. 74).

7. "Communication," Life Hack, accessed May 8, 2018, https://www.lifehack.org/articles/communication/sometimes-have-let-whats-killing.html.

8. K. Cherry, "Quotes from Albert Bandura on His Theories," Very Well Mind, accessed May 8, 2018, https://www.verywellmind.com/albert-bandura-quotes-2795687.

9. "Zig Ziglar Quotes," BrainyQuote, accessed May 8, 2018, https://www.brainyquote.com/quotes/zig_ziglar_617769.

10. "William Shakespeare: Quotes," Goodreads, accessed May 8, 2018, https://www.goodreads.com/quotes/276750-expectation-is-the-root-of-all-heartache.

11. "Tommy Lasorda Quotes," AZ Quotes, accessed December 10, 2018, https://www.azquotes.com/quote/168879.

12. G. A. Shelley, "Goal Setting: A New Way to Think About Goals and Goal-Setting—Part I," Championship Coaches Network, accessed May 8, 2018http://www.championshipcoachesnetwork.com/public/Goal_Getting_A
_New_Way_to_Think_About_Goals_and_GoalSetting_Part_One.cfm.

13. "Bruce Lee: Quotes," Goodreads, accessed May 8, 2018, https://www.goodreads.com/quotes/48713-the-great-mistake-is-to-anticipate-the-outcome.

6. ATTITUDES

1. "Attitude Is a Little Thing That Makes a Big Difference," Quote Investigator, accessed August 21, 2018, https://quoteinvestigator.com/2013/03/13/attitude-little-big/.
2. "Control Quotes," BrainyQuote, accessed August 21, 2018, https://www.brainyquote.com/topics/control.
3. "25 Quotes to Encourage You through the Storm," SkipPrichard, accessed August 21, 2018, https://www.skipprichard.com/25-quotes-to-encourage-you-through-the-storm/.
4. "55 Inspiring Quotes That Show the Power of Emotional Intelligence," Inc., accessed August 21, 2018, https://www.inc.com/gordon-tredgold/55-inspiring-quotes-that-show-the-importance-of-emotional-intelligence.html.
5. "20 Quotes to Inspire Responsibility," Habits for Wellbeing, accessed August 21, 2018, https://www.habitsforwellbeing.com/20-quotes-to-inspire-responsibility/.
6. "20 Quotes to Inspire Responsibility."
7. "Roger Crawford Quote," Quote Fancy, accessed August 21, 2018, https://quotefancy.com/quote/34749/Roger-Crawford-Being-challenged-in-life-is-inevitable-being-defeated-is-optional.
8. "Planning Quotes," Goodreads, accessed August 21, 2018,https://www.goodreads.com/quotes/tag/planning.
9. "People May Hear Your Words but They Feel Your Attitude," MBA Rendezvous, accessed August 21, 2018, https://www.mbarendezvous.com/xat/people-may-hear-your-words-but-they-feel-your-attitude/.
10. "Planning Quotes."
11. N. Johnson and C. Louis, "Failing to Plan Is Planning to Fail," EE Times, accessed August 21, 2018, https://www.eetimes.com/author.asp?section_id=36&doc_id=1286981.
12. "James Allen Quote," Quote Fancy, accessed December 10, 2018, https://quotefancy.com/quote/31910/James-Allen-Self-control-is-strength-Right-thought-is-mastery-Calmness-is-power.
13. J. Rampton, "15 Uplifting Quotes for Positive Vibes," Success, November 6, 2015, accessed August 21, 2018, https://www.success.com/15-uplifting-quotes-for-positive-vibes/.
14. "Erika Taylor: Quotes," Goodreads, accessed August 22, 2018, https://www.goodreads.com/quotes/761884-sometimes-you-have-to-take-a-step-back-to-move.
15. J. Michael, "Pause: 15 Quotes on Why You Should Take Breaks, Relax, Play," B Plans, accessed August 22, 2018, https://articles.bplans.com/pause-quotes-take-breaks-relax-play/.
16. "The Top 10 Quotes to Inspire You to Be Yourself," Goalcast, accessed August 22, 2018, https://www.goalcast.com/2017/06/22/the-top-10-quotes-to-inspire-you-to-be-yourself/.
17. "Lao Tzu: Quotes," Goodreads, accessed August 22, 2018, https://www.goodreads.com/quotes/21535-the-journey-of-a-thousand-miles-begins-with-a-single.
18. "Battle Quotes," BrainyQuote, accessed August 22, 2018, https://www.brainyquote.com/topics/battles.
19. "Ownership Quotes," AZ Quotes, accessed August 22, 2018, https://www.azquotes.com/quotes/topics/ownership.html?p=3.

20. "Deepak Chopra," Quotesville.net, accessed August 22, 2018, https://quotesville-net.wordpress.com/2014/06/27/when-you-blame-and-criticize-others-you-are-avoiding-some-truth-about-yourself-deepak-chopra/.

21. "Brené Brown: Quotes," Goodreads, accessed August 12, 2018, https://www.goodreads.com/quotes/641983-if-you-own-this-story-you-get-to-write.

22. "Quotes about Exploration," Art Quotes, accessed August 22, 2018, http://www.art-quotes.com/getquotes.php?catid=107#.W316Bi2ZOuU.

23. M. Riddick, "Today's Conveyancer," accessed August 12, 2018, https://www.todaysconveyancer.co.uk/guest-writers/if-opportunity-doesnt-knock-build-a-door-milton-berle/.

24. "Detail Quotes," BrainyQuote, accessed August 22, 2018, https://www.brainyquote.com/quotes/charles_r_swindoll_389839?src=t_detail.

25. "Hold the Vision, Trust the Process," Seed Growth, accessed August 22, 2018, https://seedgrowth.wordpress.com/2015/09/26/hold-the-visiontrust-the-process/.

26. J. DeMers, "51 Quotes to Inspire Success in Your Life and Business," Inc., accessed August 22, 2018, https://www.inc.com/jayson-demers/51-quotes-to-inspire-success-in-your-life-and-business.html.

27. "Quotes for Attitude," Motivating Quotes, accessed August 22, 2018, https://www.motivatingquotes.com/attitude.htm.

28. "Moments Sayings and Quotes," Wise Old Sayings, accessed August 22, 2018, http://www.wiseoldsayings.com/moments-quotes/ (Dan Millman).

29. "107 Challenge Quotes," Wow 4 U, accessed August 22, 2018, https://www.wow4u.com/challenges/.

30. "Jon Kabat-Zinn: Quotes," Goodreads, accessed August 22, 2018, https://www.goodreads.com/author/quotes/8750.Jon_Kabat_Zinn.

7. MINDSET

1. "T. S. Eliot Quotes," BrainyQuote, accessed August 30, 2018, https://www.brainyquote.com/authors/t_s_eliot.

2. "James Branch Cabell Quotes," BrainyQuote, accessed August 30, 2018, https://www.brainyquote.com/authors/james_branch_cabell.

3. "James Branch Cabell Quotes," BrainyQuote, accessed August 30, 2018, https://www.brainyquote.com/authors/james_branch_cabell.

4. "Charlie Chaplin: Quotes," Goodreads, accessed August 30, 2018. https://www.goodreads.com/quotes/77677-you-ll-never-find-a-rainbow-if-you-re-looking-down.

5. "Sarah Dessen: Quotes," Goodreads, accessed August 30, 2018, https://www.goodreads.com/quotes/228925-if-you-expect-the-worst-you-ll-never-be-disap-pointed.

6. "Dwight D. Eisenhower Quotes," BrainyQuote, accessed August 30, 2018, https:/ /www.brainyquote.com/quotes/dwight_d_eisenhower_149110.

7. "Martin Luther King, Jr. Quotes," BrainyQuote, accessed August 30, 2018, https://www.brainyquote.com/quotes/martin_luther_king_jr_297522.

8. "Roy T. Bennet: Quotes," Goodreads, accessed August 30, 2018, https://www.goodreads.com/quotes/7536187-if-you-want-to-be-happy-do-not-dwell-in.

9. "Albert Einstein: Quotes," Goodreads, accessed August 30, 2018, https://www.goodreads.com/quotes/424937-failure-is-success-in-progress.

10. "Leonardo da Vinci Quote," Goodreads, accessed August 30, 2018, https://www.goodreads.com/quotes/8684-one-can-have-no-smaller-or-greater-mastery-than-mastery.

11. "Chaos Quotes," BrainyQuote, accessed December 10, 2018, https://www.brainyquote.com/topics/chaos.

12. "Roy T. Bennett: Quotes," Goodreads, accessed August 30, 2018, https://www.goodreads.com/quotes/7708835-it-s-only-after-you-ve-stepped-outside-your-comfort-zone.

13. "Chinese Proverb," accessed August 30, 2018, https://me.me/i/pearls-dont-lie-at-the-sea-shore-if-you-want-one-18209759.

14. "Denis Waitley Quotes," BrainyQuote, accessed August 30, 2018, https://www.brainyquote.com/quotes/denis_waitley_146949.

15. "Muhammad Ali Quotes," BrainyQuote, accessed August 30, 2018, https://www.brainyquote.com/quotes/muhammad_ali_148633.

16. "Ralph Waldo Emerson: Quote," Goodreads, accessed August 30, 2018, https://www.goodreads.com/quotes/375347-do-not-be-too-timid-and-squeam ish-about-your-actions.

17. "Margaret Spellings Quote," Quote Fancy, accessed August 30, 2018, https://quotefancy.com/quote/1745785/Margaret-Spellings-If-all-you-ever-do-is-all-you-ve-ever-done-then-all-you-ll-ever-get.

18. "David Nicholls: Quotes," Goodreads, accessed August 30, 2018, https://www.goodreads.com/quotes/295765-this-is-where-it-all-begins-everything-starts-here-today.

19. "Mark Twain Quote," PassItOn.com, accessed August 30, 2018, https://www.passiton.com/inspirational-quotes/7114-twenty-years-from-now-you-will-be-more.

20. "John Burroughs Quotes," BrainyQuote, accessed August 30, 2018, https://www.brainyquote.com/quotes/john_burroughs_119899.

8. MENTAL MUSCLES

1. "C. G. Jung: Quotes," Goodreads, accessed July 5, 2018, https://www.goodreads.com/quotes/50795-i-am-not-what-happened-to-me-i-am-what.

2. "Franklin D. Roosevelt Quote," Quote Fancy, accessed December 10, 2018, https://quotefancy.com/quote/31137/Franklin-D-Roosevelt-The-only-limit-to-our-real-ization-of-tomorrow-will-be-our-doubts.

3. "Lena Horne Quote," Pinterest, accessed December 10, 2018, https://www.pinterest.com/pin/199354720980549952/?lp=true.

4. "Samuel Johnson Quotes," BrainyQuote, accessed June 4, 2018, https://www.brainyquote.com/quotes/samuel_johnson_122529.

5. "Marcus Garvey Quotes," Goodreads, accessed June 4, 2018, https://www.goodreads.com/quotes/108316-if-you-haven-t-confidence-in-self-you-are-twice-defeated.

6. "Arthur Ashe Quotes," BrainyQuote, accessed July 5, 2018, https://www.brainyquote.com/quotes/arthur_ashe_109755.

7. "Nicholas Cage Quotes," AZ Quotes, accessed November 11, 2016, http://www.azquotes.com/quote/1178912.

8. "Ruth Fishel Quote," MeMe, accessed December 10, 2018, https://me.me/i/brain-wave-tests-prove-that-when-we-use-positive-words-8564685.

9. "Charles B. Newcomb Quotes and Quotations," Famous Quotes and Authors, accessed December 10, 2018, http://www.famousquotesand authors.com/authors/charles_b_newcomb_quotes.html.

10. J. Scearce, "22 Quotes about Self-Confidence That Will Brighten Up Your Life," Lifehack, accessed November 11, 2016, http://www.lifehack.org/articles/communication/22-quotes-about-self-confidence.html.

11. A. Meah, "35 Inspirational Walt Disney Quotes on Success," accessed July 7, 2018, http://awakenthegreatnesswithin.com/35-inspirational-walt-dis ney-quotes-on-success/.

12. andysinpiration, "Charles Noble Quote," Instagram, accessed June 4, 2018, https://www.instagram.com/p/BBcrwouGKTH/.

13. "George Horace Lorimer: Quotes," GoodReads, accessed June 4, 2018, http:// www.goodreads.com/quotes/274879-you-ve-got-to-get-up-every-morn ing-with-determination.

14. Unknown quote, Board of Wisdom, accessed June 4, 2018, https://boardofwisdom.com/togo/Quotes/ShowQuote?msgid=178561#.WxWiu0gvzDc.

15. Unknown quote, Inspired to Reality, accessed June 4, 2018, https:// www.inspiredtoreality.com/pin/stop-overthinking-youre-only-creating-prob lems-that-arent-there/.

16. Unknown quote, Pinterest, accessed June 4, 2018, https://in.pinterest .com/pin/545498573588197615/?lp=true.

9. PREPARATION

1. "Johann Wolfgang von Goethe Quote," Faust.com, accessed September 8, 2018, https://www.faust.com/books/authors/johann-wolfgang-von-goethe/.

2. "Clarity Quotes," BrainyQuote, accessed September 8, 2018, https:// www.brainyquote.com/topics/clarity.

3. "Optimism and Pessimism Quotes," AZ Quotes, accessed September 8, 2018, http://www.azquotes.com/quote/307099?ref=optimism-and-pessimism.

4. "Steve Maraboli Quotes," Goodreads, accessed September 8, 2018, https:// www.goodreads.com/quotes/319245-it-s-a-lack-of-clarity-that-creates-chaos-and-frus-tration.

5. "Beyond Quotes," BrainyQuote, accessed September 8, 2018, https:// www.brainyquote.com/quotes/denis_waitley_146953?src=t_beyond.

6. Q. Seale, "Quotes about Creativity, Imagination, and Innovation," KeepInspiring.me, accessed September 8, 2018, http://www.keepinspir ing.me/quotes-about-creativity-imagination-and-innovation/.

7. "Uncertainty Quotes," BrainyQuote, accessed September 8, 2018, https:// www.brainyquote.com/quotes/jim_carrey_360647?src=t_uncertainty.

8. "Decisiveness Quotes," Goodreads, accessed September 8, 2018, https:// www.goodreads.com/quotes/tag/decisiveness.

9. "Daniel Kahneman Quotes," BrainyQuote, accessed September 8, 2018, https:// www.brainyquote.com/quotes/daniel_kahneman_567118.

10. "Daniel Kahneman Quotes," BrainyQuote, accessed September 8, 2018, https:// www.brainyquote.com/quotes/daniel_kahneman_446049.

11. "Albert Einstein Quotes," Goodreads, accessed September 8, 2018, https:// www.goodreads.com/quotes/966500-the-framing-of-a-problem-is-often-far-more-essential.

12. "Assemble Quotes," BrainyQuote, accessed September 8, 2018, https://www.brainyquote.com/quotes/tim_gunn_493188?src=t_assemble.

13. "Patience Quotes," BrainyQuote, accessed September 8, 2018, https://www.brainyquote.com/quotes/saadi_155337?src=t_patience.

14. L. Sweatt, "18 Motivational Quotes about Successful Goal Setting," Success, December 29, 2016, accessed September 8, 2018, http://www.success.com/article/18-motivational-quotes-about-successful-goal-setting.

15. "Mark Victor Hansen Quotes," BrainyQuote, accessed September 8, 2018, https://www.brainyquote.com/quotes/mark_victor_hansen_160469.

Bibliography

INTRODUCTION

Bernstein, J. *Crisis Manager Internet Newsletter about Crisis Management*, October 15, 2002. https://www.bernsteincrisismanagement.com/newsletter/crisismgr021015.html.

BrainyQuote. "Viktor E. Franl Quotes." https://www.brainyquote.com/quotes/viktor_e_frankl_160380.

Business Dictionary. S.v. "opportunity." http://www.businessdictionary.com/definition/opportunity.html.

Course Hero. "Response: A Crisis Is Defined as a Time of Intense Difficulty, Trouble, or Danger." https://www.coursehero.com/file/p7lkm5kj/Response-A-crisis-is-defined-as-a-time-of-intense-difficulty-trouble-or-danger/.

Dictionary.com. S.v. "opportunity." http://www.dictionary.com/browse/opportunity.

The Free Dictionary. S.v. "crisis." https://www.thefreedictionary.com/crisis.

Merriam-Webster. S.v. "opportunity." https://www.merriam-webster.com/dictionary/opportunity.

Oxford Dictionaries. S.v. "crisis." https://en.oxforddictionaries.com/definition/crisis.

TeachingHistory.org. "The Only Thing We Have to Fear Is Fear Itself." http://teachinghistory.org/history-content/ask-a-historian/24468.

CHAPTER 1

Call, J. A. "The Anatomy of Fear: Prepare to Deal with Your Fear Response to a Crisis." *Psychology Today*, July 28, 2008. https://www.psychologytoday.com/blog/crisis-center/200807/the-anatomy-fear.

Dahlitz, M. "Prefrontal Cortex." *Neuropsychotherapist*, January 4, 2017. https://www.neuropsychotherapist.com/prefrontal-cortex/

Dictionary.com. S.v. "thrive [Def. 1 and 2]." (n.d.). In *Dictionary Online*. Retrieved August 13, 2018, from https://www.dictionary.com/browse/thrive?s=t.

Etymonline Online. S.v. "possess (v.)." https://www.etymonline.com/word/possess.

Merriam-Webster. S.v. "self-possession." https://www.merriam-webster.com/diction-ary/self-possession.

———. S.v. "survival [Def. 1b]." https://www.merriam-webster.com/dictionary/survi-val.

Military Factory Online. "Course of Action [Def. 1]." https://www.militaryfactory.com/dictionary/military-terms-defined.asp?term_id=1374.

Taylor, J. "Is Our Survival Instinct Failing Us?" *HuffPost,* June 13, 2012. https://www.huffingtonpost.com/dr-jim-taylor/is-our-survival-instinct-_b_1588157.html.

Wikipedia. S.v. "amygdala." https://en.wikipedia.org/wiki/Amygdala.

CHAPTER 2

De Becker, G. *The Gift of Fear.* New York: Dell, 1997.

Flanagan, C. "Holding Out for a Hero—5 Misconceptions about Courage." *Baby Proof Your Life* (blog). https://www.babyproofyourlife.com/misconceptions-courage/.

Google Dictionary. S.v. "equanimity." https://www.google.com/search?q=equanimity+definition&rlz=1C1CHFX_enUS757US758&oq=equanit&aqs=chrome.2.69i57j0l5.3641j0j9&sourceid=chrome&ie=UTF-8.

Haikem, M. "More Than 10,000 Suicides Tied to Economic Crisis, Study Says." *Forbes,* July 12, 2014. https://www.forbes.com/sites/melaniehaiken/2014/06/12/more-than-10000-suicides-tied-to-economic-crisis-study-says/#4fa31c2a7ae2.

Medina, J. J. "The Genetics of Temperament—An Update." *Psychiatric Times,* March 10, 2010. http://www.psychiatrictimes.com/cultural-psychiatry/genetics-tempera-ment-update.

Medicine Encyclopedia. S.v. "perceived control—processes of control." http://medi-cine.jrank.org/pages/377/Control-Perceived-Processes-control.html.

Merriam-Webster. S.v. "courage." https://www.merriam-webster.com/dictionary/cou-rage.

Wikipedia. S.v. "United Airlines Flight 93." https://en.wikipedia.org/wiki/Unit-ed_Airlines_Flight_93.

CHAPTER 3

The American Institute of Stress. https://www.stress.org/emotional-and-social-support/

Bhardwaj, N. "Crisis Management." SlideShare. https://www.slideshare.net/nupsb/cri-sis-management-types-and-examples.

Dictionary.com. S.v. "panic." http://www.dictionary.com/browse/panic.

Donne, J. "No Man Is an Island." Poetry. https://web.cs.dal.ca/~johnston/poetry/is-land.html.

Klass, P. "Why Handwriting Is Still Essential in the Keyboard Age." *Well* (*New York Times* blog), June 20, 2016. https://well.blogs.nytimes.com/2016/06/20/why-hand-writing-is-still-essential-in-the-keyboard-age/.

Mayo Clinic Staff. "Stress Relief from Laughter? It's No Joke." Mayo Clinic. https://www.mayoclinic.org/healthy-lifestyle/stress-management/in-depth/stress-relief/art-20044456.

Sleep Foundation. "National Sleep Foundation Recommended New Sleep Times." Press release, February 2, 2015. https://sleepfoundation.org/press-release/national-sleep-foundation-recommends-new-sleep-times.

Study.com. "Buffering Hypothesis: Definition & Examples." https://study.com/acade-my/lesson/buffering-hypothesis-definition-examples.html.

———. "Mass Hysteria & Moral Panic: Definitions, Causes & Examples." https://study.com/academy/lesson/mass-hysteria-moral-panic-definitions-causes-examples.html.

CHAPTER 4

Bodytomy. "Functions of the Cerebral Cortex." https://bodytomy.com/cerebral-cortex-function.

Brannigan, P. *This Is a Call: The Life and Times of Dave Grohl*. Boston, MA: Da Capo Press, 2011.

Business Dictionary. S.v. "values." http://www.businessdictionary.com/definition/values.html.

Cambridge Dictionary. S.v. "values." https://dictionary.cambridge.org/us/dictionary/english/values.

Creswell, J. D., Welch, W. T., Taylor, S. E., Sherman, D. K., Gruenewald, T. L., and Mann, T. Affirmation of Personal Values Buffers Neuroendocrine and Psychological Stress Responses. *Psychological Science* 16, no. 11 (2005): 846–51.

Descartes, R. *Discourse on Method; and, Meditations on First Philosophy*. Indianapolis, IN: Hackett, 1993.

Dictionary.com. S.v. "adaptable." http://www.dictionary.com/browse/adaptability?s=t.

———. S.v. "courage." http://www.dictionary.com/browse/courage?s=t.

———. S.v. "resolve." http://www.dictionary.com/browse/resolve?s=t.

Ernst, M., Maheu, F. S., Schroth, E., Hardin, J., Golan, L. G., Cameron, J., Allen, R., et al. "Amygdala Function in Adolescents with Congenital Adrenal Hyperplasia: A Model for the Study of Early Steroid Abnormalities." *Neuropsychologia* 45, no. 9 (2007): 2104–113.

Hayes, S. C. *Get out of Your Mind and into Your Life: The New Acceptance and Commitment Therapy*. Oakland, CA: New Harbinger Publications, 2005.

Hayes, S. C., Levin, M. E., Plumb-Vilardaga, J., Villatte, J. L., and Pistorello, J. "Acceptance and Commitment Therapy and Contextual Behavioral Science: Examining the Progress of a Distinctive Model of Behavioral and Cognitive Therapy." *Behavior Therapy* 44, no. 2 (2013): 180–98.

Kaipa, P. "What Wise Leaders Always Follow." *Harvard Business Law Review*, January 18, 2012. https://hbr.org/2012/01/what-wise-leaders-always-follow.

Merriam-Webster. S.v. "resilience." https://www.merriam-webster.com/dictionary/resilience.

Pavlina, S. "List of Values." *Steve Pavlina* (blog), November 29, 2004. https://www.stevepavlina.com/blog/2004/11/list-of-values/.

Positively Positive. "PositiveQuotes." https://www.positivelypositive.com/quotes/fall-seven-times-stand-up-eight/.

Verplanken, B., and Holland, R. W. Motivated Decision Making: Effects of Activation and Self-Centrality of Values on Choices and Behavior." *Journal of Personality and Social Psychology* 82, no. 3 (2002): 434.

CHAPTER 6

Barkham, P. "The Extraordinary Story behind Danny Boyle's 127 Hours." *Guardian*, December 15, 2010. https://www.theguardian.com/film/2010/dec/15/story-danny-boyles-127-hours.

Barney, L. "Bethany Hamilton: Surfing with Only One Arm Isn't as Hard as Beating the Stigma." *Guardian*, August 25, 2016. https://www.theguardian.com/sport/2016/aug/25/bethany-hamilton-surfing-espy-award.

Beilock, S. "The Power of Expressing Yourself." *Psychology Today*, September 19, 2012. https://www.psychologytoday.com/us/blog/choke/201209/the-power-expressing-yourself.

BrainyQuote. "Epictetus Quotes." https://www.brainyquote.com/quotes/epictetus_149126.

Bruce, E. "The Devil Is in the Details." Historically Speaking, May 31, 2018. https://idiomation.wordpress.com/2014/01/22/the-devil-is-in-the-details/.

Foster, J. "Whether You Think You Can . . . or Whether You Think You Can't . . . You're Right!" Wall Street Insanity, February 25, 2013. https://wallstreetinsanity.com/whether-you-think-you-can-or-whether-you-think-you-cant-youre-right/.

Google Dictionary. S.v. "attitude." https://www.google.com/search?rlz=1C1CHFX_enUS757US758&ei=hKbsWprmIYiZ0gK9xLOoDg&q=attitude+definition&oq=attitude+def&gs_l=psy-ab.3.0.35i39k1j0j0i20i264k1j0l7.2470.5009.0.6592.12.8.4.0.0.0.100.657.7j1.8.0..2..0...1.1.64.psy-ab..0.12.687...0i67k1j0i131i67k1j0i10k1j0i22i30k1.0.O-mCReN-cRU4.

McLeod, S. "Attitudes and Behaviors." SimplyPsychology, updated 2018. https://www.simplypsychology.org/attitudes.html.

Newman, R. "What We Can All Learn from Steve Jobs." *US News*, August 25, 2011. https://www.usnews.com/news/blogs/rick-newman/2011/08/25/what-we-can-all-learn-from-steve-jobs.

Pinterest. Quote saved from Lisa Marie. https://www.pinterest.com/pin/8373949282618610/?lp=true.

University of Wisconsin–Milwaukee. "Christian Avery." March 24, 2016. https://uwm.edu/education/life-changing-illness-leads-to-a-new-career-in-counseling/.

CHAPTER 7

Better Life Coaching Blog. "The Two Travelers: A Story about Optimism." July 30, 2010. https://betterlifecoachingblog.com/2010/07/30/the-two-travellers-a-story-about-optimism/.

Dictionary.com. S.v. "optimism." http://www.dictionary.com/browse/optimism
———. S.v. "risk." http://www.dictionary.com/browse/risk.

Google Dictionary. S.v. "optimism." https://www.google.com/search?rlz=1C1CHFX_enUS757US758&ei=iFL7WuuHPMGT0wKHtLyADA&q=optimism+definition&oq=optimism+definition&gs_l=psy-ab.3..35i39k1l2j0i7i30k1l2j0j0i7i30k1l5.3204.4146.0.5269.8.8.0.0.0.0.115.522.7j1.8.0....0...1.1.64.psy-ab..2.6.381...0i67k1.0.VHt-GPwQnx0.
———. S.v. "pessimissm." https://www.google.com/search?q=pessimism+definition&rlz=1C1CHFX_enUS757US758&oq=pessimism&aqs=chrome.3.69i57j0l5.6742j1j7&sourceid=chrome&ie=UTF-8.

Owens, L. "8 Strategies for Boosting Your Optimism." LethiaOwens.com, 2018. http://lethiaowens.com/8-strategies-for-boosting-your-optimism/.

Oxford Dictionary. S.v. "despair." https://en.oxforddictionaries.com/definition/despair.

Paul, A. M. "The Uses and Abuses of Pessimism." *Psychology Today*, November 1, 2011. https://www.psychologytoday.com/us/articles/201111/the-uses-and-abuses-optimism-and-pessimism.

Rabahi, N. "What Is the Difference between an Error of Omission and an Error of Commission?" Bayt, April 24, 2016. https://www.bayt.com/en/specialties/q/285213/what-is-the-difference-between-an-error-of-omission-and-an-error-of-commission/.

RealBuzz.com. "11 Ways to Become an Optimist." https://www.realbuzz.com/articles-interests/health/article/11-ways-to-become-an-optimist/.

Steinhibur, B. "How to Train Your Brian to Be More Optimistic." NBC News, August 14, 2017. https://www.nbcnews.com/better/health/how-train-your-brain-be-more-optimistic-ncna795231.

Study.com. "How Seligman's Learned Helplessness Theory Applies to Human Depression and Stress." https://study.com/academy/lesson/how-seligmans-learned-helplessness-theory-applies-to-human-depression-and-stress.html.

CHAPTER 8

Cambridge Dictionary. S.v. "determination." https://dictionary.cambridge.org/us/dictionary/english/determination.

Collins Dictionary. S.v. "determination." https://www.collinsdictionary.com/us/dictionary/english/determination.

Redmond, B. F. "Goal Setting Theory." Confluence. https://wikispaces.psu.edu/display/PSYCH484/6.+Goal+Setting+Theory.

CHAPTER 9

Cialdini, R. "Are Human Decisions Eminently Rational, Hopelessly Irrational, or Neither?" https://www.influenceatwork.com/inside-influence-report/are-human-decisions-eminently-rational-hopelessly-irrational-or-neither/.

DC Database. "Htrae." http://dc.wikia.com/wiki/Htrae.

Delventhal, S. "One Thing to Never Do When the Stock Market Goes Down." Investopedia, June 5, 2018. https://www.investopedia.com/articles/investing/030716/one-thing-never-do-when-stock-market-goes-down.asp.

Frye, M. *The Politics of Reality: Essays in Feminist Theory*. Berkeley: Crossing Press, 2007.

Haggarty-Weir, C. "Cognitive Biases and 'Doing Your Own Research,' Part 1—Decision Making, Belief and Behavioural Biases." Mostly Science, February 25, 2013. https://mostlyscience.com/2013/02/doing-your-own-research-cognitive-biases-and-you-part-1-decision-making-belief-and-behavioural-biases/.

Kahneman, D., D. Lovallo, and O. Sibony. "Before You Make That Big Decision." *Harvard Business Review*. https://hbr.org/web/2013/06/assessment/before-you-make-that-big-decision.

Latham, G. P. "Goal-Setting Theory: Causal Relationships, Mediators, and Moderators." Oxford Research Encyclopedias: Psychology. http://psychology.oxfordre.com/view/10.1093/acrefore/9780190236557.001.0001/acrefore-9780190236557-e-12.

Reimann, M., and A. Bechara. "The Somatic Marker Framework as a Neurological Theory of Decision-Making: Review, Conceptual Comparisons, and Future Neuroeconomics Research." *Journal of Economic Psychology* 31 (2010): 767–76.

Simon, D. J., and C. F. Chabris. "Gorillas in Our Midst: Sustained Inattentional Blindness for Dynamic Events." *Perception* 28 (1999): 1059–74.

Soll, J. B., K. M. Milkman, J. W. Payne, M. C. Mankins, J. Beshears, S. Frederick, F. Gino, D. Kahneman, D. Lovallo, and O. Sibony. "Outsmart Your Own Biases."

Harvard Business Review, November 16, 2015. https://hbr.org/2015/05/outsmart-your-own-biases.

Wikipedia. S.v. "cognitive bias." https://en.wikipedia.org/wiki/Cognitive_bias.

———. S.v. "list of cognitive biases." https://en.wikipedia.org/wiki/List_of_cognitive_biases.

Index

Zone and, 78
Ovid, 48
ownership attitude: controllables in,
114; details in, 114–115; as
essential, 113; expression of, 112;
mind and, 113; planning in, 115;
rent attitude compared to, 111–115;
understanding in, 114
ownership of self, 15

Palmer, Parker, 66
panic, ix, xxi; as contagious, 53;
defined, 53; purpose compared to,
52–55
parenthood, 116, 169
patience, 29–30, 86, 118, 121, 195
Pausch, Randy, 28
pause, 19
Peale, Norman Vincent, 47
perception, 11; perceptual blindness,
181
perseverance, 29–30, 112, 121, 157
persistence, 15, 29–30, 64, 118, 155
personal values, 62
perspective: in devastation and
disappointment, 28–29; evolving
from primitive times, 29; in
optimism mindset, 132
pessimism mindset: challenging, 134;
crisis mentality and, 124; defined,
125; optimism mindset compared to,
124–135; questions to determine,
124; research on, 125; seeking
problems, 133; signs of, 126–128
pity party, 102
planning: fallacy, 182; madness
compared to method, 188–193; in
master attitudes, 106–107; in
ownership attitude, 115; for
purpose, 55; response to crisis, 35;
self-esteem and, 86; uncertainty
compared to decisiveness, 179–187
Plato, 109
positive, process, present, progress
(four Ps), 170

practical support, 57
praise, 87
preparation: blurry compared to 20/20
vision, 174–179; confidence bred
by, 152; forks in the road, 173;
master attitudes and, 104–105;
overview, 173; purpose and, 54–55
pressure, 91–92
process attitude: defined, 116;
embracing, 120; for focus, 167;
outcome attitude compared to,
116–122; shifting toward, 117,
119–121; staying in the now,
121–122; understanding of,
118–119
process focus, 166–167
process goals, 93–94, 193
progress, 92; in four Ps, 170; in
optimism mindset, 133
psychic integrity, 27, 82
psychological investment, 75
purpose: panic compared to, 52–55;
plan for, 55; preparation and, 54–55

Rania, Queen, 8
rational actors, 180
reaction instinct: amygdala and, 16, 43;
change and, 17; self-possession
instinct compared to, 16–20
realistic goals, 190
realistic optimism, 129–130
reconstructing values, 67–68
recorded goals, 191
reflection, 88; components of, 19–20;
opportunity mindset and, 19–20; of
self, 27–28; self-possession instinct
and, 19–20
relaxation: for focus, 168–169; stress
and, 49
reminders, 169
rent attitude, 111–115
resilience, 27, 30, 72, 130, 139
resources: for crisis emotions, 23;
increasing, 47–48; for resolution,
70; for response to crisis, 34

62; inhibiting nature of, 63; lost
compared to North Star, 68–70;
nourishing of, 64–65; overview,
61–62; personal, 62; reconstructing,
67–68; shaky compared to solid,
64–68; social, 62; spiritual, 62;
types of, 62
victim attitudes: capabilities and, 103;
focus in, 102, 103; master attitudes
compared to, 101–110; pity party
and, 102
virtuous cycle, 55
Voltaire, 20

Waitley, Denis, 140, 178
Ward, William Arthur, 175
The War of the Worlds (Wells), 53

Watson, Emma, 102
Waze, 71
Weatherford, David, 121
weight vest, 128, 132
Wells, H. G., 53
wide-eyed, 177–178
Williams, Venus, 14
Williamson, Marianne, 29
The Wizard of Oz, 32
worry, 128, 132, 165; counteracting,
191; freedom from, 196; stability
and, 135; uncertainty and, 179
writing by hand, 52

YouTube, 161

Ziglar, Zig, 89, 157

About the Author

Jim Taylor, PhD, is internationally recognized for his work in the psychology of crisis and critical performance and has been a consultant to numerous businesses, schools, and sports organizations.

He is a former associate professor in the School of Psychology at Nova University in Ft. Lauderdale, a former clinical associate professor at the University of Denver, and a current adjunct faculty at the University of San Francisco. He is the author of nineteen books and the editor of five textbooks. His books have been translated into ten languages.

Dr. Taylor has blogged for *Psychology Today*, *Huffington Post*, SFGate, the *Seattle Post-Intelligencer*, the Hearst Interactive Media group, and his own website. His posts are picked up by dozens of websites worldwide and have been read by more than ten million people. He has appeared on NBC's *Today Show*, ABC's *World News This Weekend*, Fox News Channel, and major television network affiliates around the United States and Canada. He has been interviewed for articles that have appeared in *Time*, the *Los Angeles Times*, the *New York Daily News*, the *London Telegraph*, the *Chicago Tribune*, the *Atlanta Journal-Constitution*, *Outside*, *Men's Health*, and many other newspapers, magazines, and websites.

A former internationally ranked alpine ski racer, Dr. Taylor is also a certified tennis teaching professional, second-degree black belt, certified instructor in karate, marathon runner, and Ironman triathlete. He lives north of San Francisco with his wife and daughters. To learn more, visit www.drjimtaylor.com.